Witness Is Presence

Witness Is Presence

Reading Stanley Hauerwas in a Nordic Setting

MIIKA TOLONEN

RESOURCE *Publications* • Eugene, Oregon

WITNESS IS PRESENCE
Reading Stanley Hauerwas in a Nordic Setting

Copyright © 2013 Miika Tolonen. All rights reserved. Except for brief quotations in critical publications or reviews, no part of this book may be reproduced in any manner without prior written permission from the publisher. Write: Permissions, Wipf and Stock Publishers, 199 W. 8th Ave., Suite 3, Eugene, OR 97401.

Resource Publications
An Imprint of Wipf and Stock Publishers
199 W. 8th Ave., Suite 3
Eugene, OR 97401
www.wipfandstock.com

ISBN 13: 978-1-62564-073-4
Manufactured in the U.S.A.

First published in Finland by Åbo Akademi University Press.
Tavastgatan 13, FI-20500 Åbo, Finland
Tel. +358 (0)2-215 3478
E-mail: forlaget@abo.fi

Scripture taken from the NEW AMERICAN STANDARD BIBLE®, Copyright © 1960, 1962, 1963, 1968, 1971, 1972, 1973, 1975, 1977, 1995 by The Lockman Foundation. Used by permission.

I dedicate this book to my wife Rebekka,
and to our children Albert and Lyydia.

Contents

Foreword / ix

Chapter 1 Introduction / 1
        Background and Task
        Stanley Hauerwas
        Method, Material, and Previous Studies
        Definitions
        Outline

Chapter 2 Church as Social Ethic / 21
        Foundational Emphases
        Christian Social Ethics
        Christian, Church, and World
        Telling Examples: Hobson and Forrester
        Particular Community
        Church: Catholic and Protestant
        A Sectarian Ecclesiology?
        The Confessing Church
        A Qualified Virtue Ethic
        Summary

Chapter 3 Embodiment and Truth / 58
        Truth and Embodiment
        Christians in the Midst of Other Stories
        Inspiration from MacIntyre
        Realism, Non-realism, and Hauerwas
        Differing Premises
        Summary

Contents

Chapter 4 Constantinianism and Nonviolence / 89
  Constantinianism
  The Problem of Constantinianism
  Non-Constantinianism?
  Secularization and the Secular
  Withdrawal and Visibility
  Nonviolence
  Theological Introduction
  Role of Community
  An Active Peace
  Witnessing Politics
  Patience and Triviality
  Stout's Question
  Summary

Chapter 5 Hauerwas in a Nordic Setting / 130
  The Problem of Nordic Theology and Ethics
  Church As Social Ethics Revisited
  Christian Narration
  Political Christianity
  Grenholm's Hauerwas
  Two Regiments
  Point of Contact
  Embodiment Revisited
  Moral as Law vs. Story-Driven Ethics
  Moral as Knowledge vs. Embodiment
  Kurtén and Hauerwas
  Constantinianism and Nonviolence Revisited

Chapter 6: Conclusion / 178

Bibliography / 183

Foreword

THIS LITTLE BOOK IS the result of my time as doctoral student and researcher at Åbo Akademi University, Finland. Writing a dissertation was a great opportunity for me to, more seriously than before, begin a life of modest learning, thinking, writing, and doing theology. One of the more important things that I have learned from Stanley Hauerwas, who is obviously central to this book, is an understanding of theology as a discipline in service of the church. This is not always self-evident where I come from. It is, therefore, my hope that this book, though written "at the end of the earth," could stimulate the imaginations of people in different cultural settings. My simple prayer is that this book could, if even in some small ways, be a blessing to churches, and more importantly, to people that God calls to be church.

Miika Tolonen
Keuruu, Finland.
A surprisingly warm day in June, 2013.

Chapter 1

Introduction

BACKGROUND AND TASK

CHARACTERISTIC OF THE ROLE of "religion" in contemporary Western Europe is a condition often described in terms of the theory of secularization. Ever since the Enlightenment religion, or to be more specific, Christianity seems to have lost its credibility in many ways, both on an individual and societal level. It has been argued that the very conditions for faith in God have changed; we have arrived at a society where it is "difficult" to believe in God.[1] Parallel to this process of secularization another development can be observed, namely, an *increased* interest in various spiritualities. Sociologists of religion have, therefore, argued that secularization theory must be corrected or challenged in a way that pays attention to the empirically observable changes in religious behavior.[2] A tendency toward religious pluralism is evident, for example, in that many people see themselves as "spiritual," while not necessarily "religious" in the way that traditional religious establishments teach. The term "postsecular" has been used to capture the idea that our cultural situation is characterized both by a secularization and a new visibility of religion.[3]

---

1. Taylor, *A Secular Age*.
2. See for example Heelas, *The Spiritual Revolution*; Heelas and Woodhead, *Religion in Modern Times*.
3. Though many who study religion have felt a need to challenge the theory of secularization by introducing terms such as postsecular, resacralization and desecularization, it must still be noted that not all do so. Some continue to uphold the secularization

Witness Is Presence

I take these large-scale changes to have relevance also in the Nordic context. In the case of Finland—which is where this study is written—it must be noted that it is in many ways (ethnically, religiously, linguistically etc.) a fairly homogenous country and consequently the secular and pluralistic tendencies are not as trenchant as in some other European countries.[4] While Finland too displays an increase in individualistic religious expressions and spiritualities it is a conviction of this project that Lutheran theology still plays a role in the shaping of the life-views of Finns.[5] Because of this, Lutheran theologies play a central role in this study.[6]

What is of particular interest to me is that in a postsecular cultural situation the conditions for understanding and communicating a Christian tradition have changed. Even in the Nordic contexts with histories of vital folk or state churches one can discern factors that contribute to the altered conditions for communicating a Christian tradition. The following developments can be seen as examples of implications of a postsecular situation: Firstly, because of growing plurality in religious expressions and

---

theory as a valid way to view religion. Graham Ward instances Steve Bruce as one, referring to Bruce, *God is Dead* and Bruce, *Religion in the Modern World* (Ward, *The Politics of Discipleship*, 120–121.) The idea of the postsecular has been understood in several ways. For a good summary of the postsecular, see Ward, *The Politics of Discipleship*, 117–158. Postsecular is—like most of the "post-somethings"—a cumbersome term to which various scholars give partly differing meanings and emphases. Ward illustrates this by making the observation that "Adding 'post-' to an abstract noun does not render that noun more descriptive." (Ward, *The Politics of Discipleship*, 154.) This too can be discussed. I would suggest that while the "post" is cumbersome it can nevertheless indicate that it is an "after" or a "beyond" that we are concerned with. For the purposes of this study, however, I do not attempt to present an exhaustive review of the various views. I simply use the notion as shorthand for a cultural situation where both secularization and a new visibility of religion can be discerned.

4. The relevance of the notion of "spiritual revolution" (in Heelas's and Woodhead's sense) for the situation in Finland is discussed critically in Ketola, "Spiritual Revolution in Finland?," 29–40.

5. See for example Helander, *Muutoksen tulkkina*. In this study it is assumed that Lutheran theology has an impact on the life of the Church. The complex empirical question regarding how theology shapes the life of the Church is not pursued in this study.

6. Several of the interlocutors in this project are Finnish theologians. Occasionally other Nordic thinkers, mainly Swedish, are referred to. This is chiefly because this study is written at Åbo akademi, a Swedish speaking university in Finland. Many researchers at Åbo Akademi are involved in Nordic collaboration, see e.g. Lindfelt et al., *Mot bättre vetande*; Østnor, *Etisk pluralisme i Norden*. Many write with a Swedish readership in mind, see e.g. Vikström, *Folkkyrka i en postmodern tid*; Hagman, *Om kristet motstånd*. In this study I do not wish to make any stark distinction between theologies developed in Finland and the rest of the Nordic countries.

Introduction

life-views a Christian tradition can no longer be communicated in a way that assumes the "recipients" to have substantial prior knowledge of Christianity. Secondly, during the last couple of decades there have been serious discussions concerning moral issues in many areas of society (medicine, business and environment etc.). This return of religious language in the wider societal discourse points to religion being a cultural factor to be reckoned with.[7] Thirdly, religion emerges in new venues; it seems to have been released, partly at least, from "the religious sphere" of modernity.[8] This becomes evident, for example, in the way literature, movies and music take up religious themes, often in eclectic and non-traditional ways, without necessarily being "religious."[9]

These examples of ongoing cultural developments implicate that the role of Christian churches in society has consequently changed and none of the established religions can any more claim monopoly in the "marketplace of religions." A claim of this study is that a postsecular situation, characterized by a changing religious landscape, opens up a need to reflect on alternative ways of understanding Christianity in its context. Likewise it is, because of dwindling memberships in established Churches and a new visibility of alternative religious expressions, meaningful to rethink how communication of a Christian tradition can be understood. I suggest, in other words, that the altered context solicits a search for meaningful options with regard to the understanding of communication of a Christian tradition, traditionally called *witness*. In a postsecular context a Christian church, even a folk church, cannot assume to be in a position of majority or power. The question how to understand Christianity as a community that is neither in power nor a majority becomes relevant.

I suggest that the changes in the religious situation that I have sketched above make Stanley Hauerwas's theological perspective interesting. I will argue that Hauerwas's theology is an appealing option in an attempt to understand Christian witness in our context. There are three reasons for this. Firstly, the postsecular development has opened up a new possibility to see religions as public phenomena. Hauerwas's conception

---

7. Even Jürgen Habermas has come to "admit" this though for him religious language must in public discourse be translated into a language that is accessible to all, see e.g. Habermas *Mellan naturalism och religion*.

8. The religious sphere is a term used in descriptions of a differentiated society. See e.g. Casanova, *Public Religions in the Modern World*.

9. In the description of the case of the Nordic countries and Finland I take my cue from Bexell, *Svensk moralpolitik* and Kurtén, "Gud i Norden." See also Henriksen, *På grensen til Den andre*.

3

of ethics as necessarily social and public is contextual in that it "resonates" with this postsecular tendency.[10] In a Lutheran context, however, Christianity has often been seen as a private persuasion, largely as a result of the Lutheran idea of two regiments.[11] Hauerwas's perspective, therefore, is an amendment to typical Lutheran views in that it consents to Christianity as a public phenomenon. Secondly, Hauerwas as an American has reflected on Christianity in a society that has for a long time been more pluralistic than the Nordic contexts have been.[12] If, however, the postsecular implies that the Nordic contexts will in some ways become more like the American ones—as far as religious pluralism and the role of Christianity in society goes—then Hauerwas provides a perspective that is increasingly relevant. The reason for this is that he has discussed issues that the Nordic folk church contexts have not occasioned.[13] Thirdly, Hauerwas's theology is a meaningful contribution to Nordic theology because it carries potential to question some cherished assumptions of Nordic theology.[14]

Because of these reasons Hauerwas's perspective carries potential to provide a contribution to how Christianity, and more specifically, Christian witness, is understood in our Lutheran context. It should also be noted that I suggest that Hauerwas's theology provides an "amendment" or a "corrective" not a complete alternative to Lutheran ways of understanding

10. Hauerwas's emphasis on Christianity as a way of life (necessarily public), rather than primarily a collection of convictions that an individual may harbor (more or less private) is similarly befitting the postsecular.

11. This is not necessarily what Lutheran theology intends but I will argue that the doctrine of the two regiments and the lack of explicit "Christian narration" in fact leads to this.

12. The kind of theology that Hauerwas stands for has often not been deemed relevant in the Nordic contexts. See e.g. Gregersen, "Fluid Mission," 74–84; Henriksen, "Mission," 70–73; Grenholm, *Bortom humanismen*, 129–132.

13. Hauerwas's attempt to critique liberalism with resources from Christian tradition is an example of such an issue. See e.g. Hauerwas, *In Good Company*, 16; Hauerwas, *Truthfulness and Tragedy*, 51.

14. Vikström, *Folkkyrka i en postmodern tid*, 182. The temptation that Vikström sees with the kind of theology that Hauerwas stands for is that the emphasis on tradition-dependent rationality may lead to a posture that does not see the need to try to relate to others. I will in the following chapters try to show that this need not be the case, considering the many articles that Hauerwas has written in relation to other thinkers. In fact, I will suggest that Hauerwas's stress on the tradition-dependency of rationality is—considering the postmodern turn—the key way in which Hauerwas questions a cherished assumption of Nordic theology, that is, the modern assumption of the possibility to gain an objective perspective on human life. For the postmodern turn in theology see e.g. Sigurdson and Svenungsson, *Postmodern teologi*, 9–10.

Christianity in its context. It is not a "replacing" that I propose (whatever that might be), but rather a complementary perspective.[15] The task of this study is, therefore, to provide *a feasible account of Christian witness that pays regard to the altered conditions for the use of religious language.*

This task is approached by providing an account of some crucial elements of Hauerwas's theology. These elements are the notions of (1) church as social ethic, (2) embodiment, and (3) Constantinianism and nonviolence. These three elements stood out in my reading of Hauerwas's material as recurring emphases.[16] These elements are then related to some emphases that are typical to Nordic Lutheran theology and ethics.[17] I must, however, be explicit in that I do not want to stress the word "typical" too heavily, since it is difficult to delineate what is, and to what degree, typical Nordic Lutheran theology. The obvious reason for this is that there are many Lutheran theologies in the Nordic countries. A further reason is that this study does not give attention to all the Nordic countries. I have limited my discussion to mainly Finnish and Swedish theologians, with only sporadic Danish and Norwegian remarks. A more cautious way to express my task is, therefore, to say that I relate my account of Hauerwas to "some voices" in the choir of Nordic Lutheran theology.[18]

It should also be note that I bring the aforementioned elements of Hauerwas's theological perspective into conversation with Nordic Lutheran theologies for a purpose. I use Hauerwas's theology as a means to illuminate some elements that are meaningful to consider in a contemporary understanding of witness. In this study I, therefore, limit the amount of discussion with secondary literature on Hauerwas's project.[19] My aim

---

15. Other complimentary perspectives could be found among so-called free church traditions (such as Pentecostals and Baptists). The perspective developed in this study is, however, somewhat critical of the pietistic stress on the individual's experience that free churches often display.

16. Church as social ethic as well as Constantinianism/nonviolence are clearly central themes for Hauerwas. The idea that Hauerwas stresses embodiment (of Christian convictions) may not be as evident as is the stress on the other two elements. I am, however, not alone in making the observation that embodiment is central to Hauerwas. See e.g. Nation and Wells, *Faithfulness and Fortitude*, 11; Reinders, "The Meaning of Sanctification," 141–172, especially 147–149.

17. By Nordic Lutheran I refer to Lutheran theology that is done in the Nordic countries.

18. "The Church's voice" in Finland has been described as a choir with many, at times even disharmonious, voices. (Hytönen, *Kirkko*, 50.)

19. Since I am "reading Hauerwas" in a Nordic context I mainly interact with theologians who in the Nordic context have engaged Hauerwas. Because of this, my focus

is not to do "Hauerwas study" *per se* but to provide an account of witness that is relevant in a Nordic postsecular setting. I have, however, included interaction with secondary sources at certain points where I have considered it clarifying. Hauerwas's role in what follows is to be the central inspirer; his project provides a distinct angle on how to understand witness in a situation in which churches cannot assume a position of power.

One may also enquire what the role and position of the researcher is in this study. Some studies describe the researcher and his or her position at some length. This is presumably done not to satisfy the addressees' curiosity but in order to orient the reader. I take this to be a commendable idea, but I am not convinced that it in effect will do much good. I remain unconvinced that the researcher's biography, including his or her theological stance, could be described in such detail that it would "validate" or "accredit" the study in some decisive way. Despite this reservation it can be noted that if the theological task is understood as one of describing and clarifying the use of the language used by Christian communities then the researcher's theological biography is of relevance: familiarity with such language could then be an asset rather than a threat to theological credibility. I should, therefore, say that I consider myself a Christian living (willingly but critically) at the fringes of the "symbol universe(s)" of Finnish Pentecostals. This means that I am familiar with conceptions of church that understand the church as mission. Finnish Pentecostals tend to assume that they are custodians of the gospel that is to be "preached to all nations." Therefore, the idea of communicating the gospel to others, often termed "evangelization," is an idea that is central to the form of life that I have been initiated into and associated with ever since my conversion some 20 years ago.

This study does not, however, stress *communication* of a Christian tradition primarily because of reasons that somehow stem from my religious biography. The reason for this is that the church (which I consider Finnish Pentecostals part of) has a missionary mandate: church is always a church in mission.[20] Witness is one crucial aspect of mission. Concomitant with the conviction of this project that thinking necessarily takes place within some tradition the following is an attempt to discuss a topic that is central to the self-understanding of churches: witness. Witness and mission are

---

is on how Hauerwas has been received in the Nordic context, not on exegeting what he "really means."

20. See e.g. Newbigin, *The Open Secret*; Brunner, *The Word and the World*; Bosch, *Transforming Mission*; Bevans and Schroeder, *Constants in Context*.

here understood in a wide sense: they include the life of any Christian local church wherever it may find itself—not just the verbal proclamation of Christian convictions.

Since witness is a notion that is at home in the context of a Christian tradition it has some important consequences for this study. These will be further discussed when the method of this study is described. The attempt to relate central emphases of Hauerwas's theology to some Lutheran ideas is not done simply because it might lead to new knowledge about the issue of witness. Since this is an attempt to think through a theme that is central to the church, in a way that seeks to be in service of the church, this study includes an ulterior motive that approaches practical theology. This is the hope that the insights that this study arrives at may in some small ways be resources for churches that seek to act in our context.

STANLEY HAUERWAS

To introduce the central interlocutor of this study, Stanley Hauerwas, I will focus on the theological approach that he stands for. Though my interest lies in some features of Hauerwas's theology it is also in order to provide a compendious biography of the man.[21]

Stanley Hauerwas (born 1940) is a Christian theologian and ethicist. He was raised in Pleasant Grove, Texas in a working class family.[22] The Hauerwas family attended Pleasant Mound Methodist Church.[23] At age fifteen, failing to "be saved" he "dedicated himself to the Lord" thinking

---

21. I share the feeling of Mark Thiessen Nation when he asks "How does one describe Stanley Hauerwas?" (Nation and Wells, *Faithfulness and Fortitude*, 19.) Dropping a few "facts" about a person with as long a career as Hauerwas's does not seem to say much. It has been suggested that some biographical data may be important, for example, that the pietism that Hauerwas grew up with may have fueled his critique of the need for some "inner experience." (Cavanaugh, "Stan the Man," 24.) I take it that some biographical data may shed light on a person's work but I also think it rather problematic to name such "causalities." For further basic introduction to Hauerwas see, for example, Nation and Wells, *Faithfulness and Fortitude*, 19–36; Berkman and Cartwright, *The Hauerwas Reader*, 17–32; Jones et al., *God, Truth, and Witness*; Pinches et al., *Unsettling Arguments*; Hauerwas, *Hannah's Child*.

22. His father was a bricklayer, a fact that Hauerwas often mentions as well as draws on in his thought on Christianity as a craft. See Hauerwas, *Hannah's Child*, 17–20, 27–33.

23. Hauerwas, *Hannah's Child*, 1–3.

"that if God was not going to save me, I could at least put God in a bind by being one of his servants in the ministry."[24]

He has received his education in Southwestern University, and Yale University. In 2001 he delivered the prestigious Gifford Lectures and the same year *Time* magazine named him "America's best theologian."[25] His teaching career has taken him to Augustana College in Rock Island (Illinois), the University of Notre Dame, and since 1984, the Divinity School of Duke University.[26] In addition to this Hauerwas has lectured extensively on several continents.[27] He has authored or co-authored 37 books and published close to 500 articles and reviews.[28]

In his theology Hauerwas draws on a wide array of thinkers. Influences that Hauerwas himself names include but are not limited to thinkers such as Reinhold and H. Richard Niebuhr, Karl Barth, Paul Ramsey, James Gustafson, John-Howard Yoder, Alasdair MacIntyre, Aristotle, Aquinas, Augustine, Calvin, but also thinkers such as John Dewey, Robin George Collingwood, Ludwig Wittgenstein and Plato.[29] Hauerwas's theology is not easily accounted for because he does not seek to arrange his thinking into "a system"; the main part of his writing consists of articles on a wide range of topics.[30] Seeking to sift out "the ecclesiology of Hauerwas,"

---

24. Hauerwas, *Hannah's Child*, 3. See also Cavanaugh, "Stan the Man," 19, 24. It seems that already at a young age Hauerwas had trouble with a pietistic stress on "being saved."

25. Hauerwas, *Hannah's Child*, 261. It has been reported that Hauerwas responded that "Best is not a theological category! Faithful or unfaithful are the right categories. The last thing in the world I'd want to be is the best." (McCarthy, "America's best theologian," 1.). Hauerwas maintains that he was simply responding to the absurdity of *Time*'s label. See Hauerwas, *Hannah's Child*, ix. I agree that "best" is a strange adjective when attributed to a theologian. Hauerwas has, however, been a much-discussed theologian already before *Time* gave him wider popular publicity. This, in combination with the fact that Hauerwas has not been extensively discussed in the Nordic context make him a meaningful inspirator for the account of witness that I will provide in the following chapters.

26. Hauerwas, *Hannah's Child*, 173, 17. Hauerwas, *curriculum vitae* (Quoted with permission).

27. Hauerwas, *curriculum vitae*, 2–6.

28. In addition to these Hauerwas has edited 10 books. (Hauerwas, *curriculum vitae*) Most of the books are collected previously published articles. There is, therefore, considerable overlap in these figures.

29. Hauerwas, *The Peaceable Kingdom*, xix.

30. It is, therefore, easy to agree with the claim that "engaging Hauerwas is frustrating because he spends far more time writing occasional essays than he does displaying the coherence of his thought in rigorous, book-length exposition. (Jones et al., *God,*

therefore, entails a construction of what seems to be the central elements in his understanding of the church.

The kind of theology that Hauerwas stands for can be called postliberal theology.[31] This theological school of thought can be described by attending to the foundational difference in approach between so-called liberal theology and postliberal theology. Liberal theology is a notion that has been used in many ways. Hauerwas, however, describes the liberal theologian as one who assumes a universal experience that can be described as religious: the different religions in the world are all manifestations of this universal experience.[32] This universal experience is, on this view, something that transcends the particular religions.[33] Applied to the field of ethics this suggests that there is "a strong continuity between Christian and non-Christian morality, especially in a liberal society."[34]

The postliberal theologian, however, has a different approach to the theological task. On this view theology does not seek to describe some universally available human experience. For an enquiry in ethics this implies that "Christian ethics does not simply confirm what all people of good will know, but require a transformation both personally and socially if we are to be true to the nature of our convictions."[35]

To describe the liberal and postliberal approaches to theology Hauerwas draws on George Lindbeck's *The Nature of Doctrine*.[36] Lindbeck contends that liberal theology is more likely to conform to current philosophical and scientific trends than is postliberal theology.[37] The reason is that liberals tend to begin with an account of reality (which is more or less influenced by current paradigms) and then seek to adjust their

---

Truth, and Witness, 7–8.)

31. Hauerwas, *Against the Nations*, 1–9.

32. Hauerwas, *Against the Nations*, 2. On this point I agree with Davaney's and Brown's description: "Postliberalism is a contemporary theological movement that distinguishes itself from both the projects of the Enlightenment and Schleiermachian liberalism with its assumptions of an unmediated religious experience common to all humans. In their stead, postliberals advocate a return to religious tradition and to the task of interiorizing the values of particular communities. To postliberals, this approach flows from the historical and traditioned nature of life." (Davaney and Brown, "Postliberalism," 456.)

33. Hauerwas, *Against the Nations*, 2.

34. Hauerwas, *Against the Nations*, 2.

35. Hauerwas, *Against the Nations*, 2.

36. Lindbeck, *The Nature of Doctrine*, 142.

37. Lindbeck, *The Nature of Doctrine*, 125–126.

understanding of the kingdom of God into that "reality."[38] Again, the postliberal approach does the opposite: it seeks to begin with the biblical stories and understand current "extrascriptural categories" from that perspective.[39] The liberal tends to "use" new approaches and insights if they seem to be scientific advancements, whereas the postliberal, according to Hauerwas, is neither traditionalist nor progressive.[40] Because of this the postliberal might be perceived as a traditionalist since she might not appear so eager to affirm new intellectual approaches.[41]

In *Against the Nations* Hauerwas describes a liberal theological approach in a very generalizing manner to make a point, namely, to describe the differences in a liberal and a postliberal approach. Making use of current intellectual trends in theology should not, however, be understood to be necessarily mistaken. Since any observer is contextually conditioned it seems obvious that even a postliberal observer will be forced to utilize intellectual means available, which may include currently fashionable expressions. The point of embarkation is, however, different in these two approaches: the liberal goes from "world to text" whereas the postliberal goes from "text to world."[42]

What is common to both approaches is the use of argumentation in describing the process of observation/research. Argumentation is based on some form of rationality, but these two views of theological method might in some cases have different understandings of the role of rationality in religion, and more specifically Christianity. In my interpretation of Hauerwas this is closely linked to his larger project of dealing critically with modern Enlightenment inspired thinking. Central to his approach

---

38. Lindbeck, *The Nature of Doctrine*, 125–126.
39. Lindbeck, *The Nature of Doctrine*, 125–126.
40. Hauerwas, *Against the Nations*, 3.
41. Hauerwas, *Against the Nations*, 3.
42. There are difficulties involved with the idea of interpreting the world "through the text." One can, for example, ask what it in effect means. If theology begins reflection from the central Christian conviction that God acted in the life, death and resurrection of Jesus, how does that inform enquiry? It seems very limited what can be "deduced" out of such a premise. It does not, as far as I can see, give much sustenance for thought when it comes to concrete questions and phenomena such as, for example, religious terrorism or immigration. As I see it the postliberal approach that "goes from text to world" makes an important conceptual point, but it also keeps theologians busy in figuring out concrete implications. It is, to reiterate, by no means clear what to think about e.g. current political issues even if one would endorse a Hauerwasian interpretation of Christian convictions.

is the acknowledgement of rationality as necessarily tradition-bound and the need to begin reflection from how the biblical texts describe the world.

Hauerwas "attempts to provide a Christian interpretation of our social situation, as well as suggest why it is so socially important to maintain the integrity of the church—both of which open up possibilities that otherwise would simply not exist."[43] Hauerwas is, in other words, suggesting that Christianity provides a perspective that no other religion or outlook includes. He is, therefore, critical of the idea that one could translate the claims of Christian proclamation into more "neutral language." The postliberal "no more believes that religions can be translated into another medium than that one can learn French by reading translations. Religions, like languages, can only be understood in their own terms."[44]

Despite this understanding of the character of religion a rational account of Christian particularities is not impossible. An "antifoundationalist" approach, such as Hauerwas's, does not have to be irrational simply because it does not seek to establish its rationality on a foundation that every rational person could affirm. The antifoundationalist perspective questions the possibility of a "neutral" context-free language that would be capable of describing a universal foundation that could in turn provide standards for rationality in or between various fields of enquiry. Hauerwas takes his cue from Aristotle for whom reasonableness "is more like a skill than a universal principle. Rationality resides not in the mind but in intelligent practices which we must learn."[45] Hauerwas's writing reflects a conceptual shift to a form of thinking where rationality is tradition-bound, and as such, receives its intelligibility in the praxis of a particular and concrete community. This is what I like to call a late modern "trait" in Hauerwas's theology.

To recap my presentation of postliberal theology I refer to one description of this kind of theology. The following sums up well how Hauerwas's project is interpreted in the present study, but it also draws a conclusion that I do not accept as necessary:

> Three characteristics can be seen to typify postliberalism. First, it is anti-foundationalist, rejecting all assertions of ahistorical, universal foundations, be they found in reason or experience. Second, it posits a thoroughly social and communitarian vision of human life, thereby repudiating the individualism endemic

---

43. Hauerwas, *Against the Nations*, 4.
44. Hauerwas, *Against the Nations*, 5.
45. Hauerwas, *Against the Nations*, 6.

to modern life and thought. Human experience is mediated through the language and practices of particular communities, and individuals only have identity within those communal contexts. The autonomous, self-subsisting individual does not exist, morally, religiously or intellectually. Third, postliberalism is particularistic and historicist. Humans are not historical or social in general. They receive their identity and experience reality within communities that live out of inherited understandings of life.[46]

These three characteristics fit Hauerwas's theology well: antifoundationalist, communitarian and historicist. I think that these points neatly capture how Hauerwas can be meaningfully understood. What I, however, do not agree with is the claim that these characteristics imply that postliberalism does not provide any "basis for conversation among traditions."[47] Is it really the case that there are only two alternatives: to assume an ahistorical common language or not being able to converse with other traditions *at all*? The way I read Hauerwas it seems that he stands for an alternative to these extremes. While he stresses the role of tradition one can still find similarities and points of contact with other traditions, which make conversation possible.

METHOD, MATERIAL, AND PREVIOUS STUDIES

Conforming to postliberal theology this project includes a distinct perspective on *method*. More specifically, method is not given a determinative role. This is not, however, to say that method is unimportant; it is rather a way to question the optimism in the idea that a rigid method could provide a neutral or objective perspective on a matter. In the case of theology, on the view accepted here, Christian tradition shapes method in a way that cannot be overlooked. John Howard Yoder expresses well the kind of method that is assumed in these chapters: "What must replace the prolegomenal search for 'scratch' is the confession of rootedness in historical community."[48] This is, in other words, a claim that theology is a

---

46. Davaney and Brown, "Postliberalism," 455.

47. ". . . postliberalism's emphasis upon the intrasystemic nature of theology and ethics seems to provide no basis for conversation among traditions" (Davaney and Brown, "Postliberalism," 455.) This is a common critique that I will return to.

48. Yoder, *The Priestly Kingdom*, 7. See also Hauerwas, *The State of the University*, 222n.

discipline that cannot be done in an allegedly objective mode; all theology is contextual.⁴⁹ On this view, theological method should not expect to find a foundation for thought that all humans necessarily share.⁵⁰ Instead, it is necessary for the theologian to acknowledge that he or she stands in and engages a tradition of thought. This implies that there is no one right place to "begin thinking"; theology is an ongoing conversation where mastering a tradition's language allows for rationality and informed judgment.⁵¹

If one were to assume that an objective perspective is somehow possible and that theology should be based on such a perspective the scope of this study may seem rather modest. Despite this I will have to agree with Lutheran theologian Robert Jenson in his claims on the limits of method in theology:

> The most prolegomena to theology can appropriately do is provide readers an advance description of the enterprise. Even this cannot be a pre-theological beginning, for every attempt to say what sort of thing theology is implies material theological propositions, and so is false if the latter are false.⁵²

From this premise it follows that I will not try to provide any "pre-theological beginning" that allegedly would assure an objective standpoint. In this study I will, consistent with these methodological considerations, give

---

49. This study involves a critique of "methodological atheism" and this for two reasons: Firstly, this is an account of Christian theology and Christians have traditionally "believed in God." (I do not here make any claims as to what such "believing" might entail.) Secondly, methodological atheism does not, from the perspective assumed in this study, seem to be free from assumptions, which could somewhat maliciously be called in itself a form of "belief." In any case, this study does not make claims to "neutrality."

50. This approach to rationality is similar to the one that Alasdair MacIntyre represents. See MacIntyre, *Whose Justice?*.

51. George Lindbeck is also critical of the idea of "some neutral, framework-independent language" and suggests that "In short, intelligibility comes from skill, not theory, and credibility comes from good performance, not adherence to independently formulated criteria." (Lindbeck, *The Nature of Doctrine*, 130–131.)

52. Jenson, *Systematic Theology*, 3. Jenson also notes helpfully that Christian theology is still part of "the general human cognitive effort" and that it cannot "thrive without acknowledging and cultivating its place therein. (. . .) theology has its own task and is enabled within it." (Jenson, *Systematic Theology*, 3.) From this follows, among other things, that such theology is not necessarily "fideistic" in the sense that communication between traditions is altogether impossible. (For a recent survey on various forms of fideism see Vainio, *Beyond Fideism*.) As I indicate below, I do not claim to work without method, but I do not emphasize the role of method in securing the academic standard of this study.

ample space to Hauerwas's "primal speech." With this I mean that I attempt to interpret Hauerwas on his own terms without putting him into a preconceived theoretical framework.

Despite these methodological disclaimers the general method in this study can be called an analysis of language and concepts.[53] In the fifth chapter I also utilize a compare and contrast method when I relate central notions of Hauerwas's theology to some Nordic Lutheran theologies.

The *material* of this study consists of Stanley Hauerwas's relevant books and articles. Central texts that discuss Hauerwas's approach to Christian ethics, namely, the notion of church as social ethics, as well as his ideas of Constantinianism and nonviolence are analyzed. This material is where relevant complemented with secondary sources. The work of Alasdair MacIntyre is also briefly treated because it provides important inspiration to Hauerwas's theology.[54] My account of Hauerwas's theological perspective is then brought into discussion with relevant Nordic thinkers (mainly chapter five). The Nordic material that is used is chosen with the criterion that it either (1) explicitly discusses Hauerwas's project or (2) illuminates some aspect of Hauerwas's thought that without such relating might not surface—or both of these.[55]

The notable number of articles that Hauerwas has published implies that many before the present writer have felt the need to engage his writing.[56] A survey of these *previous studies* suggests that in the Nordic contexts only Arne Rasmusson has given Hauerwas's theology a book-length treatment.[57] In the United Kingdom—which is not geographically speaking too far from the Nordic countries—John Thomson has written on Hauerwas.[58] In the Nordic context two dissertations that explicitly discuss

---

53. It is a form of "systematic analysis" (as it is often called in Finland) in which the researcher looks for recurring themes in a body of literature that may help understand and arrange e.g. a theologian's thought. See e.g. Luomanen, *Teologia*, 93.

54. The work of John Howard Yoder is also a crucial inspiration to Hauerwas. I will not, however, delve into the discussion of the degree to which there is continuity or discontinuity between Hauerwas and Yoder.

55. E.g. the discussions with Grenholm and Kurtén in this study fulfill both of these criteria. It should also be noted that in this study I do not seek to differentiate between "academic theology" and "church theology." The reason for this is that when theology is seen to be in the service of the church this distinction becomes odd.

56. At least 26 books or dissertations have directly addressed aspects of Hauerwas's theology. (Hauerwas, *curriculum vitae*, 10–12.)

57. Rasmusson, *The Church as Polis*.

58. Thomson, *The Ecclesiology of Stanley Hauerwas*, 245. Thomson identifies "The trans-contextual possibilities of Hauerwas's ecclesiology" as one of the avenues for

Introduction

Hauerwas are in progress.[59] However, neither Rasmusson, Thomson, nor the forthcoming projects that I am aware of relate Hauerwas's theology to Nordic Lutheran discourse the way that the present study does.

DEFINITIONS

There are some terms and concepts that must be defined at the outset:

Witness: Robert Jenson notes that a Christian notion of witness is witness *to* something and that this something is the resurrection of Jesus.[60] In Hauerwas's material witness often refers to church being a nonviolent alternative to, for example, typical politics.[61] The word witness in the title of this study is thus to be understood as the manifold ways in which the life of the church displays, and points to, the conviction that the resurrection is a reality. This includes verbal proclamation concerning the meaning of the resurrection. In this study, however, the emphasis is on the "body-language" of the church. The reason for this is what I call the embodied character of Hauerwas's theology. I will throughout the following chapters argue that embodiment of Christian convictions is a central trait in Hauerwas's thought.

Presence: The word presence in the title of this work is burdened with many meanings. It has been used in various ways in both theology and philosophy.[62] In this study I will not, however, delve into these discourses. The term is here used to capture the embodied sense of witness that emerges from my reading of Hauerwas's theology. *Witness is*, according

---

further study (Thomson, *The Ecclesiology of Stanley Hauerwas*, 217.) The present study can be seen as a contribution to this avenue since it relates aspects of Hauerwas's theology to Nordic Lutheran discourse.

59. Silje Kvamme Bjørndal's working title is *Church in a Secular Society: A Critical Discussion of Stanley Hauerwas's Ecclesiological Position, in Dialogue with Charles Taylor's Framework for Understanding Secularity*. Andreas Østerlund Nielsen works with the title *Does the Cross Make All Things New? A Discussion of Missional Ecclesiology and Transformation Applying Stanley Hauerwas and Mission as Transformation*. (Personal correspondence.)

60. Jenson, *Systematic Theology*, 12.

61. See e.g. Hauerwas, *The Peaceable Kingdom*, 60; Hauerwas, *The State of the University*, 38.

62. In theology one can find a lot of thinking that, for example, seeks to understand how Christ is present to people or present in the Eucharist. See e.g. Mannermaa and Stjerna, *Christ Present in Faith*, 136. Martin Heidegger and Jacques Derrida's are among the philosophers who have discussed the "metaphysics of presence." (See e.g. Reynolds, "Derrida.")

15

to my interpretation of Hauerwas, *presence* in that it necessitates a concrete community that lives in service of "the neighbor." An example of this would be something as commonplace as taking the time to sit next to a terminally ill person. This can—when done in a context where efficiency is heavily emphasized—be seen as a kind of witness to an alternative orientation in life.

Meaningful resource: I suggest that the theology of Hauerwas provides meaningful resources for Nordic theology in the present situation. Meaningful is used in the sense that a Christian community takes something to be sufficient for their purposes and in line with their "story." This would mean a claim or trait in Hauerwas's theology that helps a Christian community fulfill its mandate to be witness, in a way that is not in tension with how such a community understands itself. "Meaningful," therefore, includes a pragmatic element. It does not assume a neutral perspective, something that any observer might find meaningful. It is, rather, meaningful against the backdrop provided by a continual grappling with the story of Jesus.[63]

Tradition: The notion of Christian tradition in this study refers to a community that exists through time that consists of witnesses to the resurrection.[64] It is commonplace within the fields of, for example, sociology or religious studies[65] to view religious traditions as social constructs. There is undoubtedly a sense in which this is true also for the Christian tradition. Yet I assume that the mandate of the church to be witnesses to the resurrection adds a factor to Christian tradition that some other understandings of tradition do not display. If Christian tradition is compared

---

63. Cf. Ola Sigurdson who writes about "reasonable" (*rimlig*, e.g. Sigurdson, *Det postsekulära tillståndet*, 219.) and Grenholm who talks about "acceptable" (*godtagbar*, e.g. Grenholm, *Bortom humanismen*, 34.). My use of "meaningful" stresses the role of Christian community for determining what is and what is not meaningful.

64. This is in line with Jenson: "In that the gospel always somehow makes the claim that Jesus is risen, the gospel is a message about an alleged event. That is, the gospel is a piece of *news*, even when we speak it to God; it belongs, insofar, to the same general class of utterances as 'there was an accident this morning on Main Street.' Therefore the gospel cannot occur apart from the process of its own *tradition*; the occurrence of the gospel depends on the chain of witnesses who have brought the news from the first witnesses to those who now hear." (Jenson, *Systematic Theology*, 14. Italics in the original.) This is, consequently, a more specific idea of tradition than the one Alasdair MacIntyre (who will also be discussed below) assumes. It should also be noted that it is not here suggested how "resurrection" might be understood.

65. Usually called "science of religion" (Swedish: *religionsvetenskap*; Finnish: *uskontotiede*) in the Nordic countries.

Introduction

to a typical social club one might suggest that the latter may have some kind of tradition but it does not necessarily understand itself in terms of having a mandate that the adherents seek to be faithful to.[66] Still it must be noted that on this view it cannot be objectively secured through Scripture, liturgy or creed that a church indeed is part of such a chain of witnesses to the resurrection.[67]

Regarding tradition I might also include that I speak of "*a* Christian tradition" (instead of *the*) because I want to emphasize the contextual character of Christianity. It is a contextual "take" on Christianity and calling it *the* Christian tradition would not, from this perspective, seem meaningful. "A take" does not lay claims on exhausting the tradition.[68]

Story: Story is what one resorts to if one seeks to speak about topics that can only be spoken of analogically.[69] If one, to take an example relevant to the present study, wants to talk about the "self" or "God," one cannot simply state the "facts." The reason for this is the premise that there is no "story of stories, i.e., an account that is literal and that thus provides a criterion to say which stories are true or false."[70] Proficiency in a story is what provides a person the means to navigate life and relate to other stories.[71] Story or narrative is for this study, as it is for Hauerwas, the fundamental way to talk about God: "Narrative is not secondary for our knowledge of God; there is no 'point' that can be separated from the story."[72] On this

---

66. Jenson, *Systematic Theology*, 25. I do not suggest that Christianity is unique in this regard. I assume that other substantial religions too assume mandates or elements that could be described as "historical givens" that adherents seek to be faithful to. Jenson argues that it is the property of being witness to the resurrection that makes Christian tradition peculiar: "the church's tradition sustains the community's self-identity through time only in that it sustains witness to a particular event, the Resurrection; the church's tradition has content that is not identical with the association's own historical perdurance." (Jenson, *Systematic Theology*, 25.)

67. Jenson, *Systematic Theology*, 25. Jenson further suggests that it is "faith that *God* uses the church's communal structures to preserve the gospel's temporal self-identity and so also the temporal self-identity of the gospel's community. Invoking such an activity of God, the church speaks of the *Spirit*." (Jenson, *Systematic Theology*, 25. Italics in the original.)

68. In a general meaning, however, one may speak about *the* Christian tradition, cf. the Jewish, the Islamic, the Buddhist tradition, though this kind of talk tends to involve extreme simplifications.

69. Hauerwas, *Truthfulness and Tragedy*, 78.

70. Hauerwas, *Truthfulness and Tragedy*, 78.

71. Hauerwas, *A Community of Character*, 96–97.

72. Hauerwas, *The Peaceable Kingdom*, 25–26.

account one cannot express "directly," through, for example, doctrine what stories only say "indirectly."[73] In a similar way the human self cannot be described without a telling of the persons life; self is a story.[74]

When this study speaks of "the story of Jesus" it refers to the stories found in the Bible of God's dealings with the people of Israel, Jesus and the early church. Ongoing interpretation of the Biblical stories is necessary so that people in Christian community can place their lives in those stories. On this account Christians of today can see themselves as part of the continuing story of Jesus.

Church: With church (lower case) I refer to any group of people that gather together to worship the Triune God.[75] The term Church is used to refer to particular denominations, usually the Evangelical Lutheran Church of Finland. An exception to this is "folk church" with which I denote unless otherwise stated the Evangelical Lutheran Church of Finland.

Ethics and *morality:* In this study I do not maintain a distinction between ethics and morality.[76] Neither do I make a distinction between "ethic" and "ethics." At times the word is, however, used in the plural because I see it as a helpful reminder of the fact that I am not suggesting that only "one kind of life" would follow when people seek to live faithfully to "the story of Jesus." As I provide an account of Hauerwas's notion of church as social ethic I understand it as a meta-ethical account in that it focuses on some of the foundational assumptions of Hauerwas's ethical vision, rather than on practical outworking of such an ethic.[77] I do, nevertheless, include examples of what this understanding of ethics might actually look like.

---

73. Hauerwas, *The Peaceable Kingdom*, 25–26.

74. Hauerwas, *Vision and Virtue*, 68–89.

75. Figuring out what worshipping the Triune God means is the task of Christian communities. I do not here assume that it is self-evident what it is.

76. Oftentimes morality is taken to refer to what people understand to be a good life, whereas ethics is used to denote theoretical reflection on morality, or principles or rules that are "prior to" morality. See e.g. Raunio and Luomanen, *Teologia*, 144–145.

77. Renowned Finnish philosopher of religion Simo Knuuttila categorizes "theological ethics" in the following way: "In a wide sense the term 'theological ethics' includes (a) the ethics taught by a religious community, (b) ethical theory developed within the confession of a religious community and (c) the scientific study of the ethical teaching and thought of a religious community." (Knuuttila, *Järjen ja tunteen kerrostumat*, 162. My translation.) If I were to position my account to Knuuttila's definition I would conclude that my perspective does not operate with a clear-cut distinction between "religious" and "scientific" (academic) accounts of theological ethics. The stress on the role of "initiation" in this study is the main cause for this fusion of Knuuttila's categories.

Another feature of the following account is that while it is a clarification of Hauerwas's ethical perspective it also has some features of an ecclesiological discussion. The reason is that the way Hauerwas conceives of ethics has, as I will argue in the following chapters, everything to do with embodied Christian convictions. From this follows that Hauerwas's ethical vision has ecclesiological repercussions. Consequently the following account will be concerned with the church more than many other accounts of Christian ethics.

Hauerwasian: In this study "Hauerwasian" refers to the line of thought that Hauerwas typically stands for. In some cases it refers to a person who accepts Hauerwas's theological approach. "A Hauerwasian Christian" alludes to the way that Hauerwas describes Christians.

OUTLINE

This study is divided into six chapters. *Chapter one* is the *introduction* that lays out the background, task, method, and central concepts.

Chapter two: Church as Social Ethic provides an account of this central notion of Hauerwas's. My account of church as social ethic suggests that it is a qualified virtue ethic that turns on the role assigned to "Jesus" and "church." The notion of confessing church is seen as central to the way that Hauerwas perceives Christian ethics. A feature of this perspective is that it assumes Christianity to be a tradition in its own right with its own mandate. Church as social ethic rejects the accusation that it leads to a sectarian withdrawal from society. Instead it is not a private ethic but a public one: it is a politics that is shaped by the church's narrative.

Chapter three: Embodiment and Truth displays the embodied way in which Hauerwas talks about truth. This chapter is to be read as an extended example of how Hauerwas does theology. Instead of talking about a matter such as truth in an abstract way he stresses embodied truth, or truthfulness.

Chapter four: Constantinianism and Nonviolence supplies an account of two central themes in Hauerwas's authorship. Constantinianism is understood to be any attempt to harness power structures to serve the mandate of the church. Constantinianism is seen as something that disqualifies the proclamation and witness of the church. Nonviolence, on the other hand, is the central element of a constructive alternative to constantinianism. Nonviolence, the chapter suggests, is witness in that it reflects what God is like. It is also suggested that Christian nonviolence includes the potential to widen society's imagination to see nonviolent forms of politics.

Chapter five: Hauerwas in a Nordic Setting brings central aspects of Hauerwas's thought into Nordic Lutheran theological and ethical discourse. The chapter exemplifies in what ways the notions of (1) church as social ethic, (2) embodiment, and (3) Constantinianism and nonviolence can be amendments to typical Nordic theological discourse.

Chapter six: Conclusion pulls together the study and articulates a feasible account of Christian witness that pays regard to the altered conditions for the use of religious language.

Chapter 2

Church as Social Ethic

THE CENTRAL TASK IN this chapter is to provide an account of Stanley Hauerwas's notion of church as social ethic. This is done in order to identify aspects of a relevant understanding of witness. This chapter contributes to my overall task in that it pursues the questions if and how Hauerwas's oft-made claim that the church not only has a social ethic but the church *is* a social ethic can prove such an aspect.[1]

FOUNDATIONAL EMPHASES

> "Christian ethics begins and ends with a story."[2]
> —Stanley Hauerwas—

"What makes Christian ethics Christian," for Stanley Hauerwas, "is the overriding significance of Jesus."[3] In order to unravel this claim it should be noted that Hauerwas does not assume that we can know the historical Jesus apart from how he was understood by the early church.[4] When the early church sought "to witness to the significance of Jesus for their lives they necessarily resorted to a telling of his life."[5] This is then were story,

---

1. E.g. Hauerwas, *The Peaceable Kingdom*, 99; Hauerwas, *Christian Existence Today*, 101.
2. Hauerwas, *The Peaceable Kingdom*, 97.
3. Hauerwas, *The Peaceable Kingdom*, 72.
4. Hauerwas is "quite content to assume that the Jesus we have in Scripture is the Jesus of the early church" (Hauerwas, *The Peaceable Kingdom*, 73.)
5. Hauerwas, *The Peaceable Kingdom*, 73.

or narrative, comes in. Story is for Hauerwas the form that witness necessarily takes. The life of Jesus is seen as the best example of what life in God's kingdom is like.[6] This does not, however, mean that Christological claims about "Jesus' ontological status" are unimportant, and Hauerwas explicitly acknowledges that the early church in fact made such claims.[7] It seems, nevertheless, that Hauerwas's focus lies in the narrative-bound character of such claims because Christian claims are not intelligible isolated from the context where they are at home, the church.[8] From this follows another fundamental emphasis in Hauerwas's approach to ethics. This is the conviction that the story of Jesus cannot be known abstracted from a community that is engaged in the hearing and telling of the story.[9] Hauerwas's notion of church as social ethic implies that the church is crucial for Christian ethics:

> It is from the church that Christian ethics draws its ethical substance and it is to the church that Christian ethical reflection is first addressed. Christian ethics is not written for everyone, but for those people who have been formed by the God of Abraham, Isaac, Jacob, and Jesus. Therefore Christian ethics can never be a minimalistic ethic for everyone, but must presuppose a sanctified people wanting to live more faithful to God's story.[10]

In this quote there are three aspects that I want to comment on. Firstly, what Hauerwas calls "the church" is crucial to the kind of ethics that he advocates. Church for Hauerwas names the community that seeks to hear, remember and tell the story of Jesus.[11] This strong emphasis on the church is in tension with the kinds of Christian ethics that do not assign a decisive role to community. Secondly, this quote points to the scope of Hauerwas's ethics: it is an ethic for those formed by the stories of God's acting in the lives of Israel and Jesus. As such it is in disagreement with views of Christian ethics that assume substantial continuity between Christian and "more general" human ethics. Thirdly, and in line with the second point,

---

6. Hauerwas, *The Peaceable Kingdom*, 74.

7. Hauerwas, *The Peaceable Kingdom*, 73.

8. Hauerwas refers to Janet Soskice who maintains that "When dealing with meaning, we must see that 'Words have no function save as they play a role in sentences...'" (Berkman and Cartwright, *The Hauerwas Reader*, 159, quoting Soskice, *Metaphor and Religious Language*, 135–136.)

9. Hauerwas, *The Peaceable Kingdom*, 97.

10. Hauerwas, *The Peaceable Kingdom*, 97.

11. Hauerwas, *The Peaceable Kingdom*, 103.

the notion of "sanctified people" involves the claim that Christianity is a way of life that can only be known through initiation. This means that Hauerwas does not assume that Christian ethics is necessarily intelligible to people whom are not undergoing such training in Christianity. Hauerwas does not want to make a stark partition between theology and ethics, and as a result what goes for ethics goes for theological work: The work of the theologian, on this account, is "not to make the gospel credible to the modern world, but to make the world credible to the gospel."[12] This is but another way of saying that sanctification is a prerequisite for the intelligibility of Christian ethics.

So far I have sought to identify the heart of Hauerwas's conception of Christian ethics. The role that Hauerwas assigns to "Jesus" and "church" are, according to my interpretation, the two factors that stand out as crucial elements in the kind of ethics that Hauerwas envisions. Other central factors, which will be discussed below, work out issues that follow from, or are necessitated by, these two overriding emphases. There is, however, a reason why Hauerwas not only talks about Christian ethics but rather Christian social ethics. This reason has to do with the conviction that all ethics are social.[13] Because of this Hauerwas's idea of church as social ethic involves necessarily and importantly a public aspect. The following is an account of such a social ethic.

CHRISTIAN SOCIAL ETHICS

In *A Community of Character* Hauerwas makes a constructive case for his understanding of Christian social ethics.[14] His concern is

> to reassert the social significance of the church as a distinct society with an integrity peculiar to itself. [His] wish is [to] help Christians rediscover that their most important social task is nothing less than to be a community capable of hearing the story of God we find in the scripture and living in a manner that is faithful to that story. The church is too often justified by believers, and tolerated by nonbelievers, as a potential agent for

---

12. Hauerwas and Willimon, *Resident Aliens*, 24.

13. Hauerwas and Willimon, *Resident Aliens*, 80. This same claim has also been made in a Lutheran context. E.g. Herbert Olson notes that ethics is social ethics in that people are always part of a social framework. (Olsson, *Grundproblemet i Luthers socialetik*, 8–9.)

14. Hauerwas, *A Community of Character*.

> justice or some other good effect. In contrast, [he] contend[s] that the only reason for being Christian (which may well have results that in a society's terms seem less than "good") is because Christian convictions are true; and the only reason for participation in the church is that it is the community that pledges to form its life by that truth.[15]

Central to Hauerwas's understanding of Christian social ethics is the church that is shaped by the story of God. Church is a "distinct society" because it is shaped by the story of God, a distinct story that is not identical to the stories that inform those not part of church. "Hearing the story" and learning to live in a way that is "faithful to that story" presupposes a community; it is not an individualist venture that Hauerwas promotes. In community Christians can, on this view, discover their peculiar identity as an alternative society in society. The church, furthermore, sees itself as a society shaped by Christian convictions that are understood to be true.[16]

Hauerwas further describes his view of ethics: "Every social ethic involves a narrative, whether it is concerned with the formulation of basic principles of social organization and/or concrete policy alternatives."[17] This claim implies that, for example, the categories used in societal ethical discourse (such as freedom or equality) are necessarily rooted in some narrative, typically some political philosophy. In other words, "[t]he form and substance of a community is narrative dependent and therefore what counts as 'social ethics' is a correlative of the content of that narrative."[18] This means that Christian social ethics are fundamentally shaped by a distinct narrative. This assumption puts Hauerwas at odds with perspectives that assume a natural law to form the base for Christian ethics.

Hauerwas continues: "The ability to provide an adequate account of our existence is the primary test of the truthfulness of a social ethic."[19] An ethic that cannot make the world intelligible in a way that is satisfactory to people within the tradition in question is not, on this view, a worthwhile ethic. On this point Hauerwas's "test of the truthfulness of a social ethic" has similarities to the view that Alasdair MacIntyre was later do develop

---

15. Hauerwas, *A Community of Character*, 1. This quote brings to the fore several important features of Hauerwas's approach to ethics, all of which cannot at once be elaborated on. The terminology used by Hauerwas will eventually become clearer as the chapter unfolds.

16. Hauerwas's notion of truth is discussed later in the study.

17. Hauerwas, *A Community of Character*, 9.

18. Hauerwas, *A Community of Character*, 10.

19. Hauerwas, *A Community of Character*, 10.

in *Whose Justice? Which Rationality?*.[20] MacIntyre argues that one may assess various traditions based on how well they are able to engage and explain various human phenomena. Hauerwas does not, however, embark on such a mission. Instead he claims that Christians believe that through the cross and resurrection one can most decisively delineate an adequate account of our existence.[21] Such a claim is not surprising considering that Hauerwas declares to be in the service of the Christian church and that Christianity is "a given" in the sense that we do not get to make up what it is.[22] If Christianity is understood as such a given then it involves a "matter of fact" that one as a Christian must face; not try to assess whether it is "adequate" or not.

Hauerwas's remark about "the primary test of the truthfulness of a social ethic" is, nevertheless, a somewhat unfortunate claim. At least it is a claim that would need more elaboration than what is provided in *A Community of Character*. If Hauerwas had in his overall project focused more on this angle it should have, as I see it, resulted in more work of the kind that MacIntyre displays in *Whose Justice? Which Rationality?*. In other words, one would have expected more reflection on the difficulties involved when seeking to assess different traditions and their ethics. Such reflection is not, however, a central emphasis in Hauerwas's production.

There is a further emphasis in Hauerwas's ethical project that must be brought to the fore. It is the claim that Christian social ethics "can only be done from the perspective of those who do not seek to control national or world history but who are content to live 'out of control.'"[23] Living "out of control" is a result of the conviction that God is ultimately the one who is in control of the outcome of history.[24] If Christians could see themselves as not responsible for "running the world" it might, according to Hauerwas, release them from the use of violence (such as coercion and war) in order to secure national interests.[25] The enthusiasm to control everything might be construed as a consequence of Enlightenment rationality. To the degree that this is the case Hauerwas's idea of "living out of control" might prove a valuable resource for Christianity in our present context.[26]

20. MacIntyre, *Whose Justice?*
21. Hauerwas, *A Community of Character*, 10.
22. Hauerwas, *Wilderness Wanderings*, 3.
23. Hauerwas, *A Community of Character*, 11.
24. Hauerwas, *A Community of Character*, 11.
25. Hauerwas, *A Community of Character*, 11.
26. This is a point that Tage Kurtén made me aware of. Living out of control, in the

In Hauerwas's thought, an emphasis on church as a distinct community entails certain types of social action: "For the church to be, rather than to have, a social ethic means we must recapture the social significance of common behavior, such as acts of kindness, friendship, and the formation of families."[27] Hauerwas has further developed this in his stress on the importance of the ordinary; in other words, taking the time to care for the sick, mentally challenged and elderly is a concrete example of what a Christian social ethic might mean.[28] In a culture that seems to measure most things in capitalist terms, such as effectiveness and productivity, the practices mentioned above identify a contrast society that testifies that an alternative life is possible.[29]

For Hauerwas "the first task of the church" is to provide a "critical perspective on those narratives that have captivated our vision and lives."[30] On this view the church could present an alternative paradigm for social relations, an original contribution that otherwise would not be thought to be possible.[31] Hauerwas, in other words, does not only propagate church as a critique to the wider society but also church as a constructive nonviolent alternative to social life.

An example of church as social ethic could be the church's relationship to economy: church members are to consider how they use their money and what kind of participation in the economic life of society is legitimate for Christians. For Hauerwas it is important that Christians rediscover that not all professions are necessarily open to Christians and in realizing this, churches might regain a sense of "the moral importance of . . . conscientious participation in society."[32] The call for conscientious participation in society is also an example of the fact that Hauerwas is

---

sense that Hauerwas speaks about it, seems to be linked to trusting God to make history come out "right" which in turn is linked to a "Christian configuration" of politics, which in turn involves what I have called the particularity (peculiarity) of the church. I will revisit this theme later.

27. Hauerwas, *A Community of Character*, 11. This does not mean to say that other communities cannot hold these to be important practices. For a Christian community, however, such practices can be seen to be derived from the Biblical stories, whereas for other communities they may be important for reasons that arise from other narratives.

28. Hauerwas, *Naming the Silences*, 54n; Hauerwas, *Dispatches from the Front*, 169.

29. Hauerwas often refers to the L'Arche movement as a concrete example of such a contrast.

30. Hauerwas, *A Community of Character*, 12.

31. Hauerwas, *A Community of Character*, 12.

32. Hauerwas, *Truthfulness and Tragedy*, 143.

not proposing withdrawal from society, something that he has often been accused of.[33] A local example of such conscientious participation could be the case where a refugee found asylum at a local church in the city of Turku when she was to be expelled from Finland.[34]

In *The Peaceable Kingdom* Hauerwas further maintains that "the first social ethical task of the church is to be the church—the servant community" and further that "as such the church does not have a social ethic; the church is a social ethic."[35] The service function of the church, which for Hauerwas is crucial to what it means to be church, is however not simply any type of service. It is rather a form of service to society that is shaped by the biblical text and more specifically the notion of witness: Hauerwas claims that "the church serves the world by giving the world the means to see itself truthfully."[36] Church, to the degree that it is shaped by its story, is a counter-community in society. In other words, the world only sees that it is the world if it sees a different kind of community.[37]

If this train of thought is reflected upon in the Finnish context a critical note is in place. In a folk church setting Hauerwas's idea of church as a servant community might easily be understood in terms of church as service provider: for example, counseling for people in crisis or free meals for unemployed people. While such services might be an integral part of the ministry of a church they can also be misunderstood in a way that has the potential to distort the distinctness of the church as a "community of the book." While "helping people" might be central to what a church is seeking to do, equating a church to other helping organizations fails to appreciate the self-understanding of Christianity.[38] Hauerwas writes:

> The church does not exist to ask what needs doing to keep the world running smoothly and then to motivate our people to go do it. The church is not to be judged by how useful we are as a "supportive institution" and our clergy as members of a "helping

---

33. See e.g. Stout, *Democracy and Tradition*, 147–148.
34. Reported by the newspaper Helsingin Sanomat.
35. Hauerwas, *The Peaceable Kingdom*, 99.
36. Hauerwas, *The Peaceable Kingdom*, 101, 102.
37. E.g. Hauerwas, *The Peaceable Kingdom*, 101–102; Hauerwas and Willimon, *Where Resident Aliens Live*, 46.
38. Hauerwas suggests that "there is a faithful and an unfaithful way to feed the poor" (Hauerwas and Vanier, *Living Gently*, 55.) The context for this quote is Hauerwas's claim that the world is based on speed and efficiency, while the church should offer an alternative to this.

profession." The church has its own reason for being, hid within its own mandate and not found in the world.[39]

This is not, however, to say that people who are not Christians could not help people in crisis or feed unemployed. It can also be questioned if one can meaningfully make a distinction between, for example, giving someone a loaf of bread "for the sake of Christ" and simply giving someone a loaf of bread. I would argue that from the perspective of a church that sees its ministry as part of its missionary task in the world one might make a distinction: a Christian might think that it is important to help others because it reflects something of God, or because it can be a form of witness to the kingdom of God, whereas for someone who is not a Christian, helping others might be important for some other reasons. The strength of Hauerwas's description of church as a servant community shaped by the biblical story is that it does not overlook or violate the self-understanding of the church community or its particularities in its life and mission to the wider community. In such a view the various ministries or activities of a church do not make sense without the community-shaping message of the gospel, which is seen as intrinsic to what it means to be church.[40]

In his view of Christian ethics, as in his overall project, Hauerwas is critical of the emphasis on the individual, an emphasis that has its roots in the Enlightenment. In, for example, his reading of the Sermon on the Mount Hauerwas calls for what can be called a "community premise."[41] In other words, the Sermon on the Mount should be read as a community: the recipients of the Sermon are not detached individuals but people in community. Hauerwas argues that the Sermon is understandable only if read as a vision of a community that "embodies the Kingdom" on earth.[42] On this view, the Enlightenment asks how it is possible for the individual

39. Hauerwas and Willimon, *Resident Aliens*, 39.

40. This does not have to mean that, for example, serving free meals to unemployed people would simply be a means to an end, namely, to converting people. In my view a church can have a "holistic vision" where message and activity are intimately intertwined. Still I acknowledge that there are endless theological suggestions as to what is at the heart of Christianity and what sort of response or life it should generate in the adherents. For Hauerwas discussions about the heart of the gospel are futile, because they assume that what Christians believe can be reduced down to some essential core. (Hauerwas, *Wilderness Wanderings*, 15.) Such discussions might also make too much distinction between belief and practice, or doctrine and life. Hauerwas emphasizes that Christianity is a way of life that embodies Christian convictions, instead of primarily being a set of beliefs that one then (more or less successfully) puts to practice.

41. Hauerwas and Willimon, *Resident Aliens*, 72–92.

42. Hauerwas and Willimon, *Resident Aliens*, 81.

to live up to such standards.[43] In contrast to this one should, according to Hauerwas, ask what sort of community is needed in order for non-violence, marital fidelity, forgiveness to be possible (or at least a viable alternative)?[44] He further claims that

> The Sermon on the Mount cares nothing for the European Enlightenment's infatuation with the individual self as the most significant ethical unit. In a sense, the traditional designation of "social ethics" is a tautology. All Christian ethics are social ethics because all out ethics presuppose a social, communal, political starting point—the church.[45]

This is a good example of Hauerwas's attempt to do ethics (and theology in general) in a way that is critical of modern individualistic assumptions. Calling the term "social ethics" a tautology because all Christian ethics are social ethics is central to Hauerwas's conception of ethics.[46] At the same time it also points to the inadequacy of the language of social ethics. The notion of social ethics is born in a milieu that assumes that ethics could be a personal non-social matter. Hauerwas has later explicitly observed that talking about Christian ethics in the language of social ethics is a type of concession to people who assume the autonomous individual to be the fundamental ethical unit.[47] Such "concessions" are no doubt important in order for communication, constructive attempts and critique alike, to be understandable. Despite his usage of the language of social ethics Hauerwas is generally critical towards attempts to translate Christian convictions into ways of speaking that are not rooted in the biblical narrative.[48]

---

43. Hauerwas and Willimon, *Resident Aliens*, 80.

44. Hauerwas and Willimon, *Resident Aliens*, 80.

45. Hauerwas and Willimon, *Resident Aliens*, 81. Hauerwas acknowledges that understanding ethics as a personal non-social matter is an old debate. He notes that already Augustine dealt with the Sermon on the Mount by "moving its demands from the outward and the practical to the inward and the subjective. Such interpretation is not supported by the text itself, which has as its role, not to cultivate some subjective attitude, but rather to form a visible people of God. Our ethics do involve individual transformation, not as a subjective, inner, personal experience, but rather as the work of a transformed people who have adopted us, supported us, disciplined us, and enabled us to be transformed." (Hauerwas and Willimon, *Resident Aliens*, 82.)

46. Hauerwas and Willimon, *Resident Aliens*, 81.

47. Hauerwas in conversation 2010/01/30.

48. Distinguishing between languages that are rooted in Scripture and those that are not is obviously not always easy. The distinction, furthermore, cannot always be a clear-cut either-or.

CHRISTIAN, CHURCH, AND WORLD

Thus far the account of church as social ethic that I have provided has introduced several relevant and interrelated elements of Hauerwas's thought. In the following I attempt to further clarify how Hauerwas talks about Christians, church, and world. This is done through discussing relevant texts that exemplify how Hauerwas talks about these concepts. I will also utilize examples from secondary sources to bring to the fore the way in which Hauerwas uses these notions. Then I will discuss the particular nature of Christian community. In the final section of this subchapter, I will consider whether Hauerwas writes as a Catholic or a Protestant.

The church that Hauerwas understands to be a social ethic does not primarily refer to a Church, denomination, or movement such as the Lutheran Church, Methodism, or Pentecostalism. The notion of church is rather to be seen as an image:

> The most general name we give that community is church, but there are other names for it in the history of Christianity. It is 'the way,' the body of Christ, people of God, and a plethora of images that denote the social reality of being Christian and what it means to be a distinctive people formed by the narrative of God. We should remember that the name 'church' is no less an image than 'people of God.'[49]

Hauerwas uses here the term *church* to identify groups of people who are shaped by the stories of how God has acted in the lives of Israel and Jesus.[50] This means that on this account a *Christian* is someone who seeks to situate her or his life in "the narrative of God." Church in Hauerwas's production refers, therefore, both to local groups of Christians and in a general way to all Christians.[51] Hauerwas's use of church thus reflects the

---

49. Hauerwas, *The Peaceable Kingdom*, 96.

50. Hauerwas also notes, along the lines of his notion of church as social ethic, that church does not do a kind of religious education but instead *is* a form of education that is religious. (I might add that religious must here be understood as something that does not accept the idea that religious things can be relegated to an apolitical personal sphere.) Hauerwas further worries that making a clear distinction between the church's education and the rest of church life may give the impression that there is a difference between what the church does in worship and what it does in its education. (Hauerwas and Swinton, *Critical Reflections*, 72.) This insight stems from Hauerwas's view that worship trains people to see the world "right."

51. E.g. in Hauerwas and Willimon, *Where Resident Aliens Live*, 47 church is referred to as "a people who are universally connected across the nations." Hauerwas is, however, critical of the notion of an idealized "universal church": "There is no ideal

catholic character of the church: it can be thought of as an inter-national and inter-generational[52] Christian community, but it can, however, only be seen in local gatherings. As I see it, Hauerwas emphasizes the church as a visible and concrete community. This emphasis does not have to mean that the local gathering exhausts the notion of church: one may still speak of a community that exists through time, but with Hauerwas the stress is on a visible local community.

Telling Examples: Hobson and Forrester

The following two examples are brief excerpts from two commentators of Hauerwas. These are included because they identify central issues in Hauerwas's ecclesiology, though at some points their critique also, on my reading, misfires.

Theo Hobson in his Against Hauerwas accuses Hauerwas of making the common mistake of speaking vaguely about church.[53] Hobson charges that "It is crucial that we interrogate every use of this word; that we ask whether it refers to an actual institution or an ideal."[54] I agree that in some of Hauerwas's writings there is room for specification in how he speaks about church. Let us consider the following lengthy passage as a telling example of how Hauerwas understands church.

> However, to speak of the church as a continuing miracle simply does not sound like any church we know or experience. The church is not just a "community" but an institution that has budgets, buildings, parking lots, potluck dinners, heated debates about who should be the next pastor, and so on. What do these matters pertaining to the institutional form of the church have to do with the church as the miracle of God's continuing presence in our midst?
>
> The people of God are no less an empirical reality than the crucifixion of Christ. The church is as real as his cross. There is no "ideal church," no "invisible church," no "mystically exist-

---

church, no invisible church, no mystically existing universal church more real than the concrete church with parking lots and potluck dinners." (Hauerwas, *The Peaceable Kingdom*, 107.) As a specification of this kind of talk about the universal church Hauerwas elsewhere notes that "the Christian word for universal is catholic." (Hauerwas, *The State of the University*, 144.)

52. Including those who as St. Paul puts it are "dead in Christ " (1 Thess 4:16).
53. Hobson, "Against Hauerwas," 300.
54. Hobson, "Against Hauerwas," 300.

ing universal church" more real than the concrete church with parking lots and potluck dinners. It is the church of parking lots and potluck dinners that comprises the sanctified ones formed by and forming the continuing story of Jesus Christ in the world. . . .

The church, therefore, is not some ideal of community but a particular people, who like Israel must find the way to sustain its existence generation after generation. Indeed, there are clear "marks" through which we know that the church is church. These marks do not guarantee the existence of the church, but are the means that God has given us to help us along the way. Thus the church is known where the sacraments are celebrated, the word is preached, and upright lives are encouraged and lived. Certainly some churches emphasize one of these "marks" more than others, but that does not mean that they are deficient in some decisive manner. What is important is not that each particular body of Christians does all of these things, but that these "marks" are exhibited by Christians everywhere.[55]

I suggest that Hauerwas's writing on the church is best viewed as both prescriptive and descriptive. It is prescriptive in that Hauerwas envisions what the church ought to be like in order to be truthful to its tradition and realize its calling. At the same time it is descriptive because Hauerwas does not assume that the church never lives up to its calling. On the contrary, many of Hauerwas's books include examples of people displaying, for example, kindness, nonviolence and hospitality; virtues which are taken to be some of the shapes that a faithful Christian life takes.[56] The fact that there often is a discrepancy between Hauerwas's prescription and what local churches appear to be is at least partly explained with the conviction that the church is often unfaithful.[57]

---

55. Hauerwas, *The Peaceable Kingdom*, 106–107. Hauerwas later said of *The Peaceable Kingdom* "I suspect it is all 'there' in *The Peaceable Kingdom*. Most of what I have said since, I said there." (Hauerwas, *Hannah's Child*, 136.)

56. E.g. Hauerwas and Willimon, *Resident Aliens*; Hauerwas and Willimon, *Where Resident Aliens Live*; Hauerwas, *Hannah's Child*, 111–131.

57. Hauerwas, *The Peaceable Kingdom*, 98. Niels Henrik Gregersen faults Hauerwas for not giving sufficient attention to the effects of sin: "What I miss in Hauerwas's view of church is exactly a sense of the smell of sin, a recognition of inner tensions, the fights about authority and power, the trials and errors, which characterize all human life, including church life." (Gregersen, "Fluid Mission," 80.) There may be some truth to this since Hauerwas in my view does not give prominence to wicked human tendencies. I, nevertheless, find it strange that Gregersen's olfactory modality cannot detect such an odor in Hauerwas's view of church, e.g. in light of the above and oft-quoted

Church as Social Ethic

Another reason for such a perceived discrepancy has to do with the capacity to see: if a community is or is not faithful to its story cannot always be seen objectively.[58] In some cases fluency in a tradition is needed in order for a person to see that an action or assumption is not faithful. An example of this could be a church that in its ministry inadvertently underwrites essentially capitalist strategies. Tradition-tempered insight can provide the ability to identify such incongruities. This is but another way of saying that it can be problematic to attempt to empirically and objectively see that a group of Christians is (or is not) faithful. I am not, however, proposing that what appears to be an unfaithful church really is faithful if one only could "see right." What I am suggesting is that if one were to try to find Hauerwas's church one should pay attention to the tradition-bound character of Christian faithfulness. Hauerwas claims, for example, that people trained in the ways of a Christian community can identify the saints in the community.[59] Such saints are on this account people who are recognized in the community as ones that exemplify well what Christianity is. The criteria for such insight are, however, internal to the tradition.[60]

Hobson not only identifies the importance of speaking clearly about church but also goes on to blame Hauerwas for indulging in a work of fiction: he faults Hauerwas for presenting a "utopian sectarian ecclesiology" and that "The obvious problem with this is that there is no empirical reality which corresponds to such an account of church."[61] Hobson, in other

---

passage in *The Peaceable Kingdom* (Hauerwas, *The Peaceable Kingdom*, 106–107.)

58. Though I assume that "severe" cases of faithfulness/unfaithfulness will hardly go unnoticed.

59. e.g. Hauerwas, *The Peaceable Kingdom*, 97; Hauerwas, *In Good Company*, 181. Will Willimon writes in a very Hauerwasian fashion: "If we can't point to examples, even to ourselves, we have very little to say. If every hundred years or so we cannot point to a Teresa of Calcutta, or a Martin Luther King, Jr., or a Desmond Tutu, we Christians have a problem, because the world is quite right in judging our religion by the sort of lives that it produces. Lacking changed lives, we pervert the gospel into an intellectual dilemma, some head trip, rather than a life-style trip. Being Christian is a matter of following someone who is headed somewhere I would not have gone if left to my own devices." (Willimon and Hauerwas, *Against the Nations*, 48–49. The quote is from Willimon but it relies on material from Hauerwas, which the latter acknowledges (p. 50).)

60. This is not to say that there are no similarities between traditions. I take it that e.g. kindness or hospitality can be recognized as virtues in most ways of life. Yet I think that the place or role that such virtues are given is tradition dependent.

61. Hobson, "Against Hauerwas," 304.

words, declares that Hauerwas's church in reality cannot be found.⁶² With this his whole theological project will fall, since Hauerwas himself acknowledges that his "theological position makes no sense unless a church actually exists that is capable of embodying the practices of perfection."⁶³

The merit of Hobson's sharp critique lies in that he raises and attempts to answer the question of whether the church that Hauerwas speaks such great things about actually exists. The drawback in Hobson's attempted answer lies in his disregard for the examples of church that Hauerwas provides throughout much of his writing.⁶⁴ A telling case in point is provided in *Christian Existence Today*.⁶⁵ Hauerwas writes:

> If challenged that no one knows of an empirical church that looks like the one for which I am calling, I can give the ultimate theological "out"—namely, my task as a theologian is not to say what the church is but what the church ought to be. Yet I cannot be happy with that response, as it seems finally to entail a distinction between the visible and invisible church which I think is theologically untenable.⁶⁶

The approach that Hauerwas instead resorts to is to tell stories of the life of a church, Broadway United Methodist Church, South Bend, Indiana.⁶⁷ One of the stories recounts how the church did not consider re-locating itself although the neighborhood had become quite run-down and repair and maintenance costs were high. They were determined that they had something to offer to the people living close by. Another story tells of the commitment of the church members to share meals after Sunday services with anyone who wanted to do so. This was by the church members thought to better display what they "were about" than having a soup kitchen to feed the poor and unemployed.⁶⁸ Hauerwas does not take Broadway to be a unique church but thinks that "What was done there is done in

---

62. Hobson, "Against Hauerwas," 311.

63. Hauerwas, *In Good Company*, 10. Here quoted from Hobson, "Against Hauerwas," 310.

64. E.g. Hauerwas and Willimon, *Resident Aliens*; Hauerwas and Willimon, *Where Resident Aliens Live*; Hauerwas, *With the Grain of the Universe*, 230. Hauerwas, *Hannah's Child*, 287 also provides some examples of church, but it was obviously published only some years after Hobson's critique.

65. Hauerwas, *Christian Existence Today*, 111–131.

66. Hauerwas, *Christian Existence Today*, 112.

67. Hauerwas, *Christian Existence Today*, 115–121.

68. Hauerwas, *Christian Existence Today*, 120.

every church."⁶⁹ "The crucial issue," however according to Hauerwas "is whether the church is willing to trust that God is really present among us, making us his church."⁷⁰

There is nothing spectacular about the church Hauerwas describes. Most of the members were not extraordinary in any specific way. Yet they are taken to be an example of what a life shaped by Christian convictions might turn out to be. In his recent memoir Hauerwas writes in a similar fashion:

> People often ask, "Where is the church you allege is so central for the world? Where is the church that is the necessary condition for rightly knowing the way things are? Where is the church that is the end of war?" I believe with all my heart that this church is present in congregations like Aldersgate. Aldersgate is not an exception. Such congregations exist everywhere, but we have to be able to recognize them for what they are.⁷¹

This quote brings me back to the point previously made about seeing, and the need to have one's capacity to see trained. To find such a church one would have to pay attention to the lives of ordinary Christians for whom the story of Jesus in various ways in various moments shapes their everyday lives. One would also have to keep in mind that on this account Christians may be unfaithful to their calling. Hauerwas's church, therefore, is best found in certain moments on a "grass-roots level," just to the extent that the lives of ordinary people are formed by Christian convictions. The fact that Hauerwas in his writing gives numerous examples of such Christian formation I take to be a good reason for not calling his ecclesiology utopian. It may, however, seem utopian if one does not allow for the idea

---

69. Hauerwas, *Christian Existence Today*, 121.

70. Hauerwas, *Christian Existence Today*, 121.

71. Hauerwas, *Hannah's Child*, 221–222. Aldersgate United Methodist Church, Chapel Hill, North Carolina, is the church that Hauerwas frequently attended. The following describes his participation in the church and, more importantly, gives another example of a life in which conviction entails a kind of political activity: "For many years, Paula and I gave all we had to Aldersgate. Paula often celebrated and preached. I sometimes preached. I particularly liked to preach when Paula celebrated. I even taught sixth-graders for a short period. The period was short because apparently I had no special gifts for teaching sixth-graders. We were humbled by the quiet and good lives of those who worshiped at Aldersgate. Wanda, for example, was a code breaker for the Navy during World War II. She told us on lay Sunday how in the process of teaching young Japanese women how to quilt she had discovered how horrible the bombing of Japan had been. She joined a protest movement of quilters against war. They encircle the Pentagon with peace quilts." (Hauerwas, *Hannah's Child*, 221.)

that a Christian community, including its understanding of what is (or is not) faithful, is shaped by a distinct tradition.

Duncan Forrester serves as the second clarifying example. In the following Forrester tries to clarify Hauerwas's notion of church:

> The talk here is of the calling of the church rather than its empirical reality, which is often sadly different. A church which is serious about its faith must seek to shape its life by that faith; before it addresses 'the world' about God's justice and calls for obedience, it must make serious efforts to frame its structures and its relationships so that they show something of the truth and worth of what it proclaims. A blatant and unacknowledged contradiction between the teaching and the life of the church is a scandal which makes the message implausible.
>
> Hauerwas and his allies have been deeply influenced by the Mennonite tradition, and tend by 'church' to mean the small local congregation of disciples, nurturing an absolutist ethic and existing as a kind of counter-culture, in tension with the broader society, when they speak of the church. But similar principles are true when different and broader ecclesiologies are involved. Magisterial social teaching on justice, on subsidiary, on any social issue loses credibility if the church concerned appears to make little effort to apply the teaching to its own life and structures. In this sense it is indeed necessary to be a social ethic if that ethic and the faith of which it is an expression are to be credible in broader circles.[72]

There are three comments that I want to make with regard to Forrester's reflection. The first is that without communities that struggle to embody their convictions Christian witness, or any attempt to understand a Christian tradition, even in our context, becomes unintelligible. Body language is determinative to face-to-face communication and communicating a way of life is no exception. This is an important critique toward an intellectualization and verbalization of Christianity that has been typical in our context.[73]

Secondly, I do not think that Forrester's claim that Hauerwas simply talks about the calling of the church is correct. The reason being, as alluded above that Hauerwas writes both in a prescriptive and a descriptive mode.

---

72. Forrester, "Social Justice and Welfare," 202–203.

73. Tage Kurtén has critically pointed out that an "intellectualization and verbalization of Christianity has been typical in our context." (Kurtén in conversation 2009/04/07.)

It should, furthermore, be noted that to speak about "empirical reality" might involve a problematic element. If one assumes, as Hauerwas does, that Christianity is a tradition that takes initiation and practice to appreciate, it opens up for the possibility that not all people observe empirically the same reality. Because virtues are relative to narratives one cannot identify the former extracted from the latter. In some situation it may require appropriate training in Christian tradition "to recognize [churches] for what they are."[74]

Thirdly and finally, a clarification on being "credible in broader circles": it is surely the case that a "blatant and unacknowledged contradiction between" conviction and life renders a church unintelligible. It is worth noting that these "broader circles" necessarily include the church in question, for a church with such contradictions could hardly be credible, or in the language of the Christian tradition, faithful, in its own eyes. One can, furthermore, ask in how broad circles a Hauerwasian church would be credible even when there is not such a contradiction between creed and life? It is, after all, an ethic that claims to be shaped by the story of Jesus as found in the New Testament. Hauerwas's idea is that through a faithful embodiment of its convictions a church functions as an example of an alternative life, a life that is not based on deceit and coercion.[75] Yet Hauerwas also seems to imply that such an alternative might not be effective or widely popular; he even hints that perhaps the church is better off as a minority.[76]

Particular Community

To further describe Hauerwas's understanding of church it should be mentioned that he stresses the particularity of the Christian tradition.[77] A Christian is someone who views life in light of the story of Jesus as found in the New Testament and continually interpreted by a concrete

---

74. Hauerwas, *Hannah's Child*, 222.

75. Hauerwas, *The State of the University*, 38.

76. Hauerwas suggests that Christians "don't seem to do well when we are in majority." (Hauerwas and Willimon, *Resident Aliens*, 151.) This remark can be understood in the way that it is easier to "live out of control" if one does not in the first place have any power.

77. Hauerwas, e.g., calls church "a particular people." (Hauerwas, *The Peaceable Kingdom*, 107.)

community of Christians.[78] Consequently this becomes a fundamental premise for a Christian view of life. It is fundamental in the sense that it shapes, for example, how a Christian understands human relationships, politics, and economy, in short, all of life.[79]

There is an important clarification to be made on this point. In my reading this "particularity" that Hauerwas talks about might be better expressed as "peculiar" or "distinct." What I interpret Hauerwas to mean is that the story that shapes the church is a distinct story. The Christian story is not, for example, identical with a nation's story. Though the church has a particular story in this sense it should be noted that church in the words of Cavanaugh, "has always claimed to be a universal, not merely a particular, association."[80] Cavanaugh's observation is a good corrective to or improvement of Hauerwas's use of "particular."[81] I do not consider there to be any notable theological disagreement on this point, Hauerwas simply at times uses the term to emphasize Christianity as a tradition in its own right.

Church is for Hauerwas equivalent to Christians in community. This is a community that necessitates coming together, and worship names the central gathering of Christians. It is in and through liturgy[82] that Christians are trained to see the world in light of their central convictions:

78. Without an interpreting community the Bible is, for Hauerwas, a "dead book" but when appropriately interpreted it can have a critical function in the community. (Hauerwas, *The Peaceable Kingdom*, 98.) This means, in other words, that on Hauerwas's account the Bible alone cannot tell the story of Jesus; the church is necessary in order for the story to be rightly told. (Hauerwas, *The Peaceable Kingdom*, 98.)

79. Christianity on this view involves a transformation of the imagination. (Hauerwas, *Dispatches from the Front*, 7.) An example of this is how Hauerwas frames an understanding of the family by drawing on resources in Christian tradition. (See Berkman and Cartwright, *The Hauerwas Reader*, 505–518.)

80. Cavanaugh, "Discerning," 220.

81. Another helpful corrective is that church is *not* best described as a *polis*, the Greek city-state, precisely because it is catholic. Arne Rasmusson in his *Church as Polis* rightly notes that Hauerwas's theology is better described as a theological politics than a political theology, but mistakenly calls the church that Hauerwas describes a *polis*. Church as *polis* is, furthermore, a description that Hauerwas accepts as an apt description of his understanding of church. (Hauerwas and Willimon, *Resident Aliens*, 46; Hauerwas, *In Good Company*, 6.) Cavanaugh, however, notes that "The Church is not like a territorial state, with boundaries that are policed. The Church does not occupy a fixed territory, but moves on pilgrimage through the *civitas terrena*"; the church, therefore, is neither *polis* (nor *koinon*) but *ekklesia*. (Cavanaugh, "Discerning," 220.)

82. Of talking about "liturgy as moral formation" Hauerwas notes: "I thought that very way of putting the matter was a mistake. Liturgy is not something done to provide moral motivation. The liturgy is how the church worships God and how from such worship we become a people capable of being an alternative to the world. That is why

> These rites, baptism and eucharist, are not just "religious things" that Christian people do. They are the essential rituals of our politics. Through them we learn who we are. Instead of being motives or causes for effective social work in the part of Christian people, these liturgies are our effective social work. For if the church is rather than has a social ethic, these actions are our most important social witness. It is in baptism and eucharist that we see most clearly the marks of God's kingdom in the world. They set our standard, as we try to bring every aspect of our lives under their sway.[83]

Baptism and Eucharist are not always thought of as political events.[84] Yet that is exactly what they are in that they exemplify God's kingdom. The Eucharist, for example, is political in that it non-coercively unifies people of different classes, races and nations. On Hauerwas's account baptism and Eucharist are also political in that they set a "standard" that people can strive for in their lives. Gathering for worship can, furthermore, be seen as a clash of narratives: in everyday life Christians are implicitly told, through, for example, contemporary politics, that God is not to be reckoned with to rule the world, but in worship Christians are told and trained to see that God's kingdom has come in Christ and that God will bring God's work to an eschatological closure.[85] Another way to put this would be to say that the clash of narratives is between "church and world."

Church and world in Hauerwas's production is not to be understood as the distinction between Christians and those who are not Christians. Hauerwas refers to John Howard Yoder who claims the world to be "all of that in creation that has taken the freedom not yet to believe."[86] Hauerwas further notes that

---

the language of the liturgy is so important. Nothing betrays the love of God more than the inelegance of the language Christians use in their worship. Some Christians seem to think we can attract people back to Christianity if we try to compete with TV, but when you do that you have already lost. The only result is that Christian worship becomes as banal and ugly as the rest of our lives." (Hauerwas, "Faith Fires Back.")

83. Hauerwas, *The Peaceable Kingdom*, 108.

84. Rasmusson, *The Church as Polis*, 188. Rasmusson characterizes Hauerwas's theology as "theological politics" to distinguish it from "political theology." The motivation for this is that the latter assumes politics as we know it to set the frames for Christian political activity. The former, on the contrary seeks to view the world's politics through the story of Jesus.

85. Hauerwas and Willimon, *Where Resident Aliens Live*, 50.

86. Yoder, *The Original Revolution*, 116. Yoder here quoted from Hauerwas, *The Peaceable Kingdom*, 101. It must be make explicit that Hauerwas at times uses the

> It is particularly important to remember that the world consists of those, including ourselves, who have chosen not to make the story of God their story. The world in us refuses to affirm that this is God's world and that, as loving Lord, God's care for creation is greater than our illusion of control. The world is those aspects of our individual and social lives where we live untruthfully by continuing to rely on violence to bring order. (. . .)
>
> Church and world are thus relational concepts—neither is intelligible without the other.[87]

This understanding of church and world sheds light on Hauerwas's oft-made remark that through varying phrasings makes the point that without the church the world cannot know that it is the world.[88] What follows from this is that Hauerwasian Christians cannot assume to be free from the world; it is just that they have resources to identify the world, even the world in themselves, and as such people they can seek to be witnesses to an alternative.[89] Cavanaugh also notes along the same lines that

> the boundaries of the Church are not always easy to delineate. "Church" is a crucial theological concept, but it often acts as more a prescriptive than a descriptive term. In practice, the Church is full of the world, full of what is not-Church. We hardly need reminding of the manifest sinfulness of those who gather in the name of Christ and his Church. In this light it is helpful to think of the Church not as a location or an organiza-

---

notion of world in a more neutral way, as a synonym for society, or the totality of the context in which we live.

87. Hauerwas, *The Peaceable Kingdom*, 101.

88. E.g. Hauerwas, *The Peaceable Kingdom*, 101–102; Hauerwas and Willimon, *Where Resident Aliens Live*, 46.

89. Hauerwas notes that the "reality designated 'world' is obviously an extremely complex phenomenon. In the New Testament it is often used to designate that order organized and operating devoid of any reference to God's will. This is particularly true of the Johannine corpus. Yet the world is nonetheless described as the object of God's love (John 3:16) and even in 1 John, Jesus is called the 'savior of the world' (4:14). The world, therefore, even in the Johannine literature is not depicted as completely devoid of God's presence and/or good order. The great problem, as well as temptation, is to assume that we have a clear idea what empirical subject, i.e., government, society, etc., that corresponds to the Johannine description. That is why I think Yoder so wisely locates the basis for the distinction between church and world in agents rather than ontological orders or institutions." (Hauerwas and Willimon, *Where Resident Aliens Live*, 166.)

tion, but more like an enacted drama; it is the liturgy that makes the Church.[90]

An understanding of the church such as Hauerwas's might lead a Nordic reader to associate it with what can be called "a believers' church"[91], or a "sect" *vis-à-vis* a "folk church." Yet I suggest that such a conclusion is somewhat hasty. Firstly, one should pay attention to the fact that Hauerwas's context is different from the Nordic one which also means that a term such as "believers church" may not be helpful in describing Hauerwas's ecclesiology.[92] Hauerwas is, furthermore, critical of a pietistic emphasis on "personal salvation."[93] Because of this the church that Hauerwas describes is not one that emphasizes an abrupt "conversion experience." Conversion is instead understood as a life-long process of discipleship.[94] According to Hauerwas "The salvation wrought in Christ is not 'spiritual,' but rather the creation of a new community that constitutes an alternative to the world."[95] At the same time, Hauerwas's church *does* entail a person to submit to the Christian story and be shaped by it. The main setting for this shaping on this account is the worship service: liturgy trains people to see the world in a certain way. The coming together of people to worship God is what makes church concrete, manifest.[96]

---

90. Cavanaugh, "Discerning," 220.

91. In this I include groups within the Lutheran folk church, pietistic *ecclesiolae in ecclesia* (in Swedish "*väckelsekristna*"), but also, e.g. Pentecostals and Baptists.

92. Despite this I think that one can make general distinctions such as whether membership in a Church is based on cultural habit or personal conviction, or both.

93. Hauerwas, *The Peaceable Kingdom*, 63; Hauerwas, *Sanctify Them*, 108. In an interview Hauerwas noted that "Pietism confuses personal experience with ecclesial formation" (Clapp, "What Would Pope Stanley Say?") Hauerwas further claims that "Fundamentalism and protestant liberalism are forms of Christianity, and note I assume fundamentalists and liberals are Christians, who reflect the formation of Christianity in modernity to be 'beliefs' adhered to by an 'individual.' Both are the bastard stepchildren of pietism run amuck." (Hauerwas, *The State of the University*, 38.) It has also been speculated that it was the Methodist church that Hauerwas grew up in that caused him to become so critical of pietism. (Nation and Wells, *Faithfulness and Fortitude*, 23.)

94. Hauerwas and Willimon, *Resident Aliens*, 46.

95. Hauerwas, *The State of the University*, 38.

96. Cavanaugh, "Discerning," 220.

Church: Catholic and Protestant

The notion of church in Hauerwas's theology can further be clarified by asking if he writes as a Catholic or a Protestant.[97] This is a valid question considering the many theological influences evident in Hauerwas life and work. He was raised a Methodist and trained at Yale but worked for 14 years at Notre Dame, a Catholic University.[98] In the *Peaceable Kingdom* Hauerwas comments on the issue in the following words:

> . . . do I write as a Catholic or as a Protestant? The answer is that I simply do not know. I do not believe that theology when rightly done is either Catholic or Protestant. The object of the theologians inquiry is quite simply God—not Catholicism or Protestantism. The proper object of the qualifier "catholic" is the church, not theology or theologians. No theologian should desire anything less than that his or her theology reflect the catholic character of the church. Thus I hope my theology is catholic inasmuch as it is true to those Protestants and Roman Catholics who constitute the church catholic.[99]

Hauerwas is, in other words, claiming to write for all Christians. In this he has strong similarities to Lutheran theologian Robert Jenson who sets as his task to write for "the unique and unitary church of the creeds."[100] These two both display a mode of theologizing that seeks to go beyond the divisions, for example, between East and West, Protestant and Catholic. What becomes obvious with both Hauerwas and Jenson is that despite such attempts to speak to the whole church catholic it cannot be done without reference to more specific branches of Christianity. I do not see this as a problem, but more of a matter of fact. Even if one were somehow to construct an understanding of Christianity based on the early Christian tradition before the great schisms, one would, at least to some degree, have to relate such a construct to more contemporary thought for intelligibility's sake. What I, however, think to be important is that a theologian is aware of the difficulty involved in making claims for the whole church: there is the risk that one interprets a local ecclesial peculiarity as an essential feature of the church catholic.

---

97. Catholic and Protestant are here typological descriptions.

98. Nation and Wells, *Faithfulness and Fortitude*, 23; Hauerwas, *Hannah's Child*, 94.

99. Hauerwas, *The Peaceable Kingdom*, xxvi.

100. Jenson, *Systematic Theology*, vii.

Hauerwas for one has not always been fully aware of how different meanings, for example, the word church can receive in Catholic and Protestant contexts respectively—a fact that Hauerwas attributes to the influence of the church that he grew up with.[101] In this regard Hauerwas writes like a Protestant. Yet it must be noted that his ecclesiology gives an important role to the maxim *extra ecclesiam nulla salus*, commonly associated with the Catholic Church.[102] This is an example of a Catholic element in Hauerwas's thought. For Hauerwas this claim, however, refers to the formative function of a Christian community: a person cannot be shaped by the story of Jesus if he or she is not part of such a community.[103] This view on the crucial role of the church in Hauerwas's thought sets him in some tension with those Protestants who maintain that a person is "saved" by grace through faith in Christ without the mediation of church. Yet Hauerwas is "not Catholic" in that he does not equate the Roman Catholic Church with the church catholic to the degree that Catholics tend to do. The Catholic Church on the other hand does not give the Christian communities that came to be through the Reformation the title "church."[104]

Hauerwas can be accused of occasional generalizations in his attempt to write for the church catholic.[105] This should not, however, lead the reader to dismiss possible insights in his project.

A SECTARIAN ECCLESIOLOGY?

As hinted above Hauerwas's understanding of church has been criticized as a sectarian ecclesiology. At this point I do not focus on rehearsing this critique but on Hauerwas's reply. The reason for this is that it surfaces important aspects of the kind of ethics that church as social ethics is. In the following loaded quote Hauerwas responds to his critics:

---

101. Hauerwas, *Christian Existence Today*, 112.
102. Hauerwas, *After Christendom?*, 26. The question of what this maxim more specifically entails in Catholic theology is a vast one. Here I simply rely on the following: "How are we to understand this affirmation, often repeated by the Church Fathers? Re-formulated positively, it means that all salvation comes from Christ the Head through the Church which is his Body." (Pope John Paul II, *Catechism*, 846.)
103. Hauerwas, *After Christendom?*, 35–39.
104. Uskonopin kongregaatio, "Vastauksia."
105. E.g. Jeffrey Stout states that Hauerwas's "arguments and scholarship often strike[s him] as unsound." (In the "advance praise" to Berkman and Cartwright, *The Hauerwas Reader*.)

> Consider first the allegation that I am a "sectarian." What I find disconcerting about this claim is the assumption that the one making the charge has the argumentative high ground, so that the burden of proof is on me. But where is the generally agreed criterion for the use of this term, "sectarian"? Too often those making the charge assume epistemological (as well as sociological) positions that are question begging. Has it not been long recognized that Ernst Troeltsch's typology presumed the normative status of the "church type"?

That I have been critical of the moral limits of liberalism is certainly true, but I do not understand why that makes me a ready candidate for being a sectarian. Insofar as the church can reclaim its integrity as a community of virtue, it can be of great service in liberal societies. Moreover, the fact that I have written about why and how Christians should support as well as serve the medical and legal professions, Christian relations with Judaism, how we might think about justice, as well as an analysis of the moral debate concerning nuclear war seems to have no effect on those who are convinced I am a "withdrawn" sectarian. (...)

> I am certainly aware that the position that I have developed is not in the recent mainstream of Christian ethical reflection. To be candid, I often am a bit surprised by some of the implications that arise as I continue to try to think through the course on which I am set. So I do not blame anyone for approaching my work (or Yoder's) with a good deal of caution and skepticism. What I find unfair, however, is the assumption that my critic has a hold on my task by calling me "sectarian." Show me where I am wrong about God, Jesus, the limits of liberalism, the nature of the virtues, or the doctrine of the church—but do not shortcut that task by calling me a sectarian.[106]

Hauerwas's strategy here is to reject the assumption that the alleged sectarian has the burden of proof in the issue at stake, especially since it is not to him clear that Troeltsch's types "church" and "sect" are sustainable.[107] Hau-

---

106. Berkman and Cartwright, *The Hauerwas Reader*, 96–97.

107. Berkman and Cartwright, *The Hauerwas Reader*, 96. Troeltsch's account of "sect" which Hauerwas does not accept as an adequate description of his ecclesial views can be found in Troeltsch, *The Social Teaching* and reads as follows: "sect is a voluntary society, composed of strict and definitive Christian believers bound to each other by the fact that all have experienced 'the new birth.' These 'believers' live apart from the world, are limited to small groups, emphasize the law instead of grace, and in varying degrees within their own circle, set up the Christian order, based on love; all this is done in preparation for the expectation of the coming Kingdom of God"

erwas challenges his critics to specify what it is that he has gotten wrong, instead of dismissing him as a sectarian. Hauerwas furthermore notes that the critique of sectarianism often rests on questionable epistemological premises. I read this in line with Hauerwas's overall theological project in which he is critical of Enlightenment inspired theologies that seek to objectify Christian convictions. What I take Hauerwas to be saying is that his critics assume premises that *de facto* are not available.

Hauerwas is then pointing out that a church that acknowledges or rediscovers its distinctness is not a church that withdraws from society. On the contrary, such a church can be of service in the wider society despite or through its peculiar convictions. Hauerwas nowhere suggests that Christians should withdraw from the world, but rather that they act in the world as Christians, that is without letting go of their particular perspective.[108] Hauerwas's view is often not well received because it is expected that a "sectarian ecclesiology" unavoidably is "irresponsible" because it does not seek to tune down its particular perspective in order to better be able to cooperate with secular actors in society.[109] Hauerwas helpfully notes that designations such as "church, sect, and denomination are not descriptive but ideal types. They are not alternatives with which we are stuck but rather are meant to be heuristic devices which can help us understand better empirical reality."[110] Such identification, in other words, does not exhaust the actual alternatives that a living community may have.

A supposedly "responsible" approach, on the other hand, is to build on a "creation-perspective," or an allegedly shared rational base.[111] It should also be noted that to talk about a "creation perspective" (as opposed to a "redemption perspective") is often assumed to be a universally accessible concept though it usually is framed within Christian theology.[112] Hauer-

---

(11:993). Cavanaugh notes that it was only after Troeltch that "'sectarian' has taken its meaning from a sociological and not a theological criterion, i.e., the Church's attitude toward the dominant culture and its political structures." (Hauerwas and Wells, *Blackwell Companion*, 206.)

108. Hauerwas, *In Good Company*, 163.

109. e.g. Grenholm, *Bortom humanismen*, 123. For a well-argued account of why the church should not fade down its particularity, see Cavanaugh, "Discerning."

110. Hauerwas, *Christian Existence Today*, 112.

111. Grenholm e.g. suggests that an acceptable understanding of ethics is one that is in tune with what we "know" about morality through sociological studies. This sounds good but it cannot, as I see it, be assumed to be unproblematic for theology to give such an interpretative privilege to sociology. See Grenholm, *Bortom humanismen*, 35–36. I will return to this later.

112. Hauerwas similarly notes that in Lutheran theology "creation-redemption"

was argues that there are considerable problems associated with such talk about creation:

> ... creation talk often serves as a means for the domestication of the Gospel. Appeals to creation often are meant to suggest that all people, Christian or not, share fundamental moral commitments that can provide a basis for common action. These appeals to creation too often amount to legitimating strategies for the principalities and powers that determine our lives. This type of creation talk is fundamentally false to the biblical profession of faith in the Lord of creation because it implicitly underwrites the lordship of the principalities and powers. Such powers are all the more subtle exactly to the extent that we either think of them as myths or believe that we create them rather than are determined by them.[113]

It is understandable that Hauerwas is critical of such an emphasis on creation since he stresses the need for Christians to recover their distinctness. The point in Hauerwas's approach, however, lies exactly here: through its particularity Christian communities can be an alternative community that opens up for the world to see that we may be determined by powers that we without the church would not be aware of.[114] As a result of this it seems

---

has become a misleading interpretative grid: "the dualistic nature [referring to church and world] of an authentic Christian social ethic cannot be construed in terms of the classic Lutheran distinction between the order of creation and redemption. This is not simply because this position has tended historically to be socially conservative as the order of creation has been identified with the current institutional arrangements, but because such a dualism is based on a fundamental theological error. Not only does such a dualism presuppose, like natural law positions, a norm of justice apart from Christ, but it turns a condition made necessary by human sin into a theological principle that even determines the subsequent doctrine of God." (Hauerwas, *Vision and Virtue*, 205.) In a similar vein Hauerwas claims that "When nature-grace, creation-redemption are taken to be the primary data of theological reflection, once they are abstracted from the narrative and given a life of their own, a corresponding distortion in moral psychology seems to follow. Since the material content—that is, the rightness or wrongness of certain behavior—is derived from nature, Christian conviction at best only furnish a motivation for 'morality.'" (Hauerwas, *The Peaceable Kingdom*, 57.) Hauerwas continues: "The language of creation and redemption, nature and grace, is a secondary theological language, that is sometimes mistaken for the story itself. 'Creation' and 'redemption' should be taken for what they are, namely ways of helping us tell and hear the story rightly." (Hauerwas, *The Peaceable Kingdom*, 62–63.)

113. Hauerwas, *Dispatches from the Front*, 111.

114. An example of such a power might be the nation-state. For a Hauerwasian Christian the church should be more determinative than the state. In other words if what the state asks of the Christian is in conflict with what the church is about a

that a church is "responsible," that is, serves the wider society best, if it rediscovers its particular story. Doing away with the particularity, on the other hand, would on this account, result in a loss of critical insight into our cultural and social situation. To recap this in a Hauerwasian way: the world cannot see that it is the world without the church.[115]

There is one final difficulty to be considered in calling Hauerwas a sectarian. It is the fact that a great deal of his work engages in what can be seen as intellectual apologetics.[116] While Hauerwas claims that theology cannot be translated into a neutral language, he nevertheless, in his work displays a continuing attempt to express and exemplify what Christianity is.[117] This is furthermore done in a way that does not seek to translate or tune down what Christians believe. This can be seen for example in how Hauerwas does not assume that Christianity properly understood can be a personal matter: Christians have traditionally confessed Jesus to be "Lord." Reducing such a confession to a personal opinion would not do justice to how Christians speak.[118] Hauerwas consequently seeks to write with the "premise" that Christian claims have political ramifications if Christians are faithful to their Lord.

There is a seeming tension in Hauerwas's theology on this point: on the one hand he claims that Christian theology cannot be properly understood without initiation into a Christian way of life. On the other hand, despite this, he seeks to communicate his take on Christianity. One way to approach this seeming tension is to observe that a truthful account of our existence is one that is capable of narrating life in a meaningful way.[119] This does not mean that Hauerwas assumes that he can convert people through his rational efforts, but it does mean that he can use rational argumentation to show that the Christian story provides "interpretative power."[120] It must also be noted that the alternatives in this reflection (the idea of initiation or possibility to communicate) are not mutually exclusive: it is not a

---

faithful Christian would have to oppose the state. (See e.g. Berkman and Cartwright, *The Hauerwas Reader*, 315.)

115. E.g. Hauerwas, *The Peaceable Kingdom*, 101–102; Hauerwas and Willimon, *Where Resident Aliens Live*, 46.

116. Nation and Wells, *Faithfulness and Fortitude*, 160.

117. I interpret the many examples that Hauerwas gives as an expression of the conviction that Christianity cannot be exhaustively expressed, only "shown."

118. In such an understanding of "Jesus is Lord" the "grammar's all screwed up." (Hauerwas, "Burke lecture.")

119. This is a central claim in MacIntyre's *Whose Justice? Which Rationality?*

120. Hauerwas, *A Community of Character*, 89.

matter of "either or."[121] Communicating a theological perspective is necessarily a process. If theology is understood to be inextricable from a way of life, as it is for Hauerwas, then the idea of process in communicating such a perspective is all the more relevant. A further point that must be kept in mind is that Hauerwas is not assuming theology's task to be to "explain the world" for every human being, but rather to be a discipline that drawing on the Christian tradition provides some part of an account of how Christians are to live in the world.[122] As is well known, Hauerwas prefers to use articles instead of substantial systematic volumes. His hesitancy to pull it all together into a *magnum opus* can be seen as an argument for the conviction that theology is something that cannot be completed.[123]

THE CONFESSING CHURCH

To call Hauerwas's notion of church as social ethic a project that entails a sectarian ecclesiology is in my view misguided. As seen above Hauerwas is critical of Troeltsch's taxonomy of the church type and the sect type. If Hauerwas's project is not sectarian, how is one then to understand it? In the following I will describe how what can be called "the confessing

---

121. I am indebted to Arne Rasmusson for this insight.

122. To say that Hauerwas seeks to write in the service of churches, that is, to help Christians make sense of their lives, is part of the picture. This is not, however, the full story since Hauerwas also relates his thought to a wide range of non-theologians. Because of this I would argue that there is a strong undercurrent of apologetics in Hauerwas's project. This is a form of apologetics that does not accept the alleged need to tune down the theological language or translate it to some "neutral language." Hauerwas makes a distinction between Christian apologetics in the second century and modern apologetics: "the apologist of the past stood in the Church and its tradition and sought relationship with those outside. Apologetic theology was a secondary endeavour because the apologist never assumed that one could let the questions of unbelief order the theological agenda. But now the theologian stands outside the tradition and seeks to show that selected aspects of that tradition can no longer pass muster from the perspective of the outsider. Ironically, just to the extent this strategy has been successful, the more theologians have underwritten the assumption that anything said in a theological framework cannot be of much interest. For if what is said theologically is but a confirmation of what we can know on other grounds or can be said more clearly in non-theological language, then why bother saying it theologically at all? (Berkman and Cartwright, *The Hauerwas Reader*, 53.) This also illustrates nicely what Hauerwas means with his idea that the work of the theologian is "not to make the gospel credible to the modern world, but to make the world credible to the gospel." (Hauerwas and Willimon, *Resident Aliens*, 24.)

123. Hauerwas, *Sanctify Them*, 2–3; Hauerwas, *Hannah's Child*, 59.

church" is a more adequate understanding of Hauerwas's project than is "sect." This view is one that is characterized by social involvement, albeit in a way that is shaped by a peculiar narrative.

In an attempt to describe the church and its relation to the wider society Hauerwas has called church a social strategy. In *Resident Aliens* Hauerwas claims that "The church doesn't have a social strategy, the church is a social strategy."[124] This is obviously a paraphrase of Hauerwas's oft-made remark that the church does not have a social ethic but it is one. Calling church a social strategy is, however, a way to emphasize and try to recover the political and social character of Christian community.

In the American context in which Hauerwas writes Reinhold and H. Richard Niebuhr had to a large degree dictated how Christian ethics was to be framed and understood. In Niebuhrs' thought Christians were either "responsible" or "irresponsible," depending on whether they sought to be "in or out of the world."[125] Responsible Christian participation in this Niebuhrian sense would then entail participation in society through supporting political liberalism in its attempt to provide peace and justice. Any Christian community that advocated what could be called "withdrawal from society" was for Niebuhr irresponsible.[126] Christians were, in other words, to take responsibility for the wider society, in order to "Christianize" culture.

A central point in Hauerwas's critique of this Niebuhrian perspective is that church does not have to choose between these alternatives. According to Hauerwas church "need not worry about whether to be in the world. The church's only concern is how to be in the world, in what form, for what purpose."[127] Hauerwas notes that one of the greatest examples of what uncritically "serving the world" can lead to was the inadequacy of Christians in Nazi Germany to oppose Hitler. The so-called Confessing Church, however, had the resources it took to speak truth and in so doing to oppose Hitler. Hauerwas says of the 1934 "Barmen Declaration" which Karl Barth wrote, that it "stands in marked contrast to a church willing to adjust its claims to those of Caesar in service to the world."[128]

---

124. Hauerwas and Willimon, *Resident Aliens*, 43.

125. Hauerwas and Willimon, *Resident Aliens*, 43; Hauerwas, *Vision and Virtue*, 204–205.

126. In the terminology of Richard Niebuhr's classic *Christ and Culture* the position "Christ against culture" best exemplifies a withdrawal stance. (Niebuhr, *Christ and Culture*, 259.)

127. Hauerwas and Willimon, *Resident Aliens*, 43.

128. Hauerwas and Willimon, *Resident Aliens*, 44.

In an attempt to recover an understanding of church that has political and social ramifications, Hauerwas draws on John Howard Yoder's ecclesiological typology. In this typology (which Hauerwas sees as more promising than Niebuhr's or Troeltsch's) a difference is made between "the activist church, the conversionist church, and the confessing church."[129] The activist church is an understanding of church that entails a heavy emphasis on developing a better society. In this type social change is ultimately attributed to God, and Christians are encouraged to support any such positive changes in society. Hauerwas notes, however, that the weakness of such an understanding of church is that it lacks the theological insight necessary "to judge history for itself. Its politics becomes a sort of religiously glorified liberalism."[130] The prime example of this is, as already mentioned, the failure of Christians in Germany to resist Hitler.

Then there is the conversionist church that is more pessimistic regarding the possibilities to tweak structures in society for the better. The emphasis in this type in not on outward structures (of society) but on inward experience of sin and salvation. As Hauerwas puts it: "Because the church works only for inward change, it has no alternative social ethic or social structure on its own to offer the world. Alas, the political claims of Jesus are sacrificed for politics that inevitably seems to degenerate into a religiously glorified conservatism."[131] The emphasis in this type is, as the term "conversionist" suggests, on (personal) conversion. Social change is in this type mainly understood to take place if a significant enough part of the population go through a conversion. Society is understood to change only if people in it are changed "from the inside out."

The third type, the confessing church is then presented as the most viable understanding of church. It is not some form of synthesis or mediating type between the previous two types. Hauerwas, following Yoder, presents it as a radical alternative. Central to this alternative is that it rejects both the emphasis on the individual seen in the conversionist type as well as the willingness to equate "what works with what is faithful" as typical of the activist church.[132] The alternative consists in a community determined to worship God truthfully no matter what happens.

---

129. Hauerwas and Willimon, *Resident Aliens*, 44.
130. Hauerwas and Willimon, *Resident Aliens*, 45.
131. Hauerwas and Willimon, *Resident Aliens*, 45.
132. Hauerwas and Willimon, *Resident Aliens*, 45.

Church as Social Ethic

Faithfulness is in focus here rather than effectiveness, though the latter is not unimportant.[133] Hauerwas describes the type further:

> The confessing church, like the conversionist church, also calls people to conversion, but it depicts that conversion as a long process of being baptismally engrafted into a new people, an alternative polis, a countercultural social structure called church. It seeks to influence the world by being the church, that is, by being something the world is not and can never be, lacking the gift of faith and vision, which is ours in Christ. The confessing church seeks the visible church, a place, clearly visible to the world, in which people are faithful to their promises, love their enemies, tell the truth, honor the poor, suffer for righteousness, and thereby testify to the amazing community-creating power of God. The confessing church has no interest in withdrawing from the world, but it is not surprised when its witness evokes hostility from the world. The confessing church moves from the activist church's acceptance of the culture with a few qualifications, to rejection of the culture with a few exceptions. The confessing church can participate in secular movements against war, against hunger, and against other forms of inhumanity, but it sees this as part of its most credible form of witness (and the most "effective" thing it can do for the world) is the actual creation of a living, breathing, visible community of faith.[134]

In this lengthy but significant quote there are aspects that need to be made more explicit. Firstly, it must be noted that such a community, or alternative polis, is by way of its seeking to be a visible church a political factor. A community with "the gift of faith and vision" that seeks to be true to that vision cannot but be political. Politics is here, however, to be understood in a specific sense. It is a way of life that does not assume contemporary party politics to be the only way to make collective decisions and relate to others. As a form of political force it does not seek to withdraw from the world but to influence it. Yet this influence is one that is done on its own terms, informed by the biblical narrative and not by cultural assumptions. As a result the confessing church may at times appear to be noncooperative. An example of this would be a church that refuses to support a government in its attempt to work for peace, or Jehovah's Witnesses who refuse to participate in learning warfare.[135] A Hauerwasian church might

---

133. Hauerwas and Willimon, *Resident Aliens*, 46.
134. Hauerwas and Willimon, *Resident Aliens*, 46–47.
135. Jehovah's Witnesses provide an example of how convictions can function as

withhold its support from certain peace efforts because its understanding of peace is not just the absence of violence. The church might point out that peace entails recognition of wrongs and reconciliation, and cannot be forced.[136]

Secondly, the authors say that "the confessing church *seeks* the visible church." In my reading this is a way to suggest that this type called the confessing church is not "there" yet. This phrasing keeps in mind both the high calling of the church as well as the fact that Christians are oftentimes not faithful toward this calling. That Christians are not always faithful does not mean that they never are. Yet the visibility of the church goes hand in hand with the church as a political factor. The confessing church is political only to the degree that it is faithful to its calling. It is not some beautiful theological thought or abstract reality that Hauerwas understands with church but a concrete community that to varying degrees of faithfulness embodies Christian convictions in a way of life.

To sum up, Hauerwas talks about church as social strategy in a way that emphasizes the church's public, and therefore political, aspect as a community with a particular narrative. The stress on the particularity of the church does not, on this account, imply withdrawal from the wider society, but rather participation in a mode that is shaped by the church's story.

A QUALIFIED VIRTUE ETHIC

The type of ethics that Christian communities are presumes, on Hauerwas's account, that Jesus' death and resurrection has changed "the world and the Christian's relation to it," in a decisive way.[137] Because of this starting-point, the type of social ethics that Hauerwas envisions is not "anyone's" ethic but expressly a *Christian* social ethic. It is a qualified ethic in that it necessitates the qualifier "Christian."[138] On this view Christian

---

a politics: In Finland the persistent nonviolence of Jehovah's Witnesses has led the government to exempt them from military service. (Vilppula, *Suomen laki*, Tu 120, p. 2064.)

136. Hauerwas claims that "the bottom line for the way the world congregates and unifies people is violence. Politics and violence go together. Violence tends to be the predominant means for establishing community in a world that knows not a God who calls a family named church." (Hauerwas and Willimon, *Where Resident Aliens Live*, 53.) If this is the case then a politics not based on violence is a radical alternative.

137. Hauerwas, *Vision and Virtue*, 215.

138. Hauerwas, *The Peaceable Kingdom*, 17, 96.

convictions function as a lens through which moral existence, indeed all of life, is perceived. For Hauerwas, discipleship involves initiation into a way of life in which one's sight and speech is trained.[139] Consequently the world, including what is deemed good and bad, does not seem the same to all people. Morality for Christians is on this view informed by a different story than is the morality of non-Christians. The emphasis on church as the form of Christian ethics involves a stress on embodiment: Christian convictions are not to be abstract but displayed in the life of a community.

Hauerwas's ethic is not, however, only an expressly Christian ethic, but it can also be called a qualified *virtue* ethic. It is qualified in the sense that the virtues are delineated from the story of Jesus as found in the Bible.[140] Of these virtues Hauerwas writes:

> [The church] must, above all be a people of virtue—not simply any virtue, but virtues necessary for remembering and telling the story of a crucified savior. They must be capable of being peaceable among themselves and with the world, so that the world sees what it means to hope for God's kingdom.[141]

From this follows that the virtues, therefore, play a crucial role in Hauerwas's account of witness to God's kingdom. Christian communities are not different from other human communities in regard to the need for virtues: Hauerwas acknowledges the fact that all communities need some kind of virtues in order to keep them together.[142] Because of this Hauerwas notes that "there is a profound sense in which the traditional 'theological virtues' of faith, hope, and love are 'natural.' As much as any other institution the church is sustained by these 'natural virtues.'"[143] That the virtues church displays are natural in this sense does not, however, mean that notions of faith, love and hope have the same meaning in every community. The meanings that these notions receive in a Christian community is shaped by the biblical stories and further shape the people of the community in ways that are, at least to some degree, different from other communities. Hauerwas maintains that church is "a community of a new age which must

---

139. Hauerwas, *Vision and Virtue*, 20; Hauerwas, *Wilderness Wanderings*, 3; Berkman and Cartwright, *The Hauerwas Reader*, 530–531.

140. Smith notes helpfully that Hauerwas's ethic is not entirely a virtue ethic, in the sense that it would rely only on virtues; rules and such do exist but they are tradition-dependent and not abstract. (Smith, *Virtue Ethics*, 75.)

141. Hauerwas, *The Peaceable Kingdom*, 103.

142. Hauerwas, *The Peaceable Kingdom*, 103.

143. Hauerwas, *The Peaceable Kingdom*, 103.

continue to exist in the old age. Because of their existence between the times, because they are a people 'on a way,' they require, or perhaps better, make central, certain virtues that other communities do not."[144] Because of this peculiar character and self-understanding of Christian communities as eschatological witness Hauerwas names patience as an important Christian virtue.[145]

A central insight of Hauerwas's virtue ethic is that who we are determines what we do.[146] In other words a person or community shaped by a particular narrative might not consider all available options valid ways to proceed in a given situation. An example of this would be a person committed to nonviolence who refuses to use coercion, such as threat, in a situation of disagreement even if it would be a viable and perhaps convenient option for someone not sharing the commitment to nonviolence. Such an emphasis on virtue entails a critique of conceptions of ethics that either focus on norms and principles and/or make "decision-making" central to ethics. Ethics no doubt has at times to do with "difficult questions" (e.g. abortion, euthanasia) but a focus on virtue brings attention to the fact that who we are decisively forms the situations in which we find ourselves, and further, inform the decisions that we make.

The kind of ethics that Hauerwas envisions is qualified in still another way that needs to be made explicit. It can be understood as a "community ethic" in that the role of community is crucial in the shaping of people to see the world "through" the story of Jesus.[147] Hauerwas's ethics is thus not to be seen as an ethics for heroic individuals, but as something that presupposes a virtuous community.[148] This entails a critique of the types of Christian ethics that focus on the individual and ascribe a secondary role to the church.

Hauerwas's emphasis on the community as something that shapes the lives of people (desires, values, priorities) is in some regards not unlike working in the academia. Writing, for example, a dissertation involves engagement on a personal level, but at the same time it is important to

144. Hauerwas, *The Peaceable Kingdom*, 103. Italics mine.

145. Hauerwas, *The Peaceable Kingdom*, 103.

146. Hauerwas, *A Community of Character*, 13; Hauerwas, *The Peaceable Kingdom*, 116.

147. Hauerwas and Willimon, *Resident Aliens*, 77.

148. Hauerwas and Willimon, *Resident Aliens*, 80, 81. An example of this is the Sermon on the Mount that should be read assuming the Christian community to be the fundamental ethical unit, not the individual. (Hauerwas and Willimon, *Resident Aliens*, 80.)

discuss texts with others. In regular seminars researchers present parts of their work and receive feedback and constructive critique from a community of colleagues. One often finds these moments illuminating not only through receiving direct feedback but also through the example set by others. If I, for instance, read and discuss other peoples' texts I often find that I learn from their example. I might notice that a certain text is structured in a way that makes the argument clear and sharp. This in turn might lead me to desire and pursue a similar structure, method or argumentation. A community of researchers can in this way make the individual better than he or she might be without the community.

Hauerwas gives a similar example in which he compares Christianity to learning a craft such as bricklaying.[149] Christianity is not on this view something that is necessarily intelligible to any thinking person, but rather something that is understood and learned through "initiation into a community."[150] It is in Christian community, church, that one can learn the language and practices of a community that seeks to imitate Jesus.

SUMMARY

What remains to be done in this chapter is to summarize the central elements of Hauerwas's notion of church as social ethic that have surfaced in the account I have provided. In addition to this I will also tentatively suggest how Hauerwas's theology can be a resource for a meaningful understanding of witness in our present context.

In this chapter I suggested that the two foundational aspects of Hauerwas's view of ethics are the significance of "Jesus" and "church." Hauerwas talks about church as social ethic in a way that emphasizes the church's political aspect as a community with a particular narrative. Narrative is then an inescapable feature in Hauerwas's ethics. This ethics is also to be seen as expressly a Christian ethic in that it requires the qualifier "Christian."[151] Church as social ethic is not to be understood as a complete ecclesiology. It is instead better seen as an attempt to work out some of the issues that surface in an attempt to experience life through the conviction that God raised Jesus. Hauerwas's church as social ethic does, however, have ecclesiological repercussions in that it entails an understanding of the relationship between church and the wider society that is best de-

---

149. Hauerwas, *Hannah's Child*, 17–20, 27–33.
150. Hauerwas, *Unleashing the Scripture*, 35.
151. Hauerwas, *The Peaceable Kingdom*, 17, 96.

scribed with the notion of "confessing church." Central to this perspective is not sectarianism but a kind of involvement in society that is shaped by the church's narrative. This perspective can in my view be appropriated in various established ecclesial and denominational settings, while it can also provide a helpful critique to, for example, hidden violent structures or practices of an established Church or denomination.

Because Christianity, on Hauerwas's account, is a way of life and not only a way of thinking it is, therefore, inherently political. The notion of church as social ethic entails a configuration of politics that seeks to be faithful to Christian convictions. This involves a reliance on God to ultimately be in control of history, or "living out of control" to use the Hauerwasian expression. Church, for Hauerwas

> does not exist to provide an ethos for democracy or any other form of social organization, but stands as a political alternative to every nation, witnessing to the kind of social life possible for those that have been formed by the story of Christ.[152]

This means that church as social ethic is an ongoing attempt of a community to learn to live faithfully in the world that has opened up to them in or through their convictions. The account that I have provided of church as social ethic, as well as church as social strategy, sought to describe Christian participation in society as such a peculiar politics. An example of such participation could be the conviction that one should not lie. Such a disposition will sooner or later lead to conflict if one happens to be in a context in which some forms of "untruth-speaking" is accepted. In other words, such a conception of Christianity can hardly be called a personal matter.

The alternative political reality that church on this account represents is most decisively demonstrated in the gathering of people for worship. Liturgy, therefore, receives a central role in Hauerwas's take on Christian ethics: "Because the Christian story is an enacted story, liturgy is probably a much more important resource than are doctrines or creeds for helping us to hear, tell, and live the story of God."[153] Church as social ethic is, the way that the notion is interpreted here, similar to liturgy in that it is an enacted ethics; it is a way of life that embodies Christian convictions. As such it is a form of witness. The kind of "communication" that such witness is

---

152. Hauerwas, *A Community of Character*, 12.
153. Hauerwas, *The Peaceable Kingdom*, 26.

does not isolate verbal doctrinal proclamation from the "body-language" of a Christian community. It is, rather, enacted communication.

The emphasis on embodiment (instead of knowledge) in ethical matters, as well as the emphasis on the inherently public and political character of Christian community are, according to this project, meaningful resources in an attempt to understand Christian witness in our present context. These interrelated themes are meaningful because they flow from a perspective that avoids reduction of Christian language. This, I suggest, is a strength in Hauerwas's approach. Another strength of this approach to ethics is that it involves a late modern way of thinking. Hauerwas's theological project, including the notion of church as social ethic, is not operating with modern assumptions about human rationality and the possibility to gain an objective perspective on human life. This is a strength because Hauerwas's perspective corresponds with the postmodern turn that has forcefully questioned the idea of the possibility of an objective perspective.[154] Hauerwas seeks to work out some of the implications for Christian ethics that a contextual perspective involves. In such a project the role of narrative and tradition are accentuated. The premises for theological and ethical thinking do not rest on some alleged objective or universal foundation but are rooted in the Christian tradition. From this follows that Christian theology cannot claim to be intelligible to all, at least without an openness toward what Christians through the ages have believed.[155]

The type of tradition and narrative emphasizing ethics that Hauerwas's church as social ethic stands for is, according to this chapter, a valuable contribution and corrective to Nordic ethical discourse, which often is permeated by natural law approaches. A Hauerwasian perspective is valuable in that it does not assume a god's-eye viewpoint. Instead it reflects on Christian life explicitly with resources provided by Christian tradition, from the perspective *de facto* available, the context-bound perspective. Yet this is a perspective that claims to stand for a unique outlook on life: life in view of the central Christian conviction that God raised Jesus.[156] As such it is, I would argue, a constructive contribution to any discourse that reflects on how to live life well.

---

154. See e.g. Sigurdson and Svenungsson, *Postmodern teologi*, 9–13.

155. "What Christians through the ages have believed" involves on this view a continuing work of interpretation, which constitutes a Christian tradition.

156. A reference such as this to the resurrection does not claim to "explain" what the resurrection "really" is. For a credible treatment of the resurrection see Jenson, *Systematic Theology*, 194–206.

Chapter 3

Embodiment and Truth

THE QUESTION OF THE truth of theological claims is continually relevant.¹ Philosopher Ingemar Hedenius sparked a long and lively debate about truth in his native Sweden with his book *Tro och vetande* ("Belief and knowledge").² In the book Hedenius formulated a maxim according to which one should not believe something unless there are rational grounds for it.³ Protestant theology has, however, been divided over the question of whether Christ's work is "objectively real" or whether it is only "real for faith."⁴ What I aim to do in this chapter is to provide an account of Hauerwas's talk about truth. I will then enquire how such a perspective on truth might avail resources for understanding witness in a Nordic setting. In the following I will not try to assess whether or how Hauerwas's account, or indeed Christian convictions, are "true." In this project I simply do not assume to have access to some ahistorical "the way things really are." From this follows that the question of the truth of Hauerwas's account will have to remain somewhat open.⁵ These considerations also

---

1. Ola Sigurdson e.g. rightly identifies Ingemar Hedenius' demand for truth as a valid concern for theology. (Sigurdson, "Att söka sanningen," 18.)

2. Hedenius, *Tro och vetande*, 384.

3. Hedenius, *Tro och vetande*, 35. Anders Jeffner is a key theologian in the Nordic context that has done theology in the wake of Hedenius. See e.g. Jeffner, *Theology and Integration*, 73; Jeffner, *Vägar till teologi*, 107.

4. Yoder, *The Politics of Jesus*, 156. Yoder's point is that the question is problematic. On his view "History does not read itself" and the story of Jesus provides a distinct perspective on the "facts" of history (Yoder, *The Politics of Jesus*, 246–247).

5. Truth can be spoken about in many ways. One might, for example, speak about truths that one can *de facto* have access to which is not the same as speaking about

suggest that the perspective assumed in this study is critical of Hedenius' maxim: the kind of objective rational grounds that Hedenius called for is not taken to be possible. In this study, therefore, "the proof of the pudding is in the eating"; objective rational grounds for faith is not possible, because faith requires initiation in order to be rational.[6] In what follows my focus is on how Hauerwas talks about truth and how that might help articulate a meaningful notion of witness.[7]

In this chapter I present an aspect of Hauerwas's thought that is closely related to the notion of church as social ethic. Central to this aspect is an emphasis on *truthfulness*—understood as a life of embodied convictions learned through initiation into a particular tradition—*rather than* "*truth*" (in some abstract sense).

Considering the fact that there are a number of ways to approach the question of truth in theology it is important to know what one is to read into Hauerwas's talk about truth. In order to get a grip of Hauerwas's use of the word I will utilize an example: the old Christian assertion "Jesus is Lord." Asking what it means to claim such a proclamation as true rises a number of questions that I will not explicitly discuss.[8] My interest lies in

---

truth in an abstract ontological sense. This is a central theme in this chapter. Despite this I agree with Robert Jenson in the following: "We may press theology's claim very bluntly by noting that theology, with whatever sophistication or lack thereof, claims to know the one God of all and so to know the one decisive fact about all things, so that theology must be either a universal and founding discipline or a delusion." (Jenson, *Systematic Theology*, 20.) On Jenson's view Christian theology, in other words, necessarily includes a bold claim. It must be noted, however, that a claim "to know the one God" does not include far-reaching claims about how we are to live in light of this conviction. It does not, in other words, claim to provide a unanimous system of thought or way of life. I would also add to this though that speaking about a "fact" seems to preclude the need for initiation into a tradition.

6. This does not mean that one cannot critically discuss incongruities and inconsistencies in, for example, the claims that a community makes.

7. Hauerwas's claim in the previous chapter that Christian convictions are true raised the need to study further how Hauerwas's talk about truth could be meaningfully understood. This chapter can, therefore, be seen as an extended attempt to define and exemplify Hauerwas' notion of truth. My task is continually to explore and describe.

8. For example, what is meant by "Jesus" and "Lord"; what is the meaning of the claim; is it a truth that anyone can grasp or are there prerequisites for accepting such a truth; what, if any, is the role of context and community in the conviction that Jesus is Lord; what was the meaning of the claim in the early church; which theories of truth would this early creed have to fulfill in order to be trustworthy (and who gets to decide that); would it be a mistake in the first place to approach the claim with various theories of truth; is "Jesus is Lord" a claim about the world or a proclamation that has

certain emphases that Hauerwas displays in his perspective on truth. In order to describe these emphases I will both attend to specific passages in Hauerwas's writings that discuss truth as well as make some general observations about Hauerwas's theology that impact his view of truth.

TRUTH AND EMBODIMENT

In everyday life we tend to speak about truth in the sense that it is something that corresponds with "the way things really are."[9] For instance it would be true to say that Åbo Cathedral is located next to my workplace. If I, however, were to say that the Cathedral is several kilometers from my workplace it would be untrue. In a case such as this it would be easy to find out whether there is an agreement or correspondence between what I said and what really is the case. Truth, however, is not necessarily to be understood equally when religious issues are discussed, as when "things of this world" are discussed. If I say in addition to "Åbo Cathedral is located next to my workplace" that "Jesus is Lord," it is evident that these two confessions are different in kind. They might have several similarities as well as differences, but it is at least safe to say that in the case of the first statement it would be easier to verify a correspondence between statement and how things are. In the latter statement, or perhaps better, confession, it is however difficult to establish some sort of correspondence between confession and reality. There does not seem to be any equally self-evident way of "checking" (as in the first case) whether it is the case that Jesus is Lord. In the case of a religious claim there does not seem to be a way of disentangling oneself from how language is used in the claim made, in order to somehow verify its truth objectively.

Taking into consideration the fact that "things of God" are in some ways different in kind from "things of this world," how can Hauerwas still go on talking about God? To begin with it can be noted that Hauerwas considers himself a type of theological realist.[10] That fact shapes what he means with "truth." When Hauerwas says that Christianity is true he means it in the commonsensical use of the word, namely, that it is really

---

a certain meaning only to people saying it?

9. The idea of truth as correspondence goes back at least to Aristotle: "To say of what is that it is not, or of what is not that it is, is false, while to say of what is that it is, and of what is not that it is not, is true." (Aristotle, Metaphysics, 61–62.)

10. On discussing the notion of truth Hauerwas maintains "I have always been a realist." (Hauerwas in conversation 2010/01/30.)

the case that what Christianity proclaims is true. Hauerwas claims that God is Creator and that God acted in a decisive way in Jesus Christ for the redemption of the world. At the same time the question of *how* God is or exists is not the focus of Hauerwas's writing. The focus is rather on how the truth or the reality of God shapes lives. This does not, however, mean that Hauerwas is a pragmatist without any concern for whether the Christian proclamation is true. In fact, quite the opposite is true which becomes evident in the following remark by Hauerwas: "We should not want to know if religious convictions are functional; we should want to know if they are true."[11] For Hauerwas it is important that the Christian proclamation be understood as truth. This truth is, however, not to be understood as a piece of information about the actual state of things, a fragment of truth. Truth in Hauerwas's writings is rather to be viewed as embodied convictions: truth cannot be detached from a community in which the notion of truth is at home.

To call Hauerwas a theological realist, however, calls for more detailed description. Within the field of theology there are many different kinds of realisms.[12] In order to specify what kind of a realist Hauerwas is I want to call attention to the following quote:

> It has been a constant temptation for Christians to find a way to avoid the necessity of being witnesses. To be a witness seems to demand that our lives be more than we think we can be. We should like to think that what we believe could be shown to be true no matter what might be the character of our lives. It is true that what God has done in Christ is true and good even though we are unfaithful witnesses, but that does not mean that someone somewhere is not a faithful witness to Jesus. Finally the teller and the tale are one.[13]

That Hauerwas can be characterized as a realist seems obvious in his words "It is true that what God has done in Christ is true and good even though

---

11. Hauerwas, *The Peaceable Kingdom*, 15.

12. E.g. Lovin, *Christian Realism*, 231. Lovin seeks to provide an updated version of "Christian realism." It is an attempt to integrate religion and public life in a way that allows for Christians to engage "the world" responsibly from a distinct religious perspective. Lovin's Christian realism includes the notion of "moral realism" that "locates human good in objective, natural conditions that are imperfectly and fallibly comprehended by narratives, traditions." (p. 24) Hauerwas's approach to ethics is explicitly dismissed because Hauerwas anchors ethics in a narrative rather than in something objective.

13. Hauerwas, "Beyond," 8.

we are unfaithful witnesses." What God has done in Christ is consequently an "objective act" in the sense that it is not dependent on how people relate to this truth. The emphasis on witness, however, points further to what kind of realist Hauerwas is. For Hauerwas the truth of Christianity cannot be grasped without faithful witnesses that embody Christian convictions.[14] The truth of Christianity is of such a kind that one cannot verify it in any extra-lingual or objective way. The only way, according to Hauerwas, that the truth of Christianity can be assessed is through paying attention to lives that are shaped by that truth. In this sense Hauerwas's use of the notion of truth is pragmatic. His idea that "the test of a story is the kind of people it produces" also points to this.[15]

The remark that "the teller and the tale are one" is a way of pointing out that the witness cannot be separated from the message. This means, provided Hauerwas is right, that the assumption rampant in much of Western Christianity that theology/doctrine and ethics/life can be separated from one another is highly problematic. Hauerwas is very critical of viewing Christianity as knowledge or a collection of abstract convictions. Instead, he emphasizes a life of "discipleship" in which people, in and through community, learn what it might mean to be a Christian.[16]

The remark "the teller and the tale are one," however, evokes the need for clarification. If it is taken to mean that the teller is literally identical with the tale, and furthermore, that the tale is nothing more than its teller, it seems rather problematic. Certainly if one speaks about Jesus Christ one might say that the teller and the tale are one. Is Hauerwas really suggesting that the same can be said about Christian communities that seek to tell the tale? The remark about the teller and the tale being one has a parallel in Hauerwas's catchphrase "the church does not have a social ethic but it

---

14. Hauerwas also notes that similarly Christian language cannot be assessed apart from or without considering the context in which it is used: "to isolate the biblical narratives in and of themselves would be equivalent to considering the truth and falsity of sentences separate from their context of utterance." (Hauerwas, *Christian Existence Today*, 59, referring to Soskice, *Metaphor and Religious Language*, 86.)

15. Hauerwas, *Truthfulness and Tragedy*, 35; Hauerwas, *A Community of Character*, 96–97.

16. This might give the impression that Hauerwas is suggesting that true church is only "the believers' church." Such an interpretation, however, fails to acknowledge the political thrust of Hauerwas's ecclesiology. His view of church is better described as "the confessing church." The difference is that the former emphasizes the "personal faith" of the church members whereas the latter emphasizes the need for a community that exemplifies an alternative society in society.

is one."[17] Danish theologian Niels Henrik Gregersen is critical of the way Hauerwas identifies the Christian community with its message. Gregersen notes helpfully that "the church is a *fluid* community that always lingers between the visible and the invisible, between its concrete actualizations as church and its yet untold stories. The church is complex reality, rich both in failures and accomplishments."[18] The notion of the untold stories of the church implies that the teller and the tale are not necessarily one. Gregersen suggests that perhaps there can be stories that are told by others than by the church. He refers to a famous passage in Karl Barth's *Church Dogmatics*:

> God may speak to us through Russian Communism, a flute concerto, a blossoming shrub, or a dead dog. We do well to listen if he really does . . . . God may speak to us through a pagan or an atheist, and thus give us to understand that the boundary between the Church and the secular world can still take at any time a different course from that we think we discern. Yet this does not mean, unless we are prophets, that we ourselves have to proclaim the pagan or atheist thing which we have heard."[19]

On this view the message of God's kingdom is not constrained by actual Christian communities. There is also in this quote a sense of "the boundary between the Church and the secular world" being fluid.

Despite this sharp critique of Hauerwas's view Gregersen notes that elsewhere Hauerwas has expressed himself in a more cautious way. In "The Church as God's New Language" Hauerwas writes: "To be sure, like Israel, the church has a story to tell in which God is the main character. But the church cannot tell that story without becoming part of the tale."[20] "Part of the tale" is not the same as "one with the tale." I agree with Gregersen that it may be better to see the church as participant in the tale without being one with it. I do not claim to have the final truth about what Hauerwas really thinks on this matter since it is not my main task to be a Hauerwas exegete. It is, however, helpful to note that Hauerwas's theology in general emphasizes the concrete above abstractions. This becomes evident when one considers how Hauerwas talks about truth for instance: there is a strong emphasis on embodiment of truth instead of possession of some

---

17. E.g. Hauerwas, *The Peaceable Kingdom*, 99.
18. Gregersen, "Fluid Mission," 74.
19. Gregersen, "Fluid Mission," 83–84, quoting Barth, *Church Dogmatics*, 55.
20. Gregersen, "Fluid Mission," 79, quoting Berkman and Cartwright, *The Hauerwas Reader*, 149.

metaphysical[21] convictions that remain unembodied. Hauerwas, in other words, stresses the concrete and tangible aspects of Christian convictions instead of more metaphysical aspects. Likewise, witness is not so much about what is being said or claimed *verbally* as it is about embodied convictions that are *displayed* in Christian lives.

From this perspective I want to conclude that Hauerwas's remark on the teller and the tale being one can meaningfully be interpreted as yet another way of stressing embodiment. On this account there would not be a substantial difference in the quote from Hauerwas I cited and the one that Gregersen cited. The point in both is that for the tale to be intelligible and meaningful to those not participating in the tale it must be embodied by the teller. This does not, however, have to preclude a notion of the tale being something more than that what is embodied by the teller. This interpretation of Hauerwas's remark weakens Gregersen's critique considerably. By paying attention to Hauerwas's overall project one can meaningfully interpret many of the "one-liners" that Hauerwas is known for. The oft-quoted line "the church does not have a social ethic but it is one" should not according to this interpretation be read too dogmatically.[22] It can rather be viewed as a notion that emphasizes embodied convictions over a conception of ethics in which the role of knowledge is central, while it does not rule out that the church might have some "untold stories."

CHRISTIANS IN THE MIDST OF OTHER STORIES

A central emphasis for Hauerwas is also that self must be transformed in order to see the truth of Christian convictions. As a result "the Christian doctrine of sanctification is central for assessing the epistemological status of Christian convictions."[23] The example that Hauerwas gives is talk about sin: in order to understand what it is one must have already begun a new way of life.[24] The following lengthy quote further emphasizes the need for transformation of self and need for embodiment of convictions, but also contains an important reference to "reference":

21. The word is here used in Jenson's sense. He maintains that theology "claims to know elements of reality that are not directly available to the empirical sciences" (Jenson, *Systematic Theology*, 20.)

22. Hauerwas, *The Peaceable Kingdom*, 99; Hauerwas, *Christian Existence Today*, 101.

23. Hauerwas, *Christian Existence Today*, 10.

24. Hauerwas, *Christian Existence Today*, 10.

> Therefore, the most important knowledge Christian convictions involve, and there is much worth knowing for which Christians have no special claim, requires a transformation of the self. Christianity is no "worldview," not a form of primitive metaphysics, that can be assessed in comparison to alternative worldviews. Rather, Christians are people who remain convinced that the truthfulness of their beliefs must be demonstrated in their lives. There is a sense in which Christian convictions are self-referential, but the reference is not to propositions but to lives. While such a view has similarities to some pragmatic theories of truth, I suspect that the Christian sense of "fruitfulness" involves a "realism" that might make some advocates of those theories uneasy.[25]

Hauerwas notes here that Christian convictions can be seen as "self-referential." The way I read this is that if a Christian declares "Jesus is Lord," the words cannot be verified to refer to some extra-lingual reality. The only meaningful reference that the words can have is to a life or lives that have been shaped by the declaration. It is also worth noting that Hauerwas refers to pragmatic theories of truth and yet finds them inadequate in capturing an idea such as the notion of "fruitfulness." This is an example of Hauerwas's hesitancy to align himself too closely with some philosophical system or approach that might in the final analysis be foreign to the biblical narrative. It seems that there are similarities in "some pragmatic theories of truth" but it might well be, as Hauerwas here suggests, that, for example, a Christian understanding of fruitfulness might not fit into such a theory.

The observation that truth in religious matters does not seem to lend itself to verification in the same way as truth of empirical issues do, raises a question that must be voiced. The question concerns how one can know whether a community (such as a church) rests on a solid "epistemological foundation." This is not necessarily a helpful question since the language of "knowing" may be misleading when one tries to understand religious truth. Despite this it is a question that seems inevitable in a modern context that is permeated by a felt need to validate religious claims rationally or "scientifically." This is also a question that seems inevitable in a religious situation that exhibits a number of competing religious traditions.[26] One

---

25. Hauerwas, *Christian Existence Today*, 10. (In passing it can be observed that this passage has striking similarities to Hauerwas, *The Peaceable Kingdom*, 16.)

26. Hauerwas notes that when we acknowledge that we are bearers of a tradition the question that arises is "whether the tradition is more or less truthful." (Hauerwas, *The Peaceable Kingdom*, 45.) He then goes on to suggest that "At least one of the

must thus recognize that there may be other communities, for example among Jews and Muslims that also display virtuous lives. When this question is asked it seems problematic to say, "just look at what beautiful lives this community leads —they must be on to something." In other words, is there any way of "rating" or assessing traditions and communities? Hauerwas writes the following:

> . . . it may appear that Christians are left with nothing to say other than "try it—you will like it." As a result, Christians are epistemologically in the same position as Nazis or Moonies. Yet such a conclusion is false because the content of the convictions of those communities cannot stand challenge scientifically, metaphysically, or morally. However, that does not mean that disputes between all communities can be resolved by applying such tests. For example, I do not think the differences among Jews, Christians and Muslims, can be settled in terms of what we know here and now. To realize that is to begin to appreciate what it means to live eschatologically.[27]

On this view some communities can be identified as less than sufficient by drawing attention to their failure to stand certain challenges that they encounter. In some cases people from different communities might thus be able to tell that a certain community is, for example, internally incoherent or lacks resources to sustain itself. Hauerwas notes that in some cases it might not be possible to "settle differences." Various communities might have differing understandings of what kind of challenges a community or tradition should be able to face. They might further have differing views of what criteria are to be used for assessing a tradition, or how virtues are to be understood. The remark that the "content of the convictions" of certain traditions might not be able to stand against scientific, metaphysical or moral challenges is also in my reading somewhat unfortunate, particularly because Hauerwas does not at this point elaborate on what such challenges might be. If one assumes, as Hauerwas does, that there is no "view from nowhere" it is difficult to establish scientific, metaphysical or moral criteria that a tradition, if it is to be adequate, should be able to face. Elsewhere Hauerwas, however, suggests "working criteria" for assessing traditions:

---

conditions of a truthful tradition is its own recognition that it is not final, that it needs to grow and change if it is to adequately shape our futures in a faithful manner." (Hauerwas, *The Peaceable Kingdom*, 45.) I agree with Hauerwas: the work of interpretation of the Christian tradition is never-ending, and therefore, no interpretation should be given a "final" status.

27. Hauerwas, *Christian Existence Today*, 10–11.

"Any story which we adopt, or allow to adopt us, will have to display: (1) power to release us from destructive alternatives; (2) ways of seeing through current distortions; (3) room to keep us from having to resort to violence; (4) a sense for the tragic: how meaning transcends power."[28] These criteria are not to be seen as an attempt to formulate exhaustive or clear-cut standards. They are rather better seen as factors that allow a tradition to sustain a way of life. Nazism, to take Hauerwas's example, leads to violence and as such is not a sufficient ideology. Hauerwas maintains that by paying attention to how a tradition or ideology shapes the lives of its adherents one can recognize something as a distortion or less than adequate.[29] The last criterion (4) implies that an adequate tradition (or story) is one that can account for the tragic aspects of our existence. Hauerwas expounds on this criteria by contrasting "the story characteristic to Christians and Jews with one of the prevailing presumptions of contemporary culture: that we can count on technique to offer eventual relief from the human condition."[30] Hauerwas claims that contemporary (liberal) societies are not fit to face tragedy but seek to avoid it, for example through utilizing technique and technology. Hauerwas suggests that an adequate story, on the contrary, is one that can face the genuinely tragic. An example of such tragedy would be a person who is terminally ill. In Hauerwas's view the Christian story has resources to face and engross such tragedy.

In the quote above Hauerwas also seems to link epistemology to eschatology. He does not, however, develop this idea further. In my reading the reference to eschatology is simply a way of describing the Christian life as a life that does not have "all the answers." There seems, therefore, to be an inherent tension that Christians must recognize in a world with competing accounts of our existence. One might say that we do not yet have the whole story and because of that there will be issues that remain unsolved. The fact that some things simply seem to remain unsolved can also function as a resource when one faces other communities or traditions. When differing traditions meet Christians do not have to be categorically exclusive but it is valuable to seek to remain open to the other. Hauerwas notes that communication between communities or traditions should not be seen as impossible in principle: it is often the case that we must seek to encounter and understand the other, keeping an open mind,

---

28. Hauerwas, *Truthfulness and Tragedy*, 35.
29. Hauerwas, *Truthfulness and Tragedy*, 36.
30. Hauerwas, *Truthfulness and Tragedy*, 37.

because we do not in advance or in principle know what we might have to say to each other.[31]

The approach that Hauerwas takes on how to judge between traditions can seem highly problematic, at least if one assumes that there is a neutral way to judge objectively between competing communities. Hauerwas has often come under the critique that he is implicitly advocating a type of "fideism" that does not hold critical rational scrutiny. I will not at this stage go into the discussion regarding fideism. At this stage I will only note that one of the charges of this critique is that a "fideist community" cannot assess its own tradition. One of the central critics on this point has been James Gustafson.[32] Hauerwas notes:

> Moreover, contrary to Gustafson's claim that such a community lacks any means to criticize its tradition, its worship of God requires it be open to continual "reality checks." God comes to this community in the form of a stranger, challenging its smugness, exposing its temptations to false "knowledge," denying its spurious claims to have domesticated God's grace. Thus, one of the tests of the truthfulness of Christian convictions cannot help being the faithfulness of the church.[33]

---

31. Hauerwas, *Wilderness Wanderings*, 6. One way to understand how Hauerwas's work might be "in principle" intelligible to non-Christians is to draw on Ludwig Wittgenstein's idea of a "common behavior of mankind" (*die gemeinsame menschliche Handlungsweise*). (Wittgenstein, *Philosophical Investigations*, I, § 206.) This idea has been seen as a way to avoid a radical relativism ("fideism") and provide an opening for inter-traditional communication. (See Pihlström, *Uskonto*, 39; von Stosch, *Glaubensverantwortung*, 208–209) Hauerwas maintains regarding the question of relativism that "the very discription 'relativism' dependes on epistemological presuppositions that must be questioned" (Hauerwas, *In Good Company*, 158.) Hauerwas is here making the point that the "relativist challenge" is made from a perspective that assumes to be outside all tradition. (Hauerwas, *In Good Company*, 250.) I would, furthermore, argue that one should not be too eager to draw "in principle conclusions" from Hauerwas's theology. The reason for this is that Hauerwas elsewhere is reluctant in establishing fixed principles that do not look to the particularities of actual situations. (See Hauerwas, *A Better Hope*, 47–51; Hauerwas, *Sanctify Them*, 72.) Writing in a way that seeks to clarify Christian convictions even to those who do not share them has, nevertheless, a long history in Christianity—even if such activity, at least when done in a postliberal mode, can in modern times be conceived of as in principle impossible. The reasons for this concern might, I suspect, be related to typically modern views on theological method, epistemology, and the nature of Christian language. These themes will not, however, be pursued here in order to keep this study on its task.

32. See Gustafson, "The Sectarian Temptation," 83–94.

33. Berkman and Cartwright, *The Hauerwas Reader*, 101. Hauerwas states moreover that he does not identify his position in Gustafson's description. (Berkman and

Critiquing a tradition with its own resources seems to be what Hauerwas is advocating.[34] A community that does not produce virtuous people is according to this logic less than good. This is, however, a complex issue. Let us imagine a Christian community that is patriarchal and oppresses women. If such a community has gone about its life like that for as long as the members remember (thinking that it is the way Christians are supposed to behave) it might not be easy to critique its tradition with its own resources. Whether such a community desires it or not it would have to reconsider its tradition in the light of current "trends" in society. While Christian communities are told not to be conformed to things of the world (Rm. 12:2) they are not and cannot be completely cut off from the rest of society. If the rest of society comes to realize that women should have the same "rights" or status as men it cannot but impact the community. The impact can be positive in that it allows the community to reinterpret its own tradition with "new eyes" and might well discover that its own tradition might have resources that the community had not seen before. The community might also give attention to the fact that the biblical texts were written in contexts that were patriarchal and consequently the writers reflect that. What further adds to the complexity is that it is a "chicken-egg-situation" in which it is difficult to say what caused what in the interplay between cultural developments and Christianity.[35] Therefore, when encountering such "reality checks" a Christian community would have to pay attention to its collective memory and skills learned from the biblical narrative, but also to continual interpretation, while acknowledging that interpretation necessarily to some degree reflects the wider community.[36]

Cartwright, *The Hauerwas Reader*, 95.)

34. Hauerwas mentions his stress on peaceableness as a critique on Christian tradition, and wonders why Gustafson despite that suggests that critique of one's own tradition is impossible. (Berkman and Cartwright, *The Hauerwas Reader*, 97.)

35. An example of the impact of Christianity in the wider society could be the idea of hospitals: "houses of hospitality" can be seen as an extension of Christian hospitality. (Hauerwas, *Wilderness Wanderings*, 122.)

36. One might critique Hauerwas for not taking sufficiently into consideration "what we know now" (through e.g. sociology or psychology) in his reading of Christian tradition. Hauerwas's strategy in answering such accusations is to question the validity of the premises that give rise to the critique. Hauerwas repeatedly stresses that the Christian story functions as a lens that shapes how Christians view the world, including "what we know now" through various academic disciplines.

INSPIRATION FROM MACINTYRE

The discussions above have circled around the theme of justifying and assessing various traditions and stories. In a society in which various traditions and views of life coexist it seems sensible to reflect on the question of whether some traditions might provide better or more meaningful resources for living a good and satisfying life. Perhaps one tradition indeed can provide more sufficient "answers" to the tragedies and joys of life than those that competing traditions provide. Hauerwas writes as a Christian theologian. He does not only write for the academia but explicitly attempts to write in service of a concrete tradition.[37] Much theology has been done with the assumption that one must begin by establishing whether God is/exists or not and only after that can one proceed to more particular claims such as whether this God is the God of the Bible. Hauerwas is critical of the assumption that theology should be done from such a general "everyone's perspective." Instead he maintains that the task of a theologian is to help Christians make sense of the world, that is, to look for resources in the Christian tradition that can help a person encounter life and all its joys and sorrows.[38] Therefore, for Hauerwas, the task of theology is not to explain Christian convictions in some commonly understood way. Hauerwas refers to Athanasius who noted that if one wants to see a certain beautiful scenery one must go to that particular place in order to see it.[39] The requirement for theology to be done in a way that is accessible to any rational person is not something that Hauerwas accepts. Hauerwas's theology is thus a critique toward theologies that operate with an alleged detached rationality and/or try to translate Christian convictions into a "common language."

It is, however, evident that in the pluralistic context that he writes in the need to relate his writing to other traditions arises. The way Hauerwas discusses questions related to assessing traditions clearly shows that he has learned much from Alasdair MacIntyre. Hauerwas acknowledges this debt. In some situations he does it explicitly[40] but often MacIntyre's project is implicit in Hauerwas's writing.[41] Both thinkers share a debt to both Aristotle and Aquinas which explains many of the similarities between the

---

37. Hauerwas, *Sanctify Them*, 6; Hauerwas, "Testament of Friends," 213.
38. Hauerwas, *Dispatches from the Front*, 17.
39. Hauerwas, *Unleashing the Scripture*, 37.
40. Hauerwas, *The Peaceable Kingdom*, xix.
41. Hauerwas, *Character and the Christian Life*, xv.

two. MacIntyre mentions 1985 as the year when he discovered—much to his own surprise—that he is best described as a "Thomistic Aristotelian."[42] Hauerwas also identifies himself as an Aristotelian and readily acknowledges his debt to Aquinas.[43] Because of this it is in order to clarify some of the MacIntyrean backdrop of Hauerwas's theology, which also affects the question of truth which is presently under investigation.

A central question in Alasdair MacIntyre's philosophical project is if and how the claims (for example truth-claims) of a particular tradition can be more than just claims of that particular tradition. Is it possible to make universal claims from within a particular tradition? In his important book *After Virtue* MacIntyre argues that we live in a time in which several traditions coexist.[44] When these different traditions make moral arguments they are, however, incommensurable due to differing premises and rationalities.[45] MacIntyre notes that when two rival intellectual traditions meet it must be noted that one cannot establish a neutral tool for judging between the two. No neutral view of the subject matter about which the rival traditions give accounts is, according to MacIntyre, available.[46] Both traditions—provided they are large-scale traditions (such as Aristotelianism and Augustinianism)—have their own understandings of truth and knowledge, as well as of what sort of challenges ought to be met and what criteria are to be used for assessing whether a tradition meets such challenges. Though MacIntyre talks about "intellectual traditions" these are, nevertheless, to be understood in a broader sense. The intellectual enquiry is in these traditions part of a social and moral life of which the intellectual enquiry is an integral part.[47] MacIntyre suggests that for a meaningful encounter to take place (between rival intellectual traditions) "a rare gift of empathy as well as of intellectual insight for the protagonist"

---

42. MacIntyre, *Selected Essays*, vii. Bavister-Gould discusses MacIntyre's "conversion," that is his view of Aquinas, in Bavister-Gould, "The Uniqueness," 55–74. Bavister-Gould shows that MacIntyre's interpretation of Aquinas as found in *After Virtue* differs from the one after 1985. This does not, however, affect my general presentation of Hauerwas's MacIntyrean leanings.

43. Hauerwas has noted that: "I'm an Aristotelian through and through." (Hauerwas in conversation 2010/01/28.) See also Hauerwas, *The Peaceable Kingdom*, xix. Hauerwas also wrote his dissertation on Aristotle and Aquinas. (Published in revised form as Hauerwas, *Character and the Christian Life*.)

44. MacIntyre, *After Virtue*.

45. MacIntyre, *After Virtue*, 8.

46. E.g. MacIntyre, *Whose Justice?*, 367.

47. MacIntyre, *Whose Justice?*, 349; MacIntyre, *After Virtue*, 222.

is necessary.⁴⁸ Such an encounter, in other words means that the adherent of a tradition ought to put her/himself in the shoes of an adherent of the competing tradition. For this to be possible one would, at least to some degree, have to exteriorize oneself from one's own perspective and learn the views and arguments of the other tradition. MacIntyre suggests that people engaged in such encounter should "recharacterize their own beliefs in an appropriate manner from the alien perspective of the rival tradition."⁴⁹

For MacIntyre there needs to arise "an epistemological crisis" in order for a tradition to have a possibility to realize the inadequacy of its resources.⁵⁰ Such a crisis is a situation in the development of a tradition in which the enquiry of a tradition comes to a point, a situation or dilemma that cannot be absorbed or explained by the tradition in a way that is by the standards of the tradition deemed sufficient.⁵¹ Learning another tradition entails learning as it were "a new and second first language."⁵² Such language learning cannot, however, be extracted from learning the way of life in which said language is at home. As such learning the language of a competing tradition is essentially initiation into a way of life.⁵³ On MacIntyre's account an adherent of a tradition (who is also more or less fluent in a rival tradition) can in some cases of epistemological crisis rise above the shortcomings of her/his own tradition. This can be done through "The exercise of philosophical and moral imagination" in order to understand the claims of a rival tradition.⁵⁴ Such an adherent can then acknowledge that the rival tradition can on its own terms explain what the adherent's original tradition was not able to explain.⁵⁵ Even if this were to take place MacIntyre notes that fellow adherents might not recognize that the rival tradition explains a situation or problem better than the own tradition. Because of this it is no surprise if the achievement of a bilingual enquirer will not solve the epistemological crisis for all adherents of the tradition

48. MacIntyre, *Whose Justice?*, 167.
49. MacIntyre, *Whose Justice?*, 167.
50. MacIntyre, *Whose Justice?*, 366.
51. MacIntyre, *Whose Justice?*, 364.
52. MacIntyre, *Whose Justice?*, 364. Hauerwas does not assume that translation (of Christian language to some commonly understood language) is possible but notes that "To bear witness often requires that Christians acquire—to use MacIntyre's language—a second first language." (Hauerwas, "Failure of Communication," 231.)
53. MacIntyre, *Whose Justice?*, 382.
54. Knight, *The MacIntyre Reader*, 219.
55. Knight, *The MacIntyre Reader*, 219–220.

in question; the proposed solution (that draws on resources from a rival tradition) is, in other words, not available to all.[56]

The account that MacIntyre provides suggests that one could, for example, argue for the superiority of an understanding of the Christian tradition over some ideology or religious tradition though the use of rational argumentation. On this account the tradition that can best explain human existence is rationally superior to its rivals and thus the best available tradition. MacIntyre, therefore, suggests that it is possible to make universal claims from within a particular tradition.

If Hauerwas's theological project is reflected on against this central feature in MacIntyre's project some observations must be expressed. Firstly, Hauerwas does not seek to show that the Christian tradition is *rationally* superior to all other traditions and that others should, therefore, accept the claims of Christianity. Hauerwas's emphasis rather lies in his frequent assertion that Christian claims can only be known and accepted through witness and through transformation of the self.[57] As such the "superiority" of Christianity cannot be shown through rational argumentation, but it is something that must be displayed through the life of a virtuous Christian community. It can also be noted that Hauerwas hardly uses terms such as "superiority" which might in some cases bring to mind allusions of an elite forcefully submitting its rival. Instead he stresses that the witness is not in a position of power but rather someone who in a non-coercive way lives alongside others and points beyond her/himself to the truth of the tradition.[58] Secondly, though Hauerwas does not participate in trying to argue for the rational supremacy of the Christian tradition, it does not follow that he thinks that the Christian story lacks rational explaining power or that Christianity cannot meet rational challenges. Quite the contrary, Hauerwas maintains that one cannot make a general claim, for example, that "science has refuted Christianity" without pointing out which actual discoveries have allegedly done so.[59] And if or where such actual challenges are posed Hauerwas suggests that the Christian tradition might well have resources to meet such challenges.[60]

---

56. Knight, *The MacIntyre Reader*, 220.

57. E.g. Hauerwas, *With the Grain of the Universe*, 212; Hauerwas, *Christian Existence Today*, 10.

58. Hauerwas, *The State of the University*, 68.

59. Berkman and Cartwright, *The Hauerwas Reader*, 98–99.

60. Berkman and Cartwright, *The Hauerwas Reader*, 98–99. See also Hauerwas, *Christian Existence Today*, 8.

MacIntyre's view of encounters between traditions as it is portrayed primarily in *Whose Justice? Which Rationality?*, furthermore, evokes some reflections. Jack Crittenden makes an important observation: "The dilemma for MacIntyre is that this ability to step outside, to transcend, one's own tradition seems to bring him perilously close to a depiction of the liberal disengaged self."[61] Displaying traits that can be attributed to "the liberal disengaged self" that MacIntyre in his overall project is so critical of consequently seems to create a tension that does not add to the credibility of his project. I share Crittenden's impression in that MacIntyre "seems" to come close to a "disengaged self" in his talk of traditions. It must be noted, however, that MacIntyre's talk about the possibility to learn another tradition, "a second first language," takes out much of the force in Crittenden's observation.[62] The stress on "enquiry" necessarily being done from within a tradition in MacIntyre's thought, in other words, rules out assumptions of a disengaged self.[63]

Another reflection concerns MacIntyre's description of what happens when traditions meet. MacIntyre thinks, as mentioned above, that the ability to understand another tradition requires "a rare gift of empathy as well as of intellectual insight for the protagonist."[64] Despite MacIntyre calling such a disposition "rare" I wonder whether he does justice to the complexities involved in understanding, choosing and in some cases exchanging traditions. It seems as if MacIntyre comes perilously close to making some simplifications in his account of traditions. Simplification may be used in order to gain analytical clarity but they also open up for the charge that one is not sufficiently taking into consideration all relevant factors. To take an example, the case of competing religious traditions: it is not necessarily the case that one could simply exchange one's tradition to a more adequate one on a rational basis. Such a claim would give too central a place for our rational capacities. This is evident in that Macintyre writes about *choosing* a tradition, as if one's allegiance is something that can simply be given to a tradition (which seems most rational or capable of explaining the world). Perhaps this can be the case when it comes to people with a disposition accustomed to critical reflection on "the world." According to my reading of MacIntyre, he does

---

61. Crittenden, *Beyond Individualism*, 27. A similar conclusion is reached by Kingwell, *A Civil Tongue*, 137.
62. I am indebted to Arne Rasmusson for this clarification.
63. MacIntyre, *Whose Justice?*, 367.
64. MacIntyre, *Whose Justice?*, 167.

not, however, give sufficient space for situations in which a tradition is not chosen but given: in many cases one is born into and shaped by a tradition, to the degree that one sees the world in a certain way, and as a result, other interpretations might not be conceivable. Emotions, intuitions, social ties and religious experiences should also in my view be given more emphasis in MacIntyre's account.

In a similar fashion Finnish theologian Tage Kurtén inspired by Wittgenstein notes that various traditions might meet on the level of praxis, not theory.[65] Kurtén's remark can be understood to be based on the assumption that religious language is characteristically something that is not primarily grasped through rationality.[66] Kurtén suggests that it is by paying attention to the embodied convictions in a tradition, instead of focusing on differing theological constructs, that one might spot similarities and points of contact between traditions. On this point there seems to be a resemblance between Kurtén and Hauerwas in that the latter also emphasizes lives of embodied convictions over convictions in the abstract.[67] Kurtén also noted that if it was the case that we cannot rise above our own perspective *at all* then we would not be able to "talk" at all.[68] Yet in academic theology one seeks to rise above or gain a new perspective on traditions. Kurtén further noted that we might be able to detect "family resemblances" in various traditions, and therefore, understand other accounts at least to some degree.

Another example of how MacIntyre's account though multifaceted and elaborate, nevertheless, risks being a simplification is the case when one seeks to understand a rival tradition. Though it is done on the rival tradition's terms one is still inevitably doing it in a way that is shaped by one's own tradition. In other words, one can hardly completely distance oneself from one's tradition. Crittenden also notes that attempts to understand a rival tradition may lead to inventing entirely new fusions of traditions, and not necessarily to genuine understanding of the other.[69] Gerald Somerville furthermore comments on *Whose Justice? Which Rationality?* that MacIntyre

---

65. Kurtén, "Vad innebär sanning," 116.

66. This does not, in my view, necessarily mean that the role of theory or doctrine is overlooked *completely*.

67. In chapter 5 I will, however, argue that there is also a noticeable difference in the theological approaches of Kurtén and Hauerwas.

68. Kurtén in conversation 2010/05/05.

69. Crittenden, *Beyond Individualism*, 27.

does not consider the possibility that two traditions may fuse together, and both be in substantive continuity with the resultant single tradition. E.g. the conflict between the two traditions may come to be what is handed down, with the two original traditions preserved as the protagonists defined by the internalized conflict.[70]

In my reading, therefore, "choosing" between traditions is a messy enterprise in which various traditions and influences, indeed, the whole context of the choice-maker, plays parts in the equation. To characterize the role that these parts play would be close to impossible. What this adds up to is that it seems that MacIntyre is overlooking such considerations to the a degree that it takes some of the power out of his account.

A mitigating factor in MacIntyre's account of judging between traditions is, however, that he considers it "rare" that someone is sufficiently insightful about a rival tradition, that is, that he or she is fluent in more than one tradition. A further mitigating factor is that the critical remarks that I have made on MacIntyre's account have mainly faulted him for what he has left unsaid. In other words, I have suggested that MacIntyre could have discussed in greater detail some of the problems involved in interaction between traditions. This does not suggest that I am comprehensively critical of MacIntyre's perspective.

For MacIntyre it is essential and inevitable that "enquiry" is done in or from a tradition: "To be outside all traditions is to be a stranger to enquiry."[71] This is due to MacIntyre's fundamental assumption that it is "an illusion to suppose that there is some neutral standing ground, some locus for rationality as such . . . independent of all traditions."[72] In *Whose Justice? Which Rationality?* "a tradition" refers to substantial large-scale traditions such as Aristotelianism or Augustinianism. In his earlier book *After Virtue* he describes a tradition similarly as a socially embodied inter-generational argument: "A living tradition then is an historically extended, socially embodied argument, and an argument precisely in part about the goods which constitute that tradition. Within a tradition the pursuit of goods extends through generations."[73] On this point there are evident similarities between MacIntyre and Hauerwas. The assumption that there is no tradition-free or neutral way of "looking at the world" is foundational

---

70. Somerville, "On *Whose Justice?*".
71. MacIntyre, *Whose Justice?*, 367.
72. MacIntyre, *Whose Justice?*, 367.
73. MacIntyre, *After Virtue*, 222.

also for Hauerwas. Hauerwas maintains that if one tries to interpret life without a tradition that functions as an explicit interpretational grid one will simply underwrite current trends in society (American liberalism for Hauerwas).[74] For Hauerwas, similarly to MacIntyre, a tradition is a living tradition only when there is continuing discussion about what the tradition is really about. Hauerwas sees the Christian tradition as an argument that exists through time in which continual grappling with the Biblical texts is central.[75]

In addition to the emphasis on the need for a substantial tradition, Hauerwas exhibits similarities with MacIntyre's Aristotelianism. Both display an emphasis on practices, virtues and goods internal to practices. For MacIntyre a "practice" is

> any coherent and complex form of socially established cooperative human activity through which goods internal to that form of activity are realized in the course of trying to achieve those standards of excellence which are appropriate to, and partially definitive of, that form of activity, with the result that human powers to achieve excellence, and human conceptions of the ends and goods involved, are systematically extended." . . . "Bricklaying is not a practice; architecture is.[76]

MacIntyre gives a telling example of a practice. He invites the reader to consider a highly intelligent 7-year-old who is lured into discovering the goods of the game of chess through giving candy to the child.[77] First the game is played because of the candy, but after a while the child might discover some of the beauties of chess: strategy, competition, excitement and that sort of things. What I termed the beauties of chess is what Ma-

---

74. See e.g. Hauerwas, *Christian Existence Today*, 136; Hauerwas, "Testament of Friends." MacIntyre states that he is writing to "someone who, not as yet having given their allegiance to some coherent tradition of enquiry." (MacIntyre, *Whose Justice?*, 393.) Surely no one can approach any such *coherent tradition* as a tabula rasa. One will necessarily approach substantial traditions with, e.g. the assumptions of a liberal society. If one reflects on the situation in Finland I take it that most Finns, though they belong to the Lutheran folk church, do not subscribe to any coherent tradition in the MacIntyrean sense. As such they would fit into MacIntyre's intended audience.

75. Hauerwas, *A Community of Character*, 61.

76. MacIntyre, *After Virtue*, 187. Hauerwas did not learn his emphasis on virtues and practices from MacIntyre per se, but he seems to think very highly of MacIntyre's Aristotelianism, see e.g. Hauerwas, *Character and the Christian Life*, xv. An emphasis on virtue/character and practices is evident in Hauerwas as early as in *Vision and Virtue* (1974).

77. This example is given in MacIntyre, *After Virtue*, 188.

cIntyre means by goods internal to a practice. The child in the example will then through playing chess learn what is required of a good chess-player. Excelling in a practice such as chess cannot be learned in theory but only through participation and practice. MacIntyre thus distinguishes between internal and external goods. Internal goods are what can be learned through participating in a practice. External goods are what one could call "other benefits" that one might acquire through being schooled in a practice. A good chess-player might, for example, attain socially and financially enriching ties to influential people.

Many have commented that MacIntyre's understanding of practices is vague. Christopher Stephen Lutz observes that also Hauerwas has noted that it is not clear why MacIntyre thinks architecture is a practice but bricklaying is not.[78] Hauerwas has further explicitly reflected on bricklaying as a practice, or craft, that one cannot learn without a form of initiation.[79] Hauerwas is in the position to maintain this because he has, before his academic career, been trained in the craft of bricklaying, through apprenticeship to a master bricklayer.[80] Bricklaying as a craft that can only be learned through training is also a good analogy to how Hauerwas views Christianity. Christian practices for Hauerwas crucially include participation in the worship services of a local church. According to Hauerwas Christians learn to situate themselves within God's story through participation in the Christian community, in which celebrating the Eucharist is central.[81]

> We still have practices in place, in your church and ours, which can be resources for faithful renewal. But it is crucial that they be understood as practices and not simply as "beliefs." Finally, it is a matter of truth, and the truth that is gospel is known only through practices such as preaching, baptism, eucharist—in short, worship.[82]

For Hauerwas Christian practices are not, however, restricted to attending church services. A practice can be something as mundane as visiting and caring for sick people. A practice in the MacIntyrean sense, as quoted

---

78. Lutz, *Tradition*, 94 referring to Hauerwas and Wadell, "Review of *After Virtue*," 319.

79. Hauerwas, *After Christendom?*, 101. See also Berkman and Cartwright, *The Hauerwas Reader*, 528–529.

80. Berkman and Cartwright, *The Hauerwas Reader*, 528.

81. Hauerwas, *The Peaceable Kingdom*, 26, 108.

82. Hauerwas and Willimon, *Where Resident Aliens Live*, 18.

above, is an "activity through which goods internal to that form of activity are realized." When a community cares for weak or sick people it will in the process learn what love means. In this sense caring for the weak is a practice. Practices are for Hauerwas key in understanding Christianity. Taking time for practices such as the one mentioned involves learning, imitation and involvement.

On MacIntyre's account virtues are defined "in terms of their place in practices":[83] "A virtue is an acquired human quality the possession and exercise of which tends to enable us to achieve those goods which are internal to practices and the lack of which effectively prevents us from achieving any such goods."[84] Virtue is thus that which is needed in order for a person to discover the goods internal to a practice. To return to the previous example, the practice of caring for the sick would require virtues such as empathy and patience for one to discover the goods internal to that practice (identified as love in the example above). An example that Hauerwas gives is the importance of the virtues of courage and patience if one is to be able to withstand lapsing into violent behavior in a conflict situation.[85]

In Hauerwas's theology the virtues are central in another way as well. Hauerwas writes: "An ethic of virtue centers on the claim that an agent's being is prior to doing."[86] This is to be understood in the way that what we are determine what we do, or more specifically, what we might consider valid alternatives in, for example, a situation that calls for a "moral decision." Life demands us to make all kinds of decisions that have moral implications but "'Situations' are not 'out there' waiting to be seen but are created by the kind of people we are."[87] Hauerwas continues that "To be a person of virtue, therefore, involves acquiring the linguistic, emotional, and rational skills that give us the strength to make our decisions and life our own."[88] A virtuous character belongs to someone, it is as it were, the property of an individual, but it entails "living faithful to a community's history"[89] Hauerwas consequently identifies the practices of a church as the locus of Christian character-shaping. Such character demonstrates

83. MacIntyre, *After Virtue*, 193, 199.
84. MacIntyre, *After Virtue*, 191.
85. Hauerwas, *The Peaceable Kingdom*, 121.
86. Hauerwas, *A Community of Character*, 113.
87. Hauerwas, *The Peaceable Kingdom*, 116.
88. Hauerwas, *A Community of Character*, 115.
89. Hauerwas, *A Community of Character*, 116.

(in various degrees) various virtues, such as truthfulness, faithfulness and forgiveness. A person who is going through such shaping is not free to do "whatever" in a decision-situation without being in dissonance with these virtues. Acting in harmony with virtues on the other hand helps the person discover goods internal to practices. MacIntyre further describes the relationship between practices and virtues, and this might as well be said by Hauerwas, that "it is characteristic of such practices that engaging in them provides a practical education into the virtues."[90] In Hauerwas's theology such practical education might involve, for example, acknowledging that someone is kinder or more generous than oneself and then imitation of such exemplary people.[91]

Another consideration on the MacIntyrean backdrop of Hauerwas's theology has to do with *telos*. According to MacIntyre there is a need for telos in human life in order to know what the good is and what the goods are.[92] For MacIntyre the good (that is the ultimate good that is to be distinguished from goods) is "the life spent in seeking for the good life for man, and the virtues necessary for the seeking are those which will enable us to understand what more and what else the good life for man is."[93] MacIntyre is also quick to point out that the good is never something that is good only for the individual. The individual is always part of a family, tribe, network or community. In other words, we are all "bearers of a particular social identity."[94] As such MacIntyre concludes "Hence what is good for me has to be the good for one who inhabits these roles."[95] The good life is therefore necessarily something that varies depending on the historical context of the person asking what the good life is. Though this is the case, one can never, provided MacIntyre is right, search for the good life as an isolated individual. The social network (ties to family, tribe, community, tradition etc.) shapes the "moral starting point"; it gives a person her/his "moral particularity."[96]

In continuity with MacIntyre Hauerwas stresses the importance of participation in a concrete Christian community that has a sense of telos, which is to be "created to praise and glorify God" and in which the good

---

90. Knight, *The MacIntyre Reader*, 240.
91. E.g. Hauerwas, *The Peaceable Kingdom*, 97.
92. MacIntyre, *After Virtue*, 184, 203.
93. MacIntyre, *After Virtue*, 219.
94. MacIntyre, *After Virtue*, 220.
95. MacIntyre, *After Virtue*, 220.
96. MacIntyre, *After Virtue*, 220.

receives its meaning.[97] For Hauerwas it is precisely through initiation into Christian practices that one is "saved" from the violent and deceptive narratives of our time. Hauerwas, consequently, gives a very concrete meaning to the dictum *extra ecclesiam nulla salus*.

A final consideration pertaining to MacIntyre's philosophical project has to do with MacIntyre's view of contemporary politics. It may seem that this takes our MacIntyrean excursus on a side-track since this is an enquiry into Hauerwas's notion of truth. It is, however, meaningful to consider MacIntyre's description of politics in order to illuminate one central constructive Hauerwasian contribution, which in fact is linked to the notion of truthfulness. MacIntyre claims that a society that lacks consensus on the premises and aim of morality also lacks a commonly-shared view on what counts as a reasoned argument.[98] Since moral reasoning based on shared premises is ruled out protest and indignation become central to public debate.[99] As a result, on this MacIntyrean account, politics necessarily involves coercion (implicit or explicit): individuals and groups attempt to manipulate others to accept their views. For MacIntyre modern politics is, therefore, a form of civil war.[100]

Politics described in these terms helps shed light on an important aspect of Hauerwas's theology. I suggest that Hauerwas's emphasis on a nonviolent community that seeks to learn to live without violence and coercion is a constructive alternative to the coercive cultural situation that MacIntyre describes. A community that is committed to learning alternative non-coercive ways to encounter others is central to Hauerwas's understanding of Christianity. This would in practice entail learning to identify violence in its many guises, including manipulation. Manipulation is, of course, usually not expressed bluntly but "re-narrated" in more acceptable terms, such as in the language of "rights." One of the tasks of Christian community would then be to name such forms of violence for what they are, for example, forms of deception.[101] This implies that nonviolence cannot be separated from truth-telling; lying is a form of violence. As such

97. Berkman and Cartwright, *The Hauerwas Reader*, 524.
98. MacIntyre, *After Virtue*, 8, 246.
99. MacIntyre, *After Virtue*, 71.
100. MacIntyre, *After Virtue*, 253.
101. Obviously a Christian community can in itself be seen as manipulative if it suggests that its tradition is true. To such as critique it must be replied that nonviolent witness is not coercive but rather more adequately described as an invitation to a form of life, which one can accept or reject. This is not to deny the fact that much violence has been done in the name of Christendom.

Hauerwas's insistence on peaceableness and the need for Christians to learn to speak truth (even when it disturbs the apparent peace) can be seen as a constructive alternative to prevalent coercive politics.

Hauerwas's conception of Christian community as an alternative society becomes both intelligible and powerful if MacIntyre's account of incommensurable traditions and politics is correct. Hauerwas's claim that the world needs the church in order to know that it is the world is a bold claim.[102] Indeed it sounds so bold that one might easily dismiss it as an example of theological megalomania. Yet it makes sense when read with MacIntyre's account of contemporary politics in mind.

To conclude my MacIntyrean excursus I note that it is evident that Hauerwas in his understanding of Christianity draws on MacIntyre. Both men also attend to Aristotle and Aquinas. When Hauerwas talks about truth some of the key notions involved are tradition, community, virtues, and witness. Witness happens in and through a virtuous community that embodies a tradition. An enquiry into Hauerwas's notion of truth must note that truth in the Christian proclamation is explicitly something that can be seen as truth only within the Christian tradition and through witness to the reality of God. The Christian proclamation can only be recognized as truth within a concrete tradition that upholds that truth. We do not have access to some "truth in itself." Taking it to be true that God has raised Jesus Christ from the grave, which is central to what Christians have proclaimed through the ages, is not a philosophical truth that can be accepted through "rationality as such," or "independent of all traditions."[103] It requires rather, according to Hauerwas, initiation into a concrete Christian community. Through such initiation, that is or includes practices, virtues and discovering goods internal to the practices, one can then be trained to see the world as a world created and redeemed by God.

REALISM, NON-REALISM, AND HAUERWAS

As the previous subchapter tried to show, Hauerwas is not viewing truth in Christian proclamation as a "cold fact" or a "philosophical truth." What comes closest to an "epistemological foundation" in Hauerwas's thought is the idea of a virtuous community that through its life witnesses to the truthfulness of its story. In *The Peaceable Kingdom* he writes: "If we have a 'foundation' it is the story of Christ. 'For no other foundation can anyone

---

102. Hauerwas, *The Peaceable Kingdom*, 100.
103. MacIntyre, *Whose Justice?*, 367.

Embodiment and Truth

lay than that which is laid, which is Jesus Christ (1 Cor. 3:11)."[104] Though Hauerwas speaks of a foundation it must be noted that he is not seeking to establish any "objective foundation" for his theology. Indeed, a central point in Hauerwas's production is, as already noted, that the truth of Christianity can only be known through witness, and as such it cannot be secured in any objective way. For Hauerwas a God that somehow could be"proved" would not be the God that Christians worship.[105] Hauerwas has, in contrast to "foundationalism," mentioned that he is sympathetic to anti-foundationalist arguments but he does not want "to give up any possibility of some more modest realist epistemology."[106]

Claiming, as Hauerwas does, that what Christians proclaim is true, may invite various accusations of exclusivism and imperialism. These call for a thorough discussion but in this project I will simply note the following. Hauerwas's stress on "eschatological living" and openness to goodness and truth "outside Christianity" avoids some of these charges. Hauerwas's project undoubtedly has imperialistic connotations, but his insistence on categorical non-violence prevents this imperialistic tendency to turn violent.[107] In conflict-situations a Hauerwasian stance involves witness and persuasion, not coercion. Witness is something that by definition is non-violent: the witness is not in a position of power though he or she might be convinced of the truthfulness of her/his take on Christianity.

Though it was stated at the beginning of this chapter that Hauerwas is a kind of theological realist one might still seek to illuminate his way of talking about truth by relating it to the question of realism versus non-realism. Regarding the realism versus non-realism debate Rowan Williams notes helpfully that it should not be seen as a question about whether God exists but rather about how God exists.[108] Nick Trakakis further describes non-realist positions by pointing out that "'non-real' is not meant to imply 'not-real,' but a reality of a radically different sort to that examined by the

---

104. Hauerwas, *The Peaceable Kingdom*, 67.

105. Hauerwas, *With the Grain of the Universe*, 207.

106. Hauerwas, *Christian Existence Today*, 171.

107. Hauerwas calls on Frei, *The Eclipse of Biblical Narrative* to make the point that the story of the church indeed is imperial in character but that it is not to be upheld by coercion but by witness. (Hauerwas, *Christian Existence Today*, 64–65n.)

108. Williams's foreword to Crowder, *God and Reality*, v. Despite his attempt to be generous with non-realists Williams notes "I still fail to see how what the non-realist advocates can be compatible in the long run with what I understand to be Christian belief." (Crowder, *God and Reality*, ix.)

sciences."[109] Trakakis goes on to show that non-realist approaches are often misunderstood by people holding some form of realist view. Trakakis quotes John Hick as a case in point:

> Religious realism is the view that the existence or non-existence of God is a fact independent of whether you or I or anyone else believes that God exists. If God exists, God is not simply an idea or ideal in our minds, but an ontological reality, the ultimate creative power in the universe.[110]

The problem with this quote is that it implies that non-realist views suggest that God is but "an idea or ideal in our minds." Though some non-realist accounts may understand God in this way, it does not mean that is the case for all non-realist views.[111] Therefore, in non-realist views God can still be real in a very real sense, it is just that there is no way of going beyond language to verify this. This perspective thus emphasizes the utter otherness of God. This in turn can be seen—to put the matter in a Hauerwasian fashion—as a way for Christians to avoid idolatry. In contrast it can be noted that realist views (whether exclusivist, inclusivist or pluralist) risk making God an object or a being, which is not necessarily the same as the God that Christians worship.[112]

The picture that Trakakis gives of some non-realist perspectives might have some similarities to how Hauerwas talks about God. Still I would not call Hauerwas a non-realist, especially since he himself accepts the label realist. Hauerwas's notion of truth has some similarities to common theological realist perspective as well as non-realist views. Labeling him either or without careful further clarification would give a false picture of his theological project. The type of realism that Hauerwas represents might be described, for example, as non-foundational internal realism.[113] Interesting though it might be to seek to clarify in ever increasing detail what label might best fit Hauerwas, it would not in my opinion be helpful. Instead, I try to highlight how the way Hauerwas talks about truth can be a

---

109. Trakakis, *The End of Philosophy of Religion*, 74.

110. Trakakis, *The End of Philosophy of Religion*, 76 quoting Hick, "Believing," 115.

111. Trakakis, *The End of Philosophy of Religion*, 76.

112. Paul Tillich e.g. problematizes the concept of God by claiming that "God does not exist. He is being itself beyond essence and existence. Therefore, to argue that he exists is to deny him" (Tillich, *Systematic Theology*, 205. See also Marion, *God Without Being*.)

113. Tage Kurtén has used the notion of internal realism to describe Hauerwas. (Kurtén in conversation 2010/05/05.)

resource to Christians who seek to be witnesses to the truthfulness of their tradition. Giving the "right name" to Hauerwas's mode of doing theology would not further my aim.

DIFFERING PREMISES

The nonfoundationalist and tradition-emphasizing approach that Hauerwas takes raises several critical questions, some of which have been hinted at above. Hauerwas's notion of truth as well as his entire theological project seems to be characterized by a problematic circularity: Since he does not seek to write from everyone's perspective it seems that he cannot avoid falling into subjectivism and relativism. Such critical questions seem natural and unavoidable in a context colored by Enlightenment inspired thinking. Ugandan theologian Immanuel Katongole voices some of the questions that the narrative-bound character of rationality raises:

> how is one to avoid the danger of a tradition falling into complacency and solipsism about the truth of its story? Can a tradition-dependent rationality offer any useful criteria for judging between alternative stories? What form must moral reasoning within a given tradition take to ensure a sense of objectivity? And since there is no tradition-free vantage point from which questions of truth and falsity can be addressed, what sort of rational discussion can exist between two traditions? How are rival traditions themselves to be assessed short of relativism?[114]

These questions are of the kind that must have been in the mind of theologians such as Gustafson who has called Hauerwas a "sectarian, fideist, tribalist."[115] Katongole defends Hauerwas's acceptance of rationality as something necessarily tradition-dependent. He singles out four related criticisms[116]: (a) the claim that in Hauerwas's thought tradition cannot avoid lapsing into "solipsistic self-validation." Secondly, (b) such an approach is devoid of rational assessment, and thirdly, (c) cannot "account for ontological claims." The fourth critique is that (d) a tradition-dependent theology leads to relativism. Katongole constructs what can be called an adequate Hauerwasian defense against these criticisms, and attempts to show that

114. Katongole, *Beyond Universal Reason*, 122.
115. Hauerwas, *The State of the University*, 165; Hauerwas, *Dispatches from the Front*, 18.
116. Katongole, *Beyond Universal Reason*, 177.

(a) tradition (the particular) is normatively marked by a "creative tension"—phronetic attentiveness—which saves it from settling down into mere routine; (b) a social-linguistic affirmation can provide the context for rational assessment and a dynamic sense of objectivity; (c) it is possible to account for ontological claims in the absence of a 'metaphysics' or 'an absolute conception of reality'; and (d) that the nonfoundational realization of truth as historical requires the affirmation of witness as an epistemological category.[117]

What Katongole is doing here is that he is suggesting that these charges can be met adequately. He correctly notes, however, the hesitancy of Hauerwas to meet these charges on their own grounds, that is, utilizing the same premises that the criticisms do.[118] Katongole, in other words, seeks to spell out what Hauerwas might or should say if he indeed would meet these specific charges. It is not necessary here to rehearse Katongole's defense of Hauerwas in its entirety because it has already been done, and in my opinion well. What on the other hand is of importance to my project is to focus on Katongole's conclusion. This conclusion also happens to be Hauerwas's strategy in his own replies to his critics, since it is not the case that Hauerwas would not defend his views at all. The basic thrust of this strategy is to question the premises that give rise to these criticisms. Hauerwas's defense takes the form of a critique of the idea that we might establish a neutral reference point against which truth-claims can be measured. To put it briefly and perhaps roughly: Hauerwas's theology, including his view of truth, can be described as displaying a "late-modern" *ethos*, whereas his critics can be labeled "modern." Hauerwas's premises for doing theology take out much of the force of these critiques that operate with different assumptions of the perspective available to the theologian.

SUMMARY

When it comes to truth it can be concluded that Hauerwas does write about truth but the notion of truthfulness is more common in his material. A central question for him is, for example, what it would mean not to lie? Learning to live without lying is an emphasis that Hauerwas oftentimes comes back to.[119]

---

117. Katongole, *Beyond Universal Reason*, 177.
118. Katongole, *Beyond Universal Reason*, 177.
119. E.g. Hauerwas, *Sanctify Them*, 44; Hauerwas, *The State of the University*, 210.

Embodiment and Truth

In some situations it is easy to know what it is to speak truth, take the example of lying about how close to Åbo Cathedral my workplace is. Speaking truth can nevertheless be difficult, not only because we do not always want to speak truth, but also because it can be difficult to know what the truth is. And this is the case even if one does not try to understand the concept of truth in some metaphysical manner. Hauerwas does not speculate much about the concept of truth, but instead focuses on the kind of truth that is available to us.[120] Hauerwas notes that by asking what kind of person it would take to live truthfully one can get clues about how to understand a tradition that claims to be true.[121] For Hauerwas, "the test of each story is the sort of person it shapes."[122] For the question of truth this implies that there is a necessary connection between truthful behavior, for example truthful speech, and truth. "Witnesses," writes Hauerwas, "must exist if Christians are to be intelligible to themselves and hopefully to those who are not Christian, just as the intelligibility of science depends in the end on the success of the experiments."[123] In the same way truth cannot be distinguished from truthful living, that is, a life in which what is taken to be true is embodied. If this is correct then Christian theology cannot be done without paying attention to a witnessing community. Theology is not on this account immediately available and understandable without introduction to a whole way of life.

To wrap up this enquiry into Hauerwas's notion of truth I want to return to the example I gave in the opening, the proclamation "Jesus is Lord." Hauerwas has made a telling remark on this very claim. If someone were to say "Jesus is Lord . . . but it is just my personal opinion," it would be grammatically absurd; in Hauerwas's phrasing: "the grammar's all screwed-up."[124] In other words, if Jesus is Lord it cannot be only a personal opinion. What Hauerwas in this quote does is that he pays attention to how language is used in Christian communities. Through such activity one can identify possible incoherence within a tradition of thought. In addition to this Hauerwas claims it true that God indeed has altered the course of the world in Christ, in a commonsensical sense of true, while

---

120. Hauerwas is not opposed to (metaphysical) speculation about the concept of truth, but he maintains that "I just don't have a naturally metaphysical mind." (Hauerwas in conversation 2010/01/30.)

121. Hauerwas in conversation 2010/01/30.

122. Hauerwas, *Truthfulness and Tragedy*, 35.

123. Hauerwas, *With the Grain of the Universe*, 212.

124. Hauerwas, "Burke lecture."

maintaining that it is not a truth that can be established though evidence but only through witness.[125] Seeking to label Hauerwas's notion of truth "accurately" has not, however, been central here. I have rather, inspired by Hauerwas's theology, attempted to draw attention to some features of a meaningful way of talking about truth. My focus has been on how truth can be seen as something that needs to be embodied by a witnessing community in order to be purposive. For Hauerwas "What is crucial is not that Christians know the truth, but that they be the truth."[126] In the same way that church *is* a social ethic instead of simply *having* one (chapter two), witness necessitates displaying Christian convictions. Hauerwas's approach to talking about truth entails a focus on embodiment of truth, that is, truthful practices. It is not a theory-centered approach but one that necessitates a community of witness:

> if you need a theory of truth to assume that Jesus has been raised from the dead worship that theory. There can be no truth more determinative than that known through Jesus' crucifixion and resurrection. But what it means "to believe" in that cross and resurrection requires being made a participant in a community whose existence depends on the miracle of the resurrection.[127]

In the perspective that Hauerwas brings the "truth" that is "known through Jesus' crucifixion and resurrection" ought to shape how the Christian views everything else. "Believing" receives its intelligibility through participation in Christian community: its meaning is displayed in the life of the community. Truth in Hauerwas's thought is, therefore, not something abstract but something displayed and concrete.

---

125. Hauerwas, *With the Grain of the Universe*, 207.
126. Berkman and Cartwright, *The Hauerwas Reader*, 252.
127. Hauerwas, "Beyond," 9.

Chapter 4

Constantinianism and Nonviolence

IN THIS CHAPTER I will provide an account of the notions of Constantinianism and nonviolence. These are crucial elements of Hauerwas's theology. I will further ask what resources his views on Constantinianism and nonviolence might provide for a meaningful understanding of witness.

By way of introduction to this chapter it is in order to make a note on the relationship between Hauerwas and Anabaptist theologian John Howard Yoder. It must be acknowledged that in his views on Constantinianism and nonviolence Hauerwas draws extensively on Yoder. Central to my task is not to assess how Hauerwas might be developing Yoder's claims or how their perspectives may differ.[1] Hauerwas has expressed some points of concern regarding Yoder's views, as will become clear below, but my interpretation is, nevertheless, that on the whole Hauerwas complies with Yoder when it comes to Constantinianism and nonviolence.[2]

---

1. For an overview of such work, see e.g. Hauerwas et al., *The Wisdom of the Cross*; Ollenburger et al., *A Mind Patient and Untamed*, 205–245. Amos Yong suggests that Yoder is more open to the possibility of translation than is Hauerwas, see Yong, *In the Days of Caesar*, 187. I will not go into this particular discourse though I will include some critique that Hauerwas poses to Yoder. See also Nikolajsen, *Redefining the Indentity of the Church*.

2. I draw this conclusion because Hauerwas often acknowledges his debt to Yoder, e.g. "I have, of course, never pretended that I have anything to say about nonviolence that Yoder has not said and said better than any of my efforts." (Hauerwas, *Performing the Faith*, 181.)

CONSTANTINIANISM

Constantinianism in Stanley Hauerwas's literary production is shorthand for an understanding and praxis of church where the church in one way or another utilizes the "power of the 'state'" in order "to impose the Gospel on others without the vulnerability of witness."[3] The term itself comes from the emperor Constantine I who in the so-called edict of Milan (313) declared religious toleration in the Roman Empire. During the reign of Constantine I Christianity's "status" in society thus changed from an opposed and even persecuted community to that of a favored religion. Later, during the reign of Theodosius I (reigned AD 379-395) Christianity's role was further enhanced in that it was made a civil offence not to be a Christian. This altered status of Christianity can aptly be called the rise of Christendom.[4]

This alteration in the status of Christianity in society is a historical development that Hauerwas makes much of:

> Prior to Constantine, it took courage to be a Christian. After Constantine, it took courage to be a pagan. Before Constantine, no one doubted that Christians were different. After Constantine, it became increasingly unclear what difference being a Christian made.[5]

This implies, in other words, that the conditions for and self-understanding of Christianity changed during this time. As a result of this change in conditions Christianity went through a kind of internalization. As the threat of concrete persecution ceased, the battlefield for the Christian became internal in the form of temptation; temptation and holiness replaced persecution and martyrdom.[6] This does not, however, mean that Hauerwas is suggesting that the church has been categorically unfaithful since Constantine.[7] This is evident in that he maintains that even after Constantine some Christians have "found ways to dissent from the coercive measures necessary to ensure social order in the name of Christ."[8] Such dissent brings to the fore the question of violence, which for Hauerwas is a central feature of Constantinianism. To this I will return shortly.

3. Hauerwas, *The State of the University*, 103.
4. Brown, *The Rise of Western Christendom*.
5. Hauerwas and Wells, *Blackwell Companion*, 42.
6. Hauerwas and Wells, *Blackwell Companion*, 43.
7. Hauerwas and Willimon, *Resident Aliens*, 17.
8. Hauerwas and Willimon, *Resident Aliens*, 17.

What Hauerwas calls Constantinianism is, therefore, a result of this changed conception of Christianity. Critique of Constantinianism is one of the great themes in Hauerwas's authorship. It is consequently no surprise that examples of Constantinianism abound in his corpus. One common form of Constantinianism, according to Hauerwas, is the attempt to make society "more Christian" by seeking to pass laws that reflect Christian convictions.[9] For Hauerwas such a strategy for expanding the influence of Christianity in society works with the assumption that if the gospel is somehow to have an impact in our world it must be sustained through political and social institutionalization, in other words, through passing laws.[10]

Another subtler example of Constantinianism is for Hauerwas the habit of public prayer in American schools. This habit contains an element of Constantinianism in that it implies that the state is supportive of Christianity as well as imposes Christian practices even on those school children that do not share the Christian faith.[11]

The Problem of Constantinianism

For Hauerwas this shift in the status of Christianity in the wider society is problematic because before Constantine, one became a Christian through conversion, whereas after Constantine this was not necessarily the case. Hauerwas interprets this development that began with Constantine and the Edict of Milan as a *confusion* of the entities "church" and "world": the claims that Christian tradition and the New Testament lays on the Christian are not identical with the claims that a state lays on its citizens.[12]

For Hauerwas

> Constantinianism has taken many different forms throughout history, but the common thread that constitutes the family resemblance between its various forms is that the validity of the church, of Jesus Christ, and of the New Testament is to be judged by standards derived from the world.[13]

---

9. Hauerwas and Willimon, *Resident Aliens*, 38, 80.
10. Hauerwas and Willimon, *Resident Aliens*, 18.
11. Berkman and Cartwright, *The Hauerwas Reader*, 460–461.
12. Hauerwas, *Vision and Virtue*, 205. Distinguishing between church and world, it has been argued, gave early Christian asceticism its moral force, which began weakening with the conversion of Constantine. (See Hagman, *The Asceticism of Isaac of Nineveh*; Ahlqvist, *Flumen Saxosum Sonans*, 27–40.)
13. Hauerwas, *With the Grain of the Universe*, 221.

In other words, if church and world are not distinguishable from one another it leads, on this view, to a situation in which the church's legitimacy is judged by standards that are not at home in Christian tradition.

Such standards could in my view be, for example, how well a church or denomination serves the unemployed, or provides therapeutic services for anxious people. Services such as these are obviously good and can be seen as part of the church's mandate, but they are, however, not at the very center of what the church is about. I assume here that the primary task of the Christian church is to worship the Triune God. Providing services can obviously be seen as part of such worship but if it is divorced from the context that Christian worship provides, I would suggest that it risks dehistorizing the Christian faith.[14] Christian worship has traditionally centered around the Eucharist. Downplaying that would entail deemphasizing that the Triune God Christians seek to worship is "whoever raised Jesus from the dead, having before raised Israel from Egypt."[15] Christian worship, in other words, has a history. Overlooking that history risks distorting worship to something else that what Christians have considered to be worship. I am here suggesting that equating the providing of services with Christian worship would be just such disregard for how Christians have traditionally understood worship.

Hauerwas notes that "the view that what God is doing is being done primarily through the framework of society as a whole and not through the Christian community is the presumption that lies behind the Constantinian accommodation of the church to the world."[16] The way I interpret this is that Hauerwas's insistence on maintaining a distinction between church and world is key in order for Christians to be able to challenge Constantinianism. The church is, therefore, a community with a peculiar mandate; it is not on this view the same as any other helping community. The term "accommodation" implies that a Constantinian situation is taken to be a deviation from the church's mandate.

This confusion of entities has in Hauerwas's view dire consequences for the shape that Christianity takes. Firstly, the Constantinian shift has had enormous Christological and ecclesiological consequences.[17] When Christianity became the favored religion, citizens of the Empire were de-

---

14. See Hauerwas, *In Good Company*, 158.

15. Jenson, *Systematic Theology*, 63.

16. Hauerwas, *With the Grain of the Universe*, 221 referring to Yoder and Cartwright, *The Royal Priesthood*, 198.

17. Hauerwas, *The State of the University*, 66.

clared Christian, and consequently, conversion to Christ and discipleship became optional for being a Christian. The ecclesiological implications of the Constantinian shift are evident in that the "demographics" of the church changed: "citizens of the Empire" became roughly equivalent to "Christian," which is in stark contrast to earlier generations where becoming a Christian entailed some form of conversion and initiation to a new way of life. In other words, after Constantine church named a peculiar mix of those who were Christian "in name only" and those for whom the name Christian had life-shaping implications.

Secondly, another central and related consequence of the Constantinian confusion of church and world is that Constantinianism represents "an order of violence."[18] As Hauerwas sees it, when it was made a civil offence not to be Christian, Christianity was necessarily transformed from a nonviolent way of life to a coercive religion.[19] The marriage of Christianity and coercion is a central problem that Hauerwas has with Constantinianism.[20] Because of this Constantinianism, on Hauerwas's view, contradicts Christian witness. Hauerwas, furthermore, suggests that these types of Constantinianism transform the gospel into civil religion, which is not the same as Christianity.[21]

Non-Constantinianism?

What then would a non-Constantinian form of Christianity look like? If Constantinianism is contradictory with the idea of witness, and therefore not a valid option for Christians, what would a meaningful constructive alternative be? One should promptly note that this question is intrinsically problematic for Hauerwas. This has to do with the nature of Christianity as a nonviolent way of life and Constantinianism as inherently violent. Hauerwas makes the point by referring to Yoder's reflection on Christians encountering the other:

> Yoder does not try to develop or recommend a general theory or strategy for Christian conversations with other faiths or traditions. He cannot because such theories or strategies would only reproduce Constantinian habits. Yoder says 'By the nature of the

---

18. Hauerwas, *Dispatches from the Front*, 188.
19. Hauerwas, *The State of the University*, 67.
20. The same connection is made in Sigurdson, *Det postsekulära tillståndet*, 199.
21. Berkman and Cartwright, *The Hauerwas Reader*, 478.

case it is not possible to establish, either speculatively or from historical samples, a consistent anti-Constantinian model.²²

The way I read this is that the emphasis on the impossibility of a genuine anti-Constantinian model leads to at least two things: Firstly, it leads to a situation in which churches need to continually resist the temptation to resort to Constantinian practices. Constantinianism in church practices is, in other words, not a problem that can be dealt with once and for all. Instead it requires an unending effort to only utilize practices that are coherent with the Christian tradition. This implies also, in other words, a continual work of interpretation, in order to identify Constantinian traits in one's own tradition as well as in order to find non-coercive ways to go on. Resorting to violence is a real temptation because it can often seem like an easy and effective solution in conflict situations. Hauerwas suggests that it is imperative that Christians learn "habits of peace" that represent nonviolent practices and in times of conflict allow for non-coercive solutions to be discovered.²³

A second consequence of the impossibility of a coherent anti-Constantinian model is that it leads the Christian community to pay attention to the particularities displayed in a meeting with the other. More specifically this means that a rejection of Constantinian strategies implies, or carries the potential for, a heightened awareness of the claims of the other in concrete situations. To turn the argument around: it implies a reduced emphasis on general strategies and "in-principle-policies" in favor or a genuine attempt to understand the other. Hauerwas's theology includes such a perspective in relation to other religions and traditions, which becomes clear in his claim that one cannot know a priori what one might have to say to the other.²⁴ As such Hauerwas's work, the way I interpret it, utilizes the kind of *ad hoc* approach in meeting with the other that Yoder calls for.²⁵

It is a truism to note that religious convictions that include universal claims often lead to violence, and that many wrongs have been done in the name of Christ. I do not intend to claim that all such wrongs are but results of Constantinian practices, but I do suggest that they are a

---

22. Hauerwas, *The State of the University*, 69 quoting Yoder and Cartwright, *The Royal Priesthood*, 250.

23. Berkman and Cartwright, *The Hauerwas Reader*, 325.

24. Hauerwas, *Wilderness Wanderings*, 6; Hauerwas, *The State of the University*, 70.

25. Yoder and Cartwright, *The Royal Priesthood*, 250.

Constantinianism and Nonviolence

big part of the story.[26] On Hauerwas's account "for Christians to disavow Constantine requires communal repentance."[27] It seems that it is important for Hauerwas that Christians acknowledge and confess past wrongs that flow out of Constantinian assumptions: The Jesus of the Empire, the Crusades and holy places and "wars in the name of 'the Christian West' is not only something to forget but something to forgive."[28] I interpret such confession of past sins as unavoidable to any Christian community that seeks to live truthfully to its tradition. It would be less than truthful to seek to forget past wrongs without confession and possible forgiveness. Such confession would also be a truthful practice in that it truthfully implies that the violence done in the name of Christ is not necessarily intrinsic to Christianity, but often a result of Constantinianism.[29]

---

26. See Cavanaugh, "Does Religion Cause Violence?." See also Cavanaugh, *The Myth of Religious Violence*.

27. Hauerwas, *The State of the University*, 69 quoting Yoder and Cartwright, *The Royal Priesthood*, 250.

28. Hauerwas, *The State of the University*, 69 quoting Yoder and Cartwright, *The Royal Priesthood*, 250. Heidi Jokinen has reflected on what it might mean to forgive past wrongs, see Jokinen, "The Church Does (Not) Apologize," 91–111.

29. William Cavanaugh problematizes, in my view rightly, the tendency to assume religion to be violent: "The myth of religious violence helps create a blind spot about the violence of the putatively secular nation-state. We like to believe that the liberal state arose to make peace between warring religious factions. Today, the Western liberal state is charged with the burden of creating peace in the face of the cruel religious fanaticism of the Muslim world. The myth of religious violence promotes a dichotomy between *us* in the secular West who are rational and peacemaking, and *them*, the hordes of violent religious fanatics in the Muslim world. *Their* violence is religious, and therefore irrational and divisive. *Our* violence, on the other hand, is rational, peacemaking, and necessary. Regrettably, we find ourselves forced to bomb them into the higher rationality." (Cavanaugh, "Does Religion Cause Violence?," 6.) Cavanaugh argues that more violence is done in the name of the nation state than in the name of religion. A mind-boggling example of such violence that Cavanaugh gives is the "Bush Doctrine that America has access to liberal values that are 'right and true for every person, in every society,' that we must use our power to promote such values 'on every continent,' and that America will take preemptive military action if necessary to promote such values." (Cavanaugh, "Does Religion Cause Violence?," 18. (Cavanaugh is quoting The National Security Strategy of the United States of America, September 2002, prologue and page 15.) Hauerwas notes similar to Cavanaugh that "Ironically, since the Enlightenment's triumph, people no longer kill one another in the name of God but in the names of nation-states. Indeed I think it can be suggested that the political achievement of the Enlightenment has been to create people who believe it necessary to kill others in the interest of something called 'the nation,' which is allegedly protecting and ensuring their freedom as individuals." (Hauerwas, *After Christendom?*, 33.)

Secularization and the Secular

In Hauerwas's published material one can find references to "secularization" and "the secular" *vis-à-vis* the question of Constantinianism. The former is seen as a resource for non-Constantinian aspirations, whereas, interestingly, the latter can be a form of Constantinianism. To these seemingly contradictive themes we must now turn.

As mentioned above Hauerwas is critical toward the idea that it is possible to establish a coherent non-Constantinian model. Despite this Hauerwas calls for a "disavowal of Constantine."[30] Such renunciation does not, however, have to be considered only something that Christian communities should work for in their life and ministry. A large-scale development in American society that Hauerwas suggests bears relevance for the topic at hand is secularization.[31] Secularization, understood as a diminishing role of established religions, might prove a resource in the matter. In other words, secularization can be or contribute to a form of disavowal of Constantine. What Hauerwas seems to be saying is that as established religions lose their influence also the Constantinian assumptions and strategies that some of these harbor diminish. This way secularization can be interpreted to play into the hands of Christian communities that seek to renounce Constantinian strategies.

This claim is, the way I read it, reasonable because both theism and atheism lose much of their persuasiveness in a culture that is indifferent toward questions related to God. Secularization as a form of disavowal of Constantine, despite being a reasonable view, nevertheless, calls for some critical reflection. Suggesting that secularization might benefit non-Constantinian Christian communities is a bold statement and risks

---

30. Hauerwas, *The State of the University*, 66.

31. Hauerwas, *The State of the University*, 72. The kind of secularization that Hauerwas talks about here resonates with Charles Taylor's definitions of secularization, especially "secularity 1" and "secularity 2." Taylor's secularity 1 amounts to the observation that public spaces have been secularized: God has to a large degree disappeared from society and/or been pushed into what is often called a "religious sphere." A few centuries ago, however, God was interwoven with everything: the political, social, educational, and so on, aspects of life, but this is no longer the case. This development can then be called secularization. Taylor also notes a second type, secularity 2, that pinpoints in various ways the fact that in many Western countries fewer and fewer people are active church-goers. Western Europe, for example, is secularized in this way. The third type of secularity, the one Taylor focuses on in his book *A Secular Age*, is that the very *conditions* for religiosity have radically changed during the last couple of centuries. (Taylor, *A Secular Age*, 3, 15, 20.)

being rather categorical. While the disavowal of "coercive Christianities" is undoubtedly a good thing it should also be noted that secularization might simultaneously pose a challenge even to non-Constantinian forms of Christianity. Recent critiques of the secularization theory observe that while established religions seem to be in decline a new visibility of religions and spiritualities can be discerned in contemporary Western societies.[32] I think that it could be argued that these developments cause a religious situation that is more diverse than before, and perhaps an unorthodox mixture of different religions and perspectives. If this is the case, then will that not also cause confusion for Christian churches that seek to act in a non-Constantinian fashion in our context? In Nordic societies Christian churches can, however, rely on some sort of common understanding of what Christianity might be.

For Hauerwas such general and shared ideas of Christianity would be questionable considering his stress on Christianity as a way of life that requires initiation. On this view, therefore, the existence of such alleged shared understanding would be called into question. The critical question that must, notwithstanding, be presented is the following: Are remnants of Constantinian Christianity really a misrepresentation of Christianity beyond redemption? To reiterate, could Constantinian remains, nevertheless, provide a bridge for communication, and thus be a resource for churches that seek to act in this cultural situation?

In a Hauerwasian line of thinking it seems such remains are profoundly unhelpful, but I would suggest that there is room for specification. I would argue that to some degree even a misrepresentation of Christianity functions as a kind of common ground. What non-Christians happen to know about Christianity *de facto* is a kind of common ground in a situation where a community seeks to communicate a non-Constantinian form of Christianity. The reason I claim this is that in any situation where communication takes place, let us say between person X and person Y, each party will interpret the other through one's own context (past experiences, education, stereotypes etc.) If X tells of her constitutive convictions, Y might give the terms used by X meanings that X did not intend. Additional attempts at communication can, however, through specification, testing and feedback, result in Y gaining a better grasp of X's language. Such instances of communication could not only clarify what meanings X

---

32. Reflection on the issues involved has also been done by Nordic theologians, see e.g. Sigurdson, *Det postsekulära tillståndet*; Henriksen, *På grensen til Den andre*. A similar religious turn can be detected in philosophy, see e.g. Svenungsson, *Guds återkomst*.

gives the terms she used in her account of her convictions but also embody aspects of the message. An example of such embodiment could be the willingness to patiently enter into dialog with Y and listening respectfully to the views and questions of Y. This point incorporates Hauerwas's insight that what Christians believe and how they act cannot be separated. The meaning given to the notion of common ground is here not "shared common ground" but more of a "bridge for communication," that is, something that creates the possibility for more and clarifying communication.

What Y happened to know about the community that X is part of functions as a starting point for communication. Obviously it is possible that Y initially has false ideas about the meanings that X assigns to a given word. Such prior knowledge can then be unhelpful but it can also be seen as an opportunity for meaningful and clarifying dialog. It is exactly this aspect of the pontential of prior understanding—even inadequate one—that I miss in Hauerwas's dismissal of Constantinian remains. A similar categorical dismissal can be seen in Hauerwas's view that prayer in public schools is not beneficial to Christians due to the "watered down" quality of such prayers.[33] It seems strange that Hauerwas can elsewhere claim that "the ruins inherited from the past establishment of Christianity can provide imaginative ways to reclaim the visibility of the church."[34] Is there a tension in Hauerwas's thinking on this point? A mean interpretation would suggest just that. A kinder reading, however, would attribute the seeming tension to the nature of Hauerwas's writing that is often done in a provoking tone. Yet a third interpretation would be to note that it is one thing to suggest that prayer in public schools is not genuine Christian language, and quite another to claim that such "corrupt Christian language" could not under any circumstances be helpful to a community that seeks to "reclaim the visibility of the church." Due to the occasional nature of Hauerwas's writing—which also makes it difficult, as well as dubious, to approach it as if it was a coherent system of thought—I vote for the latter two readings. I have also sought to show how, in my example of the discussion between persons X and Y, how "ruins inherited from the past establishment of Christianity can provide imaginative ways to reclaim the visibility of the church."

There is another point to be made regarding the strategy to "build" on what people already know about Christianity, even Constantinian Christianity. It is the point that grounding communication on a kind of

---

33. Berkman and Cartwright, *The Hauerwas Reader*, 460–461.
34. Hauerwas, *The State of the University*, 39. Italics mine.

common ground is still to be disassociated from a liberal strategy of translation. Hauerwas suggests that:

> Christianity is in that awkwardly intermediate stage in Western culture where having once been culturally established it is still not yet clearly disestablished. Such a situation still makes liberalism seem attractive both as a pastoral and social ethical strategy. For the biblical heritage is just present enough in our culture to make redescription a useful means to keep many people vaguely related to the church. . . . Moreover the identity of many people remains influenced by the religious past; such people often insist they are as genuinely Christian as those who go to church even though the former no longer believe in God as creator or in Jesus' cross and resurrection.[35]

Hauerwas is here identifying a temptation that presents itself in contexts that have a Christian heritage. The temptation is to "redescribe" Christian language into languages of, for example, Marxism, existentialism or psychology.[36] In the Finnish context theologian Risto Saarinen has suggested that no church or denomination can claim to be in a monopoly situation in today's societies: cherishing an alleged "unitary culture" is not a meaningful strategy.[37] Saarinen notes that in such a situation churches have often responded with increasing liberalism and modernization, with the intent to be continuously relevant.[38] This is a similar analysis that Hauerwas makes in the quote above. Saarinen, however, suggests that many have found the path of liberalism to be a dead-end.[39] Saarinen mentions the rise of postliberalism as a result of liberalism's shortcomings.[40] Saarinen notes helpfully that postliberalism is a theological approach that is related to philosophical critiques of liberalism, especially to communitarianism, and that Alasdair MacIntyre is consequently a source of inspiration for postliberals.[41] MacIntyre cannot envisage a return to an idea of a unitary

---

35. Hauerwas, *Against the Nations*, 8 reflecting Lindbeck's description in Lindbeck, *The Nature of Doctrine*, 133. Lindbeck suggests that "Such attitudes are also widespread in Europe, where church attendance is much smaller than in the United States." (138)

36. Hauerwas, *Against the Nations*, 8.

37. Saarinen, *Sosiaalietiikka*, 96.

38. Saarinen, *Sosiaalietiikka*, 97.

39. Saarinen, *Sosiaalietiikka*, 97.

40. Saarinen, *Sosiaalietiikka*, 97.

41. Saarinen, *Sosiaalietiikka*, 97.

culture and, therefore, Christianity must be understood as a particular tradition in a multicultural society.[42]

Hauerwas's theology lies exactly in this vein of thought that Saarinen describes. The strengths that I see in Hauerwas's postliberal approach, when it comes to disestablishing Constantinian Christianity, is that it assigns legitimacy to primal Christian language without redescription. A Hauerwasian perspective maintains that Christian language should not and indeed cannot be translated into, for example, psychology. That would lead to reduction. In this perspective Christian language is, and opens up, an original contribution amongst the various religions and life-views perceivable in society. Another strength is the realism involved in that Hauerwas does not sustain a notion of a unitary (Christian) culture, with a corresponding (coercive) ecclesial strategy; Christianity is one tradition among other traditions. In the Nordic contexts Lutheranism is historically the majority tradition but a Hauerwasian perspective would rebuke assumptions of monopoly or a privileged position.

I would not, however, suggest as pessimistic and categorical a strategy as does Hauerwas when it comes to attempts to salvage the remains of a Christian heritage. In my view even a false idea of Christianity is, as it were, a distant echo of genuine Christian language, which carries potential for clarification and eventually orthodoxy. Hauerwas's insistence on the impossibility of translation of Christian convictions to "other languages" does not have to be understood as the impossibility of dialog with Christians that harbor Constantinian assumptions or people that are Christian "in name only."[43] In fact, I have suggested, such Constantinian remains may function as a meaningful starting-point for communication about non-Constantinian convictions.

The second issue of this subchapter still remains to be discussed, namely, the secular. Hauerwas also provides quite another perspective on Western secular culture. This perspective suggests that "the secular has become a form of Constantinianism in modernity."[44] He argues further that "the secular names an account of time crucial for the legitimation of the modern state" and that "Christians have confused our time, church time, with state time" and as a result "failed to provide an alternative to [the] world."[45] To clarify these claims it should be noted that Hauerwas

42. Saarinen, *Sosiaalietiikka*, 97.
43. e.g. Hauerwas, *Against the Nations*, 5.
44. Hauerwas, *The State of the University*, 170.
45. Hauerwas, *The State of the University*, 170.

draws on the idea that in modernity time has been homogenized, in other words, there is only one understanding of time.[46] This implies that there is no room for understandings of time other than the secular linear, chronological time. Eschatological or apocalyptic accounts of time, for instance, do not pass muster as credible views; *kairós* is ruled out by a secular *chrónos*. Drawing on Yoder Hauerwas then suggests that under Constantine Christians began losing the eschatological conviction that Christians live simultaneously in two times.[47] That Christians live in two times can, according to Hauerwas, "be distinguished only if there is a church whose life is governed by the reality of the new age."[48]

A "cure" that Hauerwas proposes to the homogenization of time is a Christian practice: prayer.[49] The point in this lies exactly in that prayer does not assume that there is only one kind of time: "Prayer takes place in liturgical time and thereby challenges the presumption that there exists no other time but the time of historical succession."[50] This cure is a good example of the way that Hauerwas draws on Christian resources to counter what he sees as liberal or secular challenges. It is also noteworthy that on Hauerwas's account a Christian response to the homogenization of time is a practice, not a verbal intellectual argument.

The perspective opened up by the claim that "the secular has become a form of Constantinianism in modernity" is, as I read it, an attempt to show that a secular understanding of time is a form of Constantinianism in that it, somehow, plays into the hands of the modern state. The homogenization of time renders an eschatological view of time implausible. This goes to show that Constantinianism in Hauerwas's thought is a multi-faceted phenomenon. In other words, it should not always be seen only as an understanding and praxis of church where the church in one way or another utilizes the "power of the 'state'" in order "to impose the Gospel on others without the vulnerability of witness," as I suggested at the beginning of my account of Constantinianism.[51] In Hauerwas's thought,

46. Hauerwas, *The State of the University*, 175 quoting Asad, *Formations of the Secular*, 5. Charles Taylor also talks about time being homogenized and suggests that it is an important secularizing factor. (Taylor, *A Secular Age*, 217.)

47. Hauerwas, *The State of the University*, 171.

48. Hauerwas, *The State of the University*, 175 referring to Yoder, *Christian Witness*, 8–13.

49. Hauerwas, *The State of the University*, 183 referring to D'Costa, *Theology in the Public Square*, 112–114.

50. Hauerwas, *The State of the University*, 183.

51. Hauerwas, *The State of the University*, 103.

therefore, not only churches but also the modern secular state can be Constantinian. If one were to pose the question "who is homogenizing time?" one would have to delve into a study of the highly complex phenomenon that is secularization.[52] This is not, however, what I intend to do at this point. My intention is rather to bring to the fore the fact that Hauerwas's talk of Constantinianism is at times highly abstract and generalizing. Despite this I suggest that Constantinianism as short-hand for coercive church attitudes and practices is a helpful heuristic tool.

Withdrawal and Visibility

There is a final observation to be made on non-Constantinianism that also tackles a critique that has often been presented to Hauerwas. It has to do with the accusation that Hauerwas is, at least implicitly, promoting withdrawal from society.[53] Hauerwas's alternative to Constantinianism is not, however, in my view, accurately described as implying withdrawal from society. Withdrawal is not an option, since Christians cannot be in the world without taking up space and interacting with non-Christians. The question for Hauerwas is, therefore, *how* Christians are in the world.[54] Hauerwas, following Yoder, suggests that non-Constantinianism entails a *visible* community that embodies and exemplifies an alternative to the world.[55] Hauerwas maintains that *anti*-Constantinianism is not the alternative to Constantinianism "but rather to develop *local* forms of life that can sustain the necessary *visibility* of the church as an alternative to the world."[56] This point regarding the locality and visibility of the church is one that I want to highlight: the church that *is* a social ethic, as was displayed in chapter two, is a visible church. It is visible in that it presupposes a distinction between church and world. In Hauerwas's account the distinction is crucial because without it church cannot be a visible alterna-

---

52. Taylor's account in *A Secular Age* identifies several crucial themes that would have to be discussed in order to take a closer look at the idea of homogenization of time with reference to Constantinianism.

53. E.g. Stout, *Democracy and Tradition*, 147–148. Kurtén rightfully notes that Stout and Hauerwas have differing understandings of "responsibility" and "withdrawal." (Kurtén, "The Christian," 98.)

54. Hauerwas, *With the Grain of the Universe*, 220. Christians are to be in the world "as he was in the world," that is nonresistant, which does not imply withdrawal from the world.

55. Hauerwas, *The State of the University*, 38.

56. Hauerwas, *The State of the University*, 4. Italics mine.

tive to the world. Central to such a visible alternative is that a Christian community "cultivate their native tongue and learn to act accordingly."[57] Such a community is not one that withdraws from the wider society but one that lives as a Christian community in society.

Hauerwas portrays locality[58] as a central feature of an alternative to Constantinianism.[59] To illuminate this I will draw on Hauerwas's critique of the modern university. A central point in this critique is that the modern university has been in the service of the nation-state.[60] Hauerwas asserts that abstractions, such as "money," "interests," and "nation," are used to justify certain kinds of knowledges—and suppressing others, such as theology—in order to legitimate the liberal state.[61] This is a similar point as is the one about time being homogenized: certain understandings of time, or in this case knowledge, are ruled out in order to reinforce the state. This is yet another example of what can be called a Constantinian feature of a nation-state.

A state that backs up its power in the manner just described is, what I would like to call, a "faceless actor." Such a state may, for example, ask a subject to fight and even die for the sake of "the nation." If the subject in question would not, for one reason or another, be inclined to die for the nation and would like to protest against the demand, whom should he or she turn to? Asking "who is the state that asks this of me?" might not produce a tangible answer.[62] The state in this example is coercive but a faceless "system." The nation-state is, according to Hauerwas, an adversary of locality.[63]

Now, what does the faceless coercive tendencies of the nation-state have to do with a non-Constantinian form of Christianity? In a similar way as a nation-state is faceless Constantinian Christianity also includes

57. Hauerwas, *Against the Nations*, 9.

58. Locality in my following discussion does not necessarily imply "small," though it may be that also. It does, however, refer to the visibility of a community and a decentralization of power, at least in the sense that a community has the freedom to embody their Christian convictions in a way that is meaningful and contextual in a locale.

59. Hauerwas, *The State of the University*, 8.

60. Hauerwas, *The State of the University*, 104.

61. Hauerwas, *The State of the University*, 8.

62. The question could obviously surface the point about nations being historical and social constructs. As such it is not self-evident that Christians should feel obligated to comply if what the nation asks of the Christian is contrarious to Christian convictions.

63. Hauerwas, *The State of the University*, 104.

an element of facelessness. An example of this is passing a law or church policy that coerces non-Christians to submit to what is taken to be a Christian conviction or value. If one would like to protest against such a law or policy, whom would one turn to? A church that is in a position that makes this type of coercion possible is in a position of power, which, I would argue, involves or allows an element of facelessness. The concreteness of a local and visible Christian community thus provides an alternative to such coercive and abstract politics. To avoid an abstract facelessness such a community would have to be one "with a face." This entails a community where people, for example in a time of conflict, can interact openly with the other, instead of having to encounter a faceless law or guideline that coerces the other into conformity. In such a community there is a sense of concreteness involved that is lacking in Constantinian projects. The need for churches to be local and visible is thus a crucial feature of an alternative to Constantinian practices.

There is one more reflection to be done with regard to the way that Christians are in the world. This is an issue that Jeffrey Stout expresses in his critique on Hauerwas's ecclesiology. Stout observes that Hauerwas in his more recent writings is not utilizing the language of "justice," whereas he did so earlier in his career.[64] Stout seems to have a strong faith in the power of justice to be something that could unite all people of good will behind its cause. Stout's claim that Hauerwas should (re?)adopt the language of justice in order for Hauerwas's critics to drop the charge regarding sectarianism seems odd: my take is that Hauerwas is not saying that justice is a bad idea, but rather questioning the assumption that if we talk about justice we would be talking about the same thing. Hauerwas, in other words, asks with Alasdair MacIntyre whose conception of justice we are talking about.[65] What I think Hauerwas means is that churches need to work for something like Stout's justice, only in a cruciform way, that is, in a way that resonates with a life of discipleship to Jesus. For Hauerwas it is important that what counts as justice is defined out of the story of God. This is important in order to avoid arbitrary uses of the word.[66]

What such a "cruciform way" might look like remains somewhat ambiguous but it is characteristically difficult to describe. It is not possible to provide a formula for what form a cruciform life takes. "Following Jesus" or "loving one's neighbor" takes different forms in various times and

---

64. Stout, *Democracy and Tradition*, 160.
65. See MacIntyre, *Whose Justice?*.
66. Berkman and Cartwright, *The Hauerwas Reader*, 323, 532.

places. A cruciform life is, consequently best described by calling attention to examples of such life.[67]

Another disturbing feature in Stout's account is what could be called a lurking Constantinianism, that is, it seems to assume that it is the task of Christians to "run the world." I assume Stout's rationale to be that since Christian's are a large group in American society they necessarily must accept responsibility in social matters (including politics and foreign policy) by voting for parties that reflect their convictions. Hauerwas does not, however, accept that the politics we know is the only kind of politics possible. He envisions a Christian community that neither assumes to be in a position of power nor to be supported by the state. Such community is, on Hauerwas's account, its own kind of politics.[68]

I conclude that the kind of "third alternative" that Stout calls for (the two others being either "ecclesiology" or "democracy") might be articulated in Hauerwasian ecclesiological terms. But it is necessarily an account in which the concept of justice receives its meaning within and from a particular community that is shaped by a particular tradition. I do not think it possible to negotiate between Stout and Hauerwas on this matter in a way that would be satisfactory to an alleged "view from nowhere."[69]

The account of Constantinianism and non-Constantinianism that I have provided identified some pertaining elements of a form of Christianity that seeks to free itself from Constantinian assumptions and practices. Though a fully coherent "once and for all" non-Constantinian account cannot, according to Yoder, be provided, it is, nevertheless, time to discuss explicitly what has only implicitly been identified as a crucial element of non-Constantinianism. This crucial element is nonviolence.

NONVIOLENCE

The task of this subchapter is to provide an account of Hauerwas's understanding of nonviolence, or peaceableness as he likes to call it. A peaceable form of Christianity can be seen as the most central characteristic

67. I interpret Hauerwas's frequent use of stories of people who in some way exemplify Christian lives as an attempt to point to witnesses.

68. This should not, however, be taken to mean that Hauerwas is suggesting that Christians should not e.g. vote or participate in various initiatives that work for the betterment of society. Cooperation with other actors is not, on Hauerwas's view ruled out. See Hauerwas, *The Peaceable Kingdom*, 101.

69. Stout has since written more about the role of grassroots movements as a way of bringing about change in society, see Stout, *Blessed Are the Organized*.

of Hauerwas's alternative to a Constantinian conception of Christianity. Violence, often in the form of subtle coercion, is emblematic for Constantinianism, and therefore, peaceableness is a decisive characteristic of a non-Constantinian church. Providing an account of the topic at hand is, however, a dubious matter in the case that Hauerwas is right: he claims that "nonviolence cannot be explained. It can only be shown by the attractiveness of the friendships that constitute our lives."[70] This exhibits the embodied character of peaceableness. It can, in other words, not be extracted from a community that practices such nonviolence, as if it was a mere intellectual position. Despite this inherent difficulty I will attempt to identify and describe central features of peaceableness.[71]

Theological Introduction

As early as in his first compilation of essays entitled *Vision and Virtue: Essays in Christian Ethical Reflection*, Hauerwas speaks for peaceableness as an intrinsic characteristic of the Christian life and witness.[72] Hauerwas laments the fact that in much theological discussion the responsibility of Christians "to work for a better society involves a denial of pacifism."[73] On this view a Christian community that seeks to oppose evil must in some instances choose the lesser evil and, in so doing, take to violence in order to minimize violence. In contrast to this assumption, Hauerwas presents a form of Christian pacifism or peaceableness.

The type of pacifism that Hauerwas promotes is distinctly a Christian pacifism in the sense that it becomes intelligible only against the backdrop of the kingdom of God inaugurated by Jesus Christ. As such it requires the qualifier "Christian," just as his take on ethics does. It is a non-violent way of life intrinsic to the life of a community that seeks to "imitate Jesus." It is not a political program that seeks to utilize politicians and states in order to make society less violent—that would be a form of Constantinianism. Such a strategy would be a theological mistake since it would confuse the

---

70. Hauerwas, *Performing the Faith*, 183.

71. The following account has, consistent with my overall method, the noble goal of exemplifying peaceableness in that it seeks to provide room for Hauerwas to speak without coercing him into a predetermined framework.

72. Hauerwas, *Vision and Virtue*. In this sub-chapter I draw extensively on Hauerwas's chapter The Nonresistant Church: The Theological Ethics of John Howard Yoder in Hauerwas, *Vision and Virtue*, 197–221.

73. Hauerwas, *Vision and Virtue*, 198.

theological entities "church" and "world." The church should not impose its pacifism on the world since it is a form of pacifism, which necessitates the conviction that Jesus is Lord. Indirectly, however, it is also a political program in that a Christian community committed to nonviolence can function as a witness to a nonresistant alternative, a kingdom that is different, and in that way affect members of the wider community. Hauerwas suggests that "Christian pacifism stated in its simplest form is that Christians cannot see how war can be an imperative of the Christian life."[74] Since this particular type of pacifism only becomes intelligible within a framework created by the gospel, it is crucial to consider the foundational theological convictions that allegedly make such pacifism plausible.[75]

At the heart of the theological framework that involves pacifism lies the conviction that God has acted in a decisive way in Jesus Christ. Jesus inaugurated the kingdom of God on earth. Hauerwas maintains that for Yoder "the essence of the incarnation is the nonresistant love that reached its most intense reality in the cross."[76] While the kingdom of God has substantial social and political implications, it was not brought about through violence but through "self-giving, non-resistant love."[77] Following this Christian pacifism is not a detached dogma or a matter of obeying a disconnected law but imitation of Jesus' life. It is intrinsic to discipleship: "as he was, so we must be in the world."[78] Consequently, Hauerwas's Christian pacifism is not based on the probability of its success but rather on a theological basis, that of imitation of Jesus. The church, or the formation of a nonresistant community that seeks to imitate the way of Jesus, is a central theological conviction in this perspective.[79]

In addition to the centrality of ecclesiology, eschatology is also crucial in understanding this pacifism. An assurance in a future judgment and conclusive justice and following complete peace that God will bring about is foundational in Yoder's thinking. Human existence is to be understood through the existence of two aeons: one refers to history before Christ and the other to history after Christ. The former centers on the fallen human being, while the latter "is the reality of redemption which can be found in

---

74. Hauerwas, *Vision and Virtue*, 200.
75. Hauerwas, *Vision and Virtue*, 200.
76. Hauerwas, *Vision and Virtue*, 201.
77. Hauerwas, *Vision and Virtue*, 201.
78. Hauerwas, *Vision and Virtue*, 202; Hauerwas, *With the Grain of the Universe*, 220.
79. Hauerwas, *Vision and Virtue*, 202–203.

a decisive way only in Jesus Christ."[80] The church, as a "first fruit" of the ultimate redemptive work of God, is the materialization of the new aeon. The old aeon takes form in society in general and in the undertakings of the state in particular. The old aeon is not replaced with the coming of Christ but rather, the new aeon "has now taken primacy over the old, explains the meaning of the old, and will finally vanquish the old."[81]

In the new aeon the state is God's vehicle in maintaining order and relative peace. This does not make violence good but to the extent that the state protects the innocent and weak, it is, according to Yoder, of service to God. Even though Yoder acknowledges that the state has a police function, it does not mean that Christians should support every kind of violence the state might resort to. Christians can affirm the police function of the state but they should recognize, nevertheless, that relative peace is acceptable only to a fallen world, while the Christian community should only pursue a peace that does not come through coercion.[82]

A way to counter Yoder's Christian pacifism would be to directly attack his theology in general and Christology in particular. Hauerwas, however, suggests that this is not the most common critique. The more common counterargument, according to Hauerwas, is the claim that Yoder fails to provide a responsible relationship between the Christian and the world (society). It seems Yoder's position calls for a passive withdrawal from the world and thus only, at best, serves as a reminder of the awfulness of violence.[83]

This argument toward Yoder can be summarized as follows: that it is a) passive (and potentially sacrificing the wellbeing of the neighbor for personal piety) and thus b) still cannot avoid violence. According to Hauerwas, Yoder counters these points of critique by arguing that Christian pacifism is not merely passive, but it seeks to promote a positive approach where the Christian community confronts the world with its violence and oppressiveness (a). The result is that this type of pacifism does not entail a withdrawal from society but nonresistant engagement with it. While violence or complicity with evil cannot completely be avoided, patience in the face of violence correlates with Jesus' attitude of nonresistance toward violence as it is revealed in the New Testament (b). Furthermore, Christian

---

80. Hauerwas, *Vision and Virtue*, 207.
81. Hauerwas, *Vision and Virtue*, 207–208.
82. Hauerwas, *Vision and Virtue*, 207–208.
83. Hauerwas, *Vision and Virtue*, 203.

pacifism is also in accord with the conviction that God will ultimately be the one who rules and sets things "right."[84]

As Hauerwas evaluates Yoder's Christian pacifism, he maintains that it should not be lightly dismissed as a sectarian ethic of withdrawal. In Hauerwas's opinion it is a well argued and solid "theological argument concerning the special nature of the Christian's responsibility for society."[85] Yoder's proposal has Lutheran traits in that it makes a distinction between the claims of a society on its members and the obligations of the gospel to the members of the kingdom of God. It has, furthermore, Calvinistic traits in that it does not "admit an ultimate separation between God's order of providence and redemption thus avoiding any suggestion that the ethic of the world is autonomous or sufficient in the light if the gospel."[86] The sectarian traits of this position are evident in that it refuses to dissolve the dialectic between these two entities, while arguing that Christians cannot withdraw from society but should actively resist violence and coercion. Hauerwas further suggests that Yoder's thinking is particularly valuable in providing an alternative to the presumption that Christians must make a choice between being "responsible" or "withdrawing" altogether. Hauerwas affirms Yoder's emphasis on the distinctness of Christianity and the critique that most of their contemporary Christian ethics is "written as if Jesus' death, resurrection, and establishment of the kingdom did not decisively change the world and the Christian's relation to it."[87]

While Hauerwas is very sympathetic toward Yoder's Christian pacifism and the theological framework that sustains it he does, however, state his concerns on a few points. Firstly, Hauerwas takes issue with Yoder's hesitancy to explicitly provide criteria for situations were Christians should oppose evil or violence. For example, when Yoder says that the church must speak against "significant forms of injustice," he does not give any criteria for "significant."[88] Hauerwas anticipates the objection from Yoder that no such criteria are necessary since Christians must engage a situation in a given historical situation within given alternatives. If this is the case then Yoder seems to be asking Christians to accept "the status quo as normative—i.e., just the problem that Yoder most wants to avoid."[89]

84. Hauerwas, *Vision and Virtue*, 202–203.
85. Hauerwas, *Vision and Virtue*, 213.
86. Hauerwas, *Vision and Virtue*, 214.
87. Hauerwas, *Vision and Virtue*, 215.
88. Hauerwas, *Vision and Virtue*, 217.
89. Hauerwas, *Vision and Virtue*, 218.

The Hauerwasian alternative to this would be to suggest that a peaceable perspective opens up for new alternatives that challenges the given ones.

Secondly, Hauerwas challenges Yoder's view that a truly Christian ethic must be based exclusively on revelation. As an example, Hauerwas mentions the ethical reflection of Christians, which cannot be entirely alienated from categories non-Christians use when they talk about justice. If Christians are to address injustices in society they will at some point have to resort to the language of justice, albeit in a transformed way. Hauerwas agrees with Yoder that language that is independent from revelation must not be accepted as normative.[90] In contrast to Yoder, Hauerwas however argues that Christians can use the "language of the world," such as the language of justice, without being limited by it.[91]

A third concern is Yoder's understanding of the two aeons. It seems that Yoder is saying that with the coming of the new aeon Christ has actually conquered the powers of the old aeon and channeled some of its violence to be at God's service. Hauerwas argues that the New Testament pictures God's work still uncompleted; it is only at the eschaton that it will be complete. Consequently, Hauerwas suggests that Yoder's view of the aeons should be more dynamic in order to embrace the abovementioned characterization of the New Testament.[92]

The final point of concern is aimed at Yoder's idea of nonresistance as the embodiment of the Christian life. Hauerwas asks what form such a life would in fact take since evil is a wider phenomenon that violence. How is a Christian to behave in the face of subtle kinds of violence and aggression?[93] Hauerwas has later in his career developed a more substantial pacifist perspective. Early on, as exemplified in *Vision and Virtue*, Hauerwas seems more critical of Yoder's position, whereas later in his career he seems more appreciative of Yoder. I do not, however, pursue further analysis of this development.

---

90. One may raise the issue regarding how to determine if something is "independent from revelation." On Hauerwasian grounds the answer would entail referring to those most adequately schooled in the tradition, that is, "saints."

91. Hauerwas, *Vision and Virtue*, 219–220. Stout may have a point in his claim that Hauerwas has later in his career spoken less optimistically about the possibilities of the language of justice. See Stout, *Democracy and Tradition*, 147–148. I do not, however, think that this observation devastates Hauerwas's overall insistence that Christian convictions cannot be adequately translated into other languages.

92. Hauerwas, *Vision and Virtue*, 220.

93. Hauerwas, *Vision and Virtue*, 221.

Constantinianism and Nonviolence

The kind of pacifism that Yoder and Hauerwas stand for involves a certain understanding of redemption and of Jesus. Learning to see oneself as a sinner in rebellion toward God is central to this way of life. Conversion to discipleship, or imitation of Jesus, is furthermore essential for peaceableness. For Hauerwas to be redeemed is to locate oneself "in God's history, to be part of God's people."[94] This does not necessitate an experience of personal salvation in a pietistic sense, but is rather an alignment of ones life with the story of God's dealings with Israel and Jesus.[95] The people of God is, furthermore called to represent and thus witness to the kingdom in order to draw new people to it. Telling the story of God is not simply telling it but it necessitates living it. It is here that peaceableness comes in; it is a crucial manifestation of the kingdom and, more specifically, of what God is like.[96]

When Hauerwas talks about imitating Jesus he acknowledges that there is no way of knowing "the historical Jesus." The only Jesus we can know is the one portrayed to us by the early church. The fact that the early church were bound by a particular cultural and social context and consequently portrayed Jesus in a way that reflects the context does not present a problem in Hauerwas's thinking. He submits that Jesus cannot be known abstracted from the response that Jesus awoke in his followers. The witness of the early church was in fact a telling of a story of the life of Jesus —not only beliefs about the ontological status of Jesus or the significance of his death and resurrection though such also occurred. Hauerwas argues that the life of Jesus is crucial to understanding the meaning of the death and resurrection. While Hauerwas stresses the importance of the life of Jesus as portrayed by the early church it is not a form of "low Christology." On the contrary, the narrative form of the Gospels displays "what it means for Jesus to be God's anointed."[97] Imitating Jesus, therefore, is done by attaining to the teachings of Jesus. Hauerwas points to Matthew 5:48 where disciples are called to "be perfect, as your heavenly Father is perfect." This perfection "comes by learning to follow and be like the man whom God has sent to be our forerunner in the kingdom."[98] It is Jesus who is the

---

94. Hauerwas, *The Peaceable Kingdom*, 33.
95. Hauerwas, *The Peaceable Kingdom*, 33.
96. Hauerwas, *The Peaceable Kingdom*, 44.
97. Hauerwas, *The Peaceable Kingdom*, 75.
98. Hauerwas, *The Peaceable Kingdom*, 75.

cue to the Christian life, and consequently, to peaceableness, since Jesus forgave his enemies and did not resist his persecutors.[99]

Regarding the premises of this kind of Hauerwasian-Yoderian theology it should be noted that it cannot but be misunderstood if it is read with the presuppositions of Troeltsch and the Niebuhrs.[100] With such presuppositions Hauerwas and Yoder seem to fall into the category "Christ-against-culture" and thus seem a "sectarian" theology. Troeltsch and the Niebuhr brothers have "dehistoricized the Christian faith in the name of 'history,'" whereas a Hauerwasian-Yoderian perspective does not assume such a dichotomy between faith and history.[101] According to Hauerwas most protestant liberals (Niebuhr as the prime example) make salvation an individualistic if not agnostic thing.[102] Yoder and Hauerwas, on the contrary, are similar to Barth in that they approach Scripture in a way that assumes that Jesus is indeed relevant to social and political matters.[103] This, therefore, "challenges all pietistic readings of salvation, whether of the left or of the right."[104]

Role of Community

The kind of nonviolence that Hauerwas's peaceableness is, is not the effort of a heroic individual.[105] The role of community in shaping nonviolent lives is crucial. For Hauerwas, the community is vital in order for a Christian to learn to imitate Jesus. It is in the church community, and more precisely in the lives of the "saints" of the church, where lives of peaceableness are exemplified and learned. The church as an alternative community cannot exist without "saints" or mature Christians who function as examples of

---

99. Hauerwas, *The Peaceable Kingdom*, 72–76.
100. Hauerwas, *A Better Hope*, 131.
101. Hauerwas, *A Better Hope*, 131.
102. Hauerwas, *A Better Hope*, 131.
103. Hauerwas, *A Better Hope*, 131.
104. Hauerwas, *A Better Hope*, 131. Hauerwas, furthermore, cannot be understood if he is read from certain presuppositions that ask for neutral arguments, or "proof," that the story of Jesus is true. Hauerwas theology is to be seen as a form of thinking that is explicitly anchored in a tradition: it does not attempt "a prolegomenal search for 'scratch'"; there is, in other words, no place to begin thinking. (Hauerwas, *A Better Hope*, 131 quoting Yoder, *The Priestly Kingdom*, 7.)
105. Hauerwas, *Christian Existence Today*, 96; Hauerwas, *Performing the Faith*, 172.

what a life shaped by the gospel might look like.[106] Hauerwas anticipates the objection that one still needs some "criterion of reason" in order to identify the saints by admitting that that is the case but also by pointing out that it is not an "extra-theological" criterion but one that arises from the believing community itself. In other words, fellow members identify the exemplary ones within their community.[107]

In A Sermon on the Sermon on the Mount Hauerwas develops further the relationship between peaceableness and the Christian community.[108] He claims that the Sermon on the Mount (Matthew 5–7) presupposes a community shaped by and committed to nonviolence. Put differently, nonviolence is not intelligible without such a community, or bluntly, "you cannot rightly read the Sermon on the Mount unless you are a pacifist."[109] For Hauerwas the Sermon on the Mount is meant to promote a community where the members are interdependent to keep each other nonviolent.[110] Such a community represents an alternative way of facing and resolving disagreements, through "confrontation, forgiveness, and reconciliation."[111] Hauerwas emphasizes that this type of nonviolence is not optimistic in the sense that "turning the other cheek" would prevent an aggressor from striking again or that such a stance would necessarily end wars.[112] It is, rather, realistic in that it is consequent with the conviction that peaceableness reflects the character of God and that "the defenceless death of the Messiah has, for all time, been revealed as the victory of faith that overcomes the world."[113] A community that is committed to nonviolence is, on Hauerwas's view, essential in order for the world to know that

---

106. Hauerwas, *The Peaceable Kingdom*, 96–97.

107. Hauerwas, *The Peaceable Kingdom*, 71.

108. Hauerwas, *Unleashing the Scripture*, 63.

109. Hauerwas, *Unleashing the Scripture*, 64. Similarly, Hauerwas notes that the New Testament (e.g. Romans 13) cannot be rightly read unless it is done through the eyes of a nonviolent community. (Hauerwas, *Dispatches from the Front*, 118.) This implies that nonviolence, for Hauerwas, is a premise for interpretation, though he acknowledges that "The text of the Bible in and of itself does not require pacifism" (Hauerwas, *Dispatches from the Front*, 118.)

110. An example of this is Hauerwas's habit of telling others that he is a pacifist in order to "create expectations in others" and to keep him accountable (Hauerwas, *Performing the Faith*, 171.)

111. Hauerwas, *Unleashing the Scripture*, 71.

112. Hauerwas, *Performing the Faith*, 181.

113. Hauerwas, *Unleashing the Scripture*, 71–72.

Witness Is Presence

God has willed peace for all of creation.[114] The role of the community, considering these remarks, is essential for a Hauerwasian understanding of witness. Indeed, a community is a witness to God's kingdom only to the extent that it is peaceable.[115]

In order to know what sin is and what it means to be sinned against it is essential for the peacemaking community to have a "language and correlative habit" about sin.[116] Through this common language and habit, in other words, through the resources of a specific tradition, the community can avoid arbitrariness in judgment.[117] For Hauerwas "the essential presupposition of peacemaking as an activity among Christians is our common belief that we have been made part of a community in which people no longer regard their lives as their own."[118] Thus, when someone is "sinned against" s/he has no right to dwell on wrongs that s/he has encountered nor to claim them as her/his "own." Grievances against a member of such a community are not directed only at an individual member but against the whole community. This is why the mistreated must involve others in the community in case the offender does not agree to be reconciled.[119]

Another important feature of peaceableness is that it is not a clear or self-evident "position" that can be "usefully contrasted to just war, 'realism,' and other alternatives that appear as 'theories' about the ethics of war."[120] The form of pacifism Hauerwas promotes is one that is unintelligible apart from Christian community: it is the qualifier "Christian" that shapes what kind of pacifism peaceableness is, indeed, Hauerwas argues that without the qualifier we cannot "know what nonviolence is."[121] It is, as I read this, in the life of Christian community that Christian nonviolence

---

114. Hauerwas, *Unleashing the Scripture*, 72.

115. Hauerwas notes that a feminist student of his had remarked that his characterization of pacifism as a minority stance in Christian tradition does not hold water since most Christians through history *have* been nonviolent. The rationale here is that the majority of Christians have been women who were prohibited from warfare. While Hauerwas does not think this is a strong argument, he notes that it nevertheless serves as a reminder of the fact that the church has always had a nonviolent witness. (Hauerwas, *Dispatches from the Front*, 122.) Still, I dare add, women can be violent without going to war.

116. Hauerwas, *Christian Existence Today*, 93.

117. Hauerwas, *Christian Existence Today*, 93.

118. Hauerwas, *Christian Existence Today*, 91.

119. Hauerwas, *Christian Existence Today*, 91.

120. Hauerwas, *Dispatches from the Front*, 117.

121. Hauerwas, *Dispatches from the Front*, 118.

receives its embodiment. As such it is not an intellectual position but a stance that ultimately can only be displayed.[122]

This understanding is in stark contrast to the idea of pacifism as an intellectual position that is assumed to be accessible to anyone, irrespective of viewpoint. Nonviolence as an intellectual position came, in America, under heavy critique from thinkers such as Reinhold Niebuhr, who asserted that pacifism so construed was optimistic and naïve.[123] For Hauerwas peaceableness is not stunned by this critique because it is taken to be intrinsic to fundamental Christian convictions.[124] The stress on embodiment that Hauerwas displays regarding pacifism is, I would argue, a further guard against the Niebuhrian critique. Pacifism, according to Hauerwas, is not a theoretical alternative to other ways of living, but a practical one: the church is not to offer an alternative but to be an alternative.[125] Christians embodied such an alternative "when they thought it a good thing to construct houses of hospitality for people who would have otherwise died alone," or "when they did not kill their children who were born deformed."[126] Peace in Hauerwas's sense is something that rests on fundamental Christian practices, and as such is not a theoretical, but a practical contribution.[127]

Hauerwas further maintains that it is our practices that show what is of great importance to us (more than our arguments or convictions):

> our theological commitments to [pacifism] are distorted insofar as our lives are shaped violently. Thus, Christian pacifism is not the result of holding certain beliefs, nor is pacifism even so much what it might mean to know these beliefs truthfully. Rather, living non-violently is in a sense the very condition for even knowing what we believe about pacifism.[128]

Nonviolence as a condition for "knowing what we believe about pacifism" is but another way of stressing peaceableness as a lived experience, in contrast to pacifism as an intellectual position. There is thus an element of discovery in peaceableness: a peaceable person does not in advance, or in principle, know what such a nonviolent stance may lead to.

122. Hauerwas, *Performing the Faith*, 183.
123. Hauerwas, *Dispatches from the Front*, 118.
124. Hauerwas, *Dispatches from the Front*, 118.
125. Hauerwas, *Wilderness Wanderings*, 122.
126. Hauerwas, *Wilderness Wanderings*, 122.
127. Hauerwas, *Wilderness Wanderings*, 122.
128. Hauerwas, *In Good Company*, 186.

An Active Peace

To further understand peaceableness it must be noted that it is characteristically "active" and not "passive." This is in contrast to the critique that Christian pacifism entails passivity or withdrawal in the face of evil. How is this active, or engaging, characteristic of peaceableness to be understood? Answering this will allow us to get a better grasp of Christian pacifism.

Christian nonviolence should not be understood simply as "not violence," that is, a simple avoidance of violence. The peace offered in Christ is, according to Hauerwas, more than just the absence of violence.[129] Peaceableness rebukes the violence in the heart of the believer: as a Christian places her/his life within the story of Jesus, he or she will be acquainted with the amount of violence stored up in her/his heart. This violence is something that a Christian must continually deal with: "recognize and lay down."[130] Despite this peaceableness is not just something that affects the life of Christians. Peaceableness is also active, even disruptive, an "unsettling peace" in Hauerwas's terms.[131] The reason is that this peace confronts deceitful undertakings wherever they are encountered and thus disturbs an eventual relative peace. From this follows that the form of pacifism that Hauerwas represents does not make the world a more peaceful place but on the contrary, it might reveal and even generate violence. This is the reason why Hauerwas says that Christian nonviolence must come to grips with the tragic in our existence.[132] It is a position that laments violence but, nevertheless, seeks to be patient in the face of aggression. This is made possible by the conviction that God will ultimately set history "right" without the help of our coercion. Because peaceableness is an active peace it might at times appear as trouble-making and at other times passive in the face of violence.[133]

In *Christian Existence Today* Hauerwas develops this aspect of peaceableness.[134] He argues that a peaceable community must consequently also be a "peacemaking" community. Hauerwas takes his cue from Matthew 18:15-22 which begins by saying that "if your brother sins against you,

---

129. Hauerwas, *Performing the Faith*, 170.
130. Hauerwas, *The Peaceable Kingdom*, 94.
131. Hauerwas, *The Peaceable Kingdom*, 145.
132. Hauerwas, *Truthfulness and Tragedy*, 35–38.
133. Berkman and Cartwright, *The Hauerwas Reader*, 323, 532.
134. Hauerwas, *Christian Existence Today*.

go and tell him his fault."¹³⁵ This implies that one cannot overlook wrongs that one faces. This conviction is an example of Hauerwas's claim that peaceableness is not a passive stance but an active venture that aims for a truthful peace. Peacemaking entails a confrontation of the wrongdoer, or "sinner" as Hauerwas following the abovementioned text calls her/him. This is, nevertheless, not done as if the "confrontator" would be "just" and the offender a "sinner" but rather the confrontator should know he or she has been forgiven. The attitude of being forgiven is crucial because if the victim does not see her/himself as forgiven a confrontation, and offer of forgiveness, is but a way to exercise power over the aggressor. Proper confrontation is, furthermore, not only to be done in order for the one wronged against to be able to "get over it" but in order to cause reconciliation between the two. Leaving a wrongdoer to her own devices would be to abandon her to her sin.¹³⁶

Confronting someone who might have caused offence is difficult, but it is, in Hauerwas's view, essential to discipleship.¹³⁷ Disciples are commanded to confront an offender (Matt 18:15–22). Such a venture might prove the offended wrong, since it might also be a case of misunderstanding, and if that is the case, a confrontation will clarify the situation and thus dissolve the conflict. This type of confrontation is not easy since "we will have to envision the possibility that, like Jonah, he or she may repent and we will therefore have to be reconciled. We will be forced to lose the subject of our hatred."¹³⁸

Peacemaking, as Hauerwas portrays it, in no way implies an absence of conflict. It, rather, aspires for a peace that is based on truth, instead of the absence of conflict. This means that wrongs that the community calls "sins" must be exposed so that the community can live truthfully. Hauerwas summarizes it as follows: "peace keeping is a virtue of the Christian community that is required if the church is to be a community of people at peace with one another in truth."¹³⁹ Truthfulness is, in other words, intimately linked to peaceableness: peaceableness does not overlook wrongs in the interest of maintaining a situation without conflict. Instead, it assumes that one cannot have genuine peace, without confronting "non-truths" and wrongs.

135. Hauerwas, *Christian Existence Today*, 89.
136. Hauerwas, *Christian Existence Today*, 92–93.
137. Berkman and Cartwright, *The Hauerwas Reader*, 323, 532.
138. Hauerwas, *Christian Existence Today*, 92
139. Hauerwas, *Christian Existence Today*, 92

This active peace is one that does not only confront current wrongs but one that rebukes both past, present and future iniquities. For Hauerwas there are things that cannot be set aright or simply forgotten, and therefore, confrontation, forgiveness and reconciliation are necessary. An example of this is the Holocaust that cannot be undone by trying to forget it, but must be faced and dealt with in order for Christians and Jews to be able to be reconciled.[140]

Peacemaking is for Hauerwas an inherent characteristic of the church. This command to confront wrongs is, however, not limited to the Christian community. While the "brother" mentioned in Matthew 18:15 refers to a fellow Christian, Hauerwas suggests that the Christian community understood itself as a community witnessing to God's peace, and as such the peacemaking aspect of church is relevant also to the wider community.[141] The church should not be any less truthful toward the world and thus the church should seek to "challenge the false peace of the world which is too often built more on power than truth."[142] If the church is not truthful toward the world in exposing wrongs, it does not have a peace to offer the world, since peace is for Hauerwas tied to truth.[143]

While peaceableness is a tragic enterprise, considering the command to confront wrongs, it also has a joyful aspect. It is the joy that the Christian can experience as he or she realizes that God has made a peaceable life possible. Hauerwas puts it as follows: "We discover that the patient hope that requires us to wait in the face of violence is not some means to a greater good, but the good itself."[144] The joy that peaceableness allegedly brings is not simply based on the hope that history will be "set right" by God, but it is a "present disposition."[145] It is a disposition based on the conviction that God has brought his peace to the world in Christ and will ultimately complete this peace in the eschaton.

In my interpretation, a peaceable disposition is "the good itself" in that it allows a person or community to take the time needed to find peaceable solutions in times of conflict. This is not to say that solutions that seem "active" or "effective" can necessarily and always be found. At times perhaps all that peaceableness amounts to is a quiet suffering in the

140. Hauerwas, *Christian Existence Today*, 94.
141. Hauerwas, *Christian Existence Today*, 96.
142. Hauerwas, *Christian Existence Today*, 95.
143. Hauerwas, *Christian Existence Today*, 95.
144. Hauerwas, *The Peaceable Kingdom*, 146.
145. Hauerwas, *The Peaceable Kingdom*, 147.

face of violence and wrongs. Yet such a disposition does not have to be belittled, because it is salvation in that it "saves" a person and a community from violent practices. Despite this it must be acknowledged that, for Hauerwas, peaceableness is not an end in itself isolated from Christian convictions, especially the practice of reconciliation.[146]

Hauerwas's peaceableness is a demanding communal conviction. It is to be seen not as the business of individual Christians as much as a conviction and institution of a peaceable community. Anyone committed to it—and every Christian ought to be so in Hauerwas's view—will be (by outsiders) seen more as a troublemaker than a peacemaker, since the form of peace that peaceableness seeks is a truthful peace. From this follows that it is an active peace that cannot be contained in modernity's alleged personal religious sphere, and as such necessarily a political venture.

Witnessing Politics

Politics is here to be understood in a certain way. It is not ordinary party politics that we are concerned with. What we are talking about is that a nonviolent community is in itself a peculiar kind of politics. A Christian community by virtue of being a body different from the world—a body that necessarily takes up space in the world—is political. It is an example of the kind of "theological politics" that Hauerwas has sought to develop.[147]

The link that Hauerwas makes between peaceableness, this peculiar politics, and community is made explicit in the claim that nonviolence is the prerequisite for a truthful politics and "the creation of nonviolent community is the means and end of all politics."[148] This seems to be an implication of Hauerwas's foundational conviction that nonviolence reflects what God is like. To reiterate, the existence of a peaceable community is necessary in order to have truthful politics, while politics should aim for a peaceable community brought about without using force.

It should be noted that this can be seen as providing a wider perspective on what I would like to call Hauerwas's "typical" talk about pacifism. Hauerwas often maintains that peaceableness is "intrinsic" to Christian community.[149] The quote above, however, suggests that it is also a means

---

146. Hauerwas, *Dispatches from the Front*, 18, 197.
147. Rasmusson, *The Church as Polis*.
148. Hauerwas, *Dispatches from the Front*, 10.
149. See e.g. Hauerwas, *Vision and Virtue*, 202; Hauerwas, *The Peaceable Kingdom*, xxiv; Hauerwas, *With the Grain of the Universe*, 220.

as well as an end. This is an important clarification to the way Hauerwas views pacifism. Though he claims that peaceableness is neither some optional add-on to Christianity nor a way to rid the world of violence, it, nevertheless, contains the aspect of being a means.

Seeing peaceableness as also a means opens up for the question of the "function"[150] of Hauerwas's pacifism. Since he does not assume that peaceableness is an effective way to do away with violence, what is then its function? I suggest that a central function of Hauerwas's peacemaking is witness to the world: it reflects the forgiving and peacemaking character of God. It is witness to the extent that it exemplifies an alternative politics. In other words, a community that rejects the use of violence in order to reach its objectives is a counter-community in a society in which coercion is considered legitimate and "normal."[151] As such peaceableness has an "educating" function in the world. It has the potential to stimulate the wider society's imagination to grasp nonviolent and peacemaking alternatives in language and habit.

What is then the shape of such witness? How can a Christian community communicate what it is about to the wider society? From the idea of Christian community as a peculiar political reality follows that witness is something that is lived *coram hominibus* ("before humanity"). It is, therefore, something that must be displayed, or embodied, by a community. On this view it is not meaningful to make any stark distinction between life *coram hominibus* and *coram Deo* ("before God"). The way I read Hauerwas, one cannot have the latter extracted from the former. In other words, life before God is not distinguishable from life before "the least of these."[152] This does not mean that a church should not also proclaim the evangel verbally, but it requires such proclamation to be part of and in tune with the "body-language" of the Christian community.

---

150. The word must be in quotation-marks because one should first and foremost see peaceableness as an intrinsic hallmark to Christian community: it is not primarily a means to some greater good, but in itself the good. Yet it, as I have tried to suggest, contains an element of it being also a means.

151. An example of such legitimated coercion is found in any democratic setting: minority views are routinely put in check with law enforced majority decisions. A Hauerwasian community is an alternative to such politics to the extent that it deals with differences without coercion. This would obviously require patience, forgiveness and ability to live with tensions.

152. "I tell you the truth, whatever you did for one of the least of these brothers of mine, you did for me." (Matt 25:40) One can, of course, make the distinction for analytical purposes or "in principle" but I am here concerned with the practical shape, or body, that life before God and humanity may take.

To return to the question of the shape of witness I must conclude that it cannot be expressed more specifically due to its inescapably *ad hoc* character. I have here interpreted Hauerwas in a way that stresses the need for embodiment of Christian convictions. There is, however, a further point to be made with regard to the ad hoc character of nonviolence and Christian witness. It is the simple point that Christian witness is inevitably contextual. Yoder maintains that we cannot escape "these skins," that is, that we are historically situated, and that whatever we say we must say "within these skins."[153] Yoder suggests that Christians cannot say anything less than "Jesus is Messiah and Lord": the question is then how to say that in a context that is, for example, pluralistic and relativistic?[154]

> Since for some even the phrase "truth claims" evokes echoes of theocratic compulsion or of pretensions to infallibility, let us use the more biblical phrases "witness" and "proclamation" as naming forms of communication which do not coerce the hearer.[155]

Yoder is suggesting that witness is a non-coercive form of communication. Peaceableness can be seen as a form of such communication, or witness, in that it exemplifies a way of life without coercing the other to adopt it. It is a form of non-coercive persuasion. Due to its embodied character it is also a peculiar politics, and at that one that is not based on violence.

Patience and Triviality

In *Christian Existence Today* Hauerwas develops yet another aspect of peaceableness, namely, the skill to take time for peace.[156] This skill can be exemplified by a peaceable Christian's response to the fact that we live in an age of nuclear weapons: Hauerwas suggests that commonly there seems to be only two alternatives for relating to said fact. The first alternative is to do everything possible in order to get rid of the nuclear threat. This would entail rallying for disarmament and seeking to inform and urge politicians

---

153. Hauerwas, *With the Grain of the Universe*, 223 quoting Yoder, *The Priestly Kingdom*, 56.

154. Hauerwas, *With the Grain of the Universe*, 223 quoting Yoder, *The Priestly Kingdom*, 56.

155. Hauerwas, *With the Grain of the Universe*, 223 quoting Yoder, *The Priestly Kingdom*, 56.

156. Hauerwas, *Christian Existence Today*.

to find means that excludes the use of nuclear weapons. The other alternative is to do nothing: to learn to "live with the bomb" and go on with life.[157]

Hauerwas proposes a third alternative, which is for Christians to do "something" in the face of the nuclear threat. This something involves learning to live peacefully by discovering "the ethical significance of the trivial."[158] Hauerwas talks about trivial in the sense of ordinary or "that which can be met anywhere."[159] The argument is that these activities have the potential to teach us to take the time needed for peace. The birth of a child is another example of this: having a child forces a person to take time to care for the child. Hauerwas maintains that this does not make sense, neither intellectually nor morally, apart from the conviction that "God has given us the time and space to be people who can rest and enjoy our creation as creatures."[160] Christians do not have to have their lives determined by threat of nuclear weapons, but instead they can trust that the outcome of history is in God's hands. Hauerwas, however, is not suggesting that Christians should not support politicians in seeking to end the nuclear armament. That support may well be given but it is hard for Hauerwas to imagine that such action would yield much result.[161]

What he is suggesting is rather that in order for us to have peace we need time to work out our disagreements, instead of a habitual lapsing into coercive behavior that often becomes the norm. Hauerwas further suggests, "peace is found within our timeful activities."[162] In other words, while we live in a violent world much of our everyday activities are nevertheless peaceful and peacemaking. Hauerwas suggests that "We know that as God's creatures we are not naturally violent."[163] Hauerwas recapitulates that "the willingness to take the time to care for the trivial is exactly the disposition that provides the basis for our learning to be peaceful people capable of finding peace as a community."[164] No other ordinary activity is for Hauerwas more peaceful and hopeful than having and raising children. It is not dissimilar to the virtues, as it is not a means to an end but contains its meaning.[165]

157. Hauerwas, *Christian Existence Today*, 253.
158. Hauerwas, *Christian Existence Today*, 256.
159. Hauerwas, *Christian Existence Today*, 263.
160. Hauerwas, *Christian Existence Today*, 257.
161. Hauerwas, *Christian Existence Today*, 257.
162. Hauerwas, *Christian Existence Today*, 259.
163. Hauerwas, *Christian Existence Today*, 95.
164. Hauerwas, *Christian Existence Today*, 259.
165. Hauerwas, *Christian Existence Today*, 264–265.

An example of such patience and peace that Hauerwas often gives is a phenomenon called *L'Arche*. What today is known as L'Arche International began in 1964 when Roman Catholic philosopher Jean Vanier (born 1928) invited two intellectually disabled men to live with him. Over the decades, what began in a small house, which Vanier named L'Arche (Ark), has grown into a movement of 131 communities that live in more than 30 countries.[166] Hauerwas suggests that L'Arche provides the place and the time necessary to discover what peace is.[167] Constancy and routine are an important aspect of life at L'Arche: "Familiarity is what makes place 'a' place."[168] L'Arche also stands for a peculiar understanding of time. It may take several hours to share a meal or to bathe someone. Patience is, therefore, an essential virtue at L'Arche. For Hauerwas the understanding of time that L'Arche operates with is an alternative to the contemporary emphasis on efficiency: "our world is based on speed—L'Arche is based on patience; L'Arche is God's time—not the world's time of speed."[169] Hauerwas, furthermore, links speed and efficiency to violence and war, whereas L'Arche with its practices is an example of peace.[170]

L'Arche is also a good example of the kind of theological politics that Hauerwas suggests that churches are called to be. Working patiently with what may appear to be trivial things are, on this view, important because they can allow us to discover what peace is. This is also why "eschatological hope" are, according to Hauerwas, among the most important virtues. Christians must learn to face violence and injustice patiently, trusting that the story of Jesus has an end where complete peace and justice will rule.[171] Alternative politics, such as L'Arche, are not a solution to the world's problems but they are a signal of the fact that there are alternative, peaceful ways to live in community.

---

166. L'Arche International, "Beginnings." Denmark is the only Nordic country in which L'Arche can be found. L'Arche is, therefore, not an example that could be claimed as typically Nordic. Despite this I find it a meaningful case for my purposes because many or the communities live in the so-called Western world. (L'Arche International, "Communities.")

167. Hauerwas and Vanier, *Living Gently*, 47. It should be noted that Hauerwas has written extensively about the mentally handicapped.

168. Hauerwas and Vanier, *Living Gently*, 47.

169. Hauerwas, "On Prayer."

170. Hauerwas and Vanier, *Living Gently*, 50.

171. Hauerwas, *The Peaceable Kingdom*, 103–104.

Stout's Question

For Hauerwas peaceableness is intrinsic to Christian discipleship because it, as mentioned above, reflects what God is like.[172] Peaceableness consequently involves a claim about God as nonviolent. This claim evokes an important critique against Hauerwas's peaceableness that in the following will be expressed in Jeffrey Stout's words. Stout suggests that Hauerwas's Christian pacifism does not rest on a comprehensive reading of the Bible:

> God's way of dealing with evil is said to be revealed definitively on Good Friday. Hence, Christians are called to deal with evil nonviolently. Who, then, authorizes the killing of the Hittites, Amorites, Canaanites, Perizzites, Hivites, and Jebusites in Deuteronomy 20? Who ordains in Matthew 25 and Revelation 20 that the accursed shall be cast into the fire on judgment day? And who says in Matthew 10:34 that he has "come not to bring peace, but a sword"? . . . Well, is God nonviolent or not?[173]

Stout's question is straight-forward: the Bible does not seem to portray God as consistently nonviolent, and yet Hauerwas is suggesting just that to the extent that peaceableness allegedly reflects God's character.

Hauerwas responds to Stout's critique in A Response to Jeff Stout's Democracy and Tradition.[174] Hauerwas begins by noting that Stout's characterization of peaceableness is somewhat off the mark in that it calls Hauerwas's pacifism "absolute pacifism" and that it is "a vocation of discipleship to Christ."[175] These terms are, according to Hauerwas, misrepresentations of peaceableness in two ways: firstly, Hauerwas does not use the language of vocation.[176] He does not, however, make a big deal out of this slight re-narration. What on the other hand seems more important for Hauerwas to express is that "absolute pacifism" does not adequately describe "christological pacifism."[177] To illustrate this Hauerwas refers to the entire book *Performing the Faith* which is an attempt to describe the

---

172. Hauerwas, *Vision and Virtue*, 202; Hauerwas, *With the Grain of the Universe*, 220.

173. Stout, *Democracy and Tradition*, 323.

174. Hauerwas, *Performing the Faith*, 215–241.

175. Hauerwas, *Performing the Faith*, 238 referring to Stout, *Democracy and Tradition*, 158.

176. Hauerwas, *Performing the Faith*, 239.

177. Hauerwas, *Performing the Faith*, 239.

kind of nonviolence that Hauerwas actually defends.[178] Central to Hauerwas's peaceableness, as well as to *Performing the Faith*, is that christological pacifism is not "a position that can be justified apart from discipleship."[179] Hauerwas, therefore, maintains that he cannot, despite Stout's requests, provide a conclusive description of what Christian pacifism entails because "we can never anticipate what we will be called on to be or do because we have disavowed the use of violence."[180]

The strategy that Hauerwas utilizes in his initial response to this particular critique made by Stout is to focus on Stout's description of what is being critiqued. The point about peaceableness not being a position is an important remark in this context, and not dissimilar to the demarcation vis-à-vis Niebuhrian and Troeltschian critiques of pacifism discussed earlier. But what about the specific charge that Hauerwas's pacifism rests on a selective reading of the Bible that omits the passages that portray God as violent? The way Hauerwas meets this direct confrontation of his peaceableness is to admit that he might be selective in his reading of the Bible: "Stout may be right about me, but I do not think he is right about the unpersuasive character of Yoder's 'biblical scholarship.'"[181] Hauerwas, in other words, considers Yoder's scholarship solid, and abides by the latter's refusal to suggest "that 'God becomes nonviolent' only in the cross.[182] By this Hauerwas implicitly answers Stout regarding God's nonviolence. Hauerwas, in turn, asks Stout to specify why he finds Yoder's biblical scholarship wanting.[183] This I take to be a valid request since Stout discards of Yoder surprisingly easily.

Interestingly, Hauerwas does not explicitly answer Stout's question about whether God is nonviolent or not. Instead, he seeks to reaffirm

178. Hauerwas, *Performing the Faith*, 239.
179. Hauerwas, *Performing the Faith*, 239.
180. Hauerwas, *Performing the Faith*, 239.

181. Hauerwas, *Performing the Faith*, 239 referring to Stout's remark "Perhaps Hauerwas feels that Yoder has dealt with these questions adequately." (Stout, *Democracy and Tradition*, 323.) Stout challenges Hauerwas for inconsistency in that pacifism is emphasized in such a rigid fashion, whereas "remarriage after divorce, for example, or the chances of a rich man to enter the kingdom of God" do not receive a similar emphasis. (Stout, *Democracy and Tradition*, 160.)

182. Hauerwas, *Performing the Faith*, 240. Hauerwas also refers to Yoder et al., *The Jewish-Christian Schism Revisited*.

183. Hauerwas, *Performing the Faith*, 240. Hauerwas notes that "For example, Stout makes no reference to Richard Hays's extremely appreciative account of Yoder's 'biblical scholarship' in [Hays, *The Moral Vision*, 239–253]." (Hauerwas, *Performing the Faith*, 240.) Hauerwas is, in other words, not alone in approving of Yoder's scholarship.

Yoder's scholarly credibility, and with it his own nonviolent project. Giving a thorough treatment of Yoder's scholarship with regard to nonviolence is, however, beyond the scope of the present study.[184] I will, therefore, in the following simply identify what I suggest is a crucial element of Yoder's take on God's alleged nonviolence.

The central point is the need to understand the historical and cultural setting of the texts in which God commands the killing of other peoples.[185] Yoder notes that a general rule of textual interpretation is to ask how the original recipients of the text would have heard it.[186] Modern readings of passages in which God appears violent are problematic because it is difficult to avoid *eisegesis*. Yoder observes that there are questions that are not "culturally conceivable" in a given context.[187] Yoder emphasizes that the bloodshed in the invasion of Canaan

> must be understood in its cultural context, i.e., cultically. Before a battle the enemy army would be "devoted to the Lord"; i.e. it was declared to be *ḥerem* or *qādōsh*, set apart, holy, taboo; it henceforth belonged to YHWH like the animal on the altar. This is why no booty was taken; neither slaves, nor cattle, nor gold. The killing was instrumental, contributing in a practical way to a political goal; it was sacrificial.[188]

This kind of cultic bloodshed is, of course, culturally *in*conceivable in our day. Yet it is through paying attention to the *contextuality* of "cultic violence" that Yoder is able to imply that the slaughters in Canaan were not as offensive as they are to the modern reader.[189] A modern day example that might illustrate the issue is killing animals for food. Many people today would not call eating animals "violent" though it involves killing. Some consider meat-eating unethical, but it is often contended on other grounds than on it being "violent." Violence is not a term we would generally apply to "culinary killing." It is in a similar way that cultic killing did not appear

---

184. It has, furthermore, recently been done in Nikolajsen, *Redefining the Indentity of the Church*.

185. Yoder, *The Politics of Jesus*, 76; Yoder, *The Original Revolution*, 94.

186. Yoder, *The Politics of Jesus*, 78.

187. Yoder, *The Politics of Jesus*, 78.

188. Yoder, *The Politics of Jesus*, 78. Italics in the original.

189. Similarly the violence found in the book of Revelations is, according to Yoder, to be understood as part of the peculiar genre of apocalyptic literature. (Yoder, *The Politics of Jesus*, 241.)

violent.[190] Yoder gives the example of the story of Abraham being told to kill his own son (Gen. 22:1-19).[191] This story is offensive today because killing one's child is simply inconceivable. Yoder notes that originally the story was not that offensive, considering that it was rather common to sacrifice one's firstborn.[192] It was, however, offensive because it was through this particular son that God had promised many descendants.

Though I have made no claims to a thorough treatment of Yoder's scholarship I must, nevertheless, report that I—in contrast to Stout—find Yoder's scholarship convincing. Yoder approaches the biblical stories with an openness, even towards what in our day is culturally inconceivable. This is necessary in order to discover how the texts were read in the context in which they came into being. When it comes to "holy wars" commanded by God one should note that Yoder also emphasizes instances were the enemy was miraculously[193] nonviolently driven away.[194] This is a valuable perspective because it helps the reader to put the holy wars into a wider perspective.

In any case I consider Yoder's view to be solid enough for Hauerwas to be able to maintain that nonviolence reflects what God is like. As he was in the world so should also his followers be.[195] Jesus was nonviolent and so should his followers be, while acknowledging that God at times acted through Israel in ways that are, when considered from today's perspective, difficult to call anything else than violent. Perhaps it would have been better for Hauerwas to say that nonviolence reflects what Jesus was like, instead of what God is like? That would, at least—apart from being a borderline modalist strategy—be an easy way out without having to show that despite modern interpretations God indeed is always nonviolent in all

---

190. I acknowledge that this may not be a fair example since I am talking about killing *animals* not humans. The point that I am trying to make is, nevertheless, that there can be forms of killing that in a given historical and cultural setting do not strike us as violent.

191. Yoder, *The Original Revolution*, 95; Yoder, *The Politics of Jesus*, 78.

192. Yoder, *The Politics of Jesus*, 78.

193. Here used the way Yoder uses the word, that is, "what the root meaning of the word accents; that it is cause for wonderment. We are not concerned here for philosophical meditations about the laws of nature, breaking the laws of nature, what miracles prove, or what is meant by miracle stories if they cannot have happened the way it says." (Yoder, *The Politics of Jesus*, 82.)

194. Yoder, *The Politics of Jesus*, 78-79. Yoder notes that the "nonmartial deliverances, which for the Israelite were part of the same picture, have been given less scholarly attention" compared to the more active invasions. (Yoder, *The Politics of Jesus*, 78.)

195. Hauerwas, *Vision and Virtue*, 202.

God's dealings. A related way to dodge the difficulty would be to maintain that in some situations God may appear to be violent but that humans do not have the same freedom and wisdom to act as does God. The nonviolent Jesus is, however, the example for Christians.

In conclusion of my account of Stout's critique I want to summarize the pros and cons of his presentation. On the positive side Stout seeks to engage Hauerwas on the latter's grounds. Stout also raises the important issue of whether Hauerwas reads the Bible selectively: some issues, namely pacifism, seem to be taken to an extreme, while other issues (for example the question of remarriage) are interpreted in a way that does not have rigid repercussions.[196] On the negative side, Stout does not give due attention to how Hauerwas in fact calls people to work for peace and justice, and also personally belongs to groups such as the Baptist Peace Fellowship, the Catholic Peace Fellowship and the Ekklesia Project.[197] Stout also, on my view, dismisses Yoder's "biblical scholarship" too easily.

SUMMARY

In conclusion to this chapter I will review the central elements of my account of the notions of Constantinianism and peaceableness. In this chapter I suggested that the notion of Constantinianism could be a resource for churches that seek to communicate a Christian tradition in our context. It is a resource in that it can function as a tool for critical self-reflection.[198] Attempting to harness existing power structures, such as the state, to work for the mandate of the church would be Constantinianism. Rejecting such strategies would, on this view, allow Christian communities to be more truthful to their nonviolent tradition. Constantinianism, I have tried to show, leads Christian communities into incoherence: the Constantinian "body language" would disqualify the verbal proclamation. To repeat, a message of God's love told coercively cannot but be self-defeating.

In what way can peaceableness then be seen as a resource? Calling peaceableness "a resource" may create the impression that nonviolence is a

---

196. Stout, *Democracy and Tradition*, 160. That Stout mentions remarriage as an example seems to be something of a potshot since Hauerwas has divorced and remarried.

197. Hauerwas, *Performing the Faith*, 239.

198. Björn Vikström notes that it is problematic to compare "theological ideals" with "empirical reality." Despite this danger he suggests, in my view rightly, that it is helpful to reflect on theological ideals in order to envision how things could be improved. (Vikström, *Folkkyrka i en postmodern tid*, 166.)

means to an end. This is not, however, how Hauerwas talks about Christian pacifism. I have argued that Hauerwasian pacifism is to be seen in itself as "the good." At the same time it might be best described as a "pragmatic good" since it also contains an element of being a means to an end, namely, to witness. Peaceableness, I have suggested, is witness in that it reflects the forgiving and peacemaking character of God. It is, furthermore, witness in the sense that it exemplifies an alternative politics. Such a politics apart from being truthful to (Hauerwas's reading of) Christian tradition, has pragmatically speaking, the potential to widen society's imagination to see nonviolent modes of operation.

Chapter 5

Hauerwas in a Nordic Setting

IN THE EARLIER CHAPTERS I have in Stanley Hauerwas's theology identified factors that have relevance for a meaningful understanding of Christian witness. The intent of this chapter is to further show *how* these features in Hauerwas's thought may provide an amendment to typical Nordic theological emphases. I will do this by bringing these relevant aspects in conversation with some Nordic Lutheran theologians. Through this resulting discussion I hope to bring to the fore some important aspects of a meaningful contextual notion of witness.

THE PROBLEM OF NORDIC THEOLOGY AND ETHICS

A claim of this study is that Hauerwas's theology provides resources for understanding witness in our context. This claim also implies that a Hauerwasian perspective provides an amendment to Nordic Lutheran theological and ethical discourse. In order to clarify this I must show *what it is an amendment to*. There are difficulties involved in this. For one it is not possible to compare and contrast two entities if it is unclear what they are. I have thus far provided an account of some central features of Hauerwas's theology. What is now needed is some account of aspects of typical Nordic theological and ethical discourse. This is where the difficulty sets in: it is far from clear if there is such a thing as *typical* Nordic theological and ethical discourse, and if there is, what it is.

Because Lutheranism has historically been dominant in the Nordic contexts it is of interest to this project to consider how Lutheran theology approaches ethics. I do, in other words, assume that one can, at least on a general level, speak of common traits in Lutheran thinking.[1] Even if one narrows the search for a typical Nordic theological and ethical discourse to Lutheran accounts it is, nevertheless, unclear who gets to speak for the Lutheran Church in, for example, Finland. It is difficult to assess to what degree, for example, an academic theologian's work reflects the Church's view because the church does not have a set "view" on everything. The Church's voice is perhaps better seen as a choir with many, at times even disharmonious, voices.[2] This makes it difficult to relate the proposed resources in Hauerwas's theology with "Nordic Lutheran theology." I will, therefore, in the following relate aspects of Hauerwas's thought to *some voices in the choir of Nordic theology*. I do not claim to provide a comprehensive sample of recent theology done in the Nordic context, or even in Finland. My intention is rather to draw on relevant Nordic Lutheran theologians in order to clarify how Hauerwas's theology can contribute with a distinct perspective in our context.[3]

Despite these difficulties in talking about Nordic theology some typical elements can, nonetheless, be identified. I will mention four relevant notions. These are the notions of folk church, creation perspective, natural law, and two regiments.[4]

Firstly, the idea of a state or folk church has been central to Nordic theology. Both "state church" and "folk church" have been described in various ways in the various Nordic countries. In the case of Sweden, Rasmusson notes that the idea of folk church is a basic part of the self-definition of the Church of Sweden.[5] This is, according to Rasmusson, widely accepted but there is no widespread consensus on what this means.[6] Björn Vikström also points out that it is difficult to present a general account of

1. By "general level" I mean in comparison to, for example, typical Catholic or Anabaptist ways of theological reasoning. Antti Raunio notes that the Lutheran Church does not have a systematic normative ethical teaching as does the Catholic Church. I agree, however, with Raunio that one can still on a more general level talk about a Lutheran way of approaching ethical questions, and as such one can talk about "the church's ethic." (Raunio, *Järki, usko ja lähimmäisen hyvä*, 28.)

2. Hytönen, *Kirkko*, 50).

3. That I focus on "some voices" and concrete examples, has some parallels to how Hauerwas does not want to create "in-principle-policies." As I have indicated above, Hauerwas attempts to pay attention to the particularities of specific situations.

4. This is not a comprehensive list of central themes share by the Nordic Churches. These are highlighted because they are relevant for my study. For a fairly recent overview of Nordic Lutheranism see Ryman et al., *Nordic Folk Churches*.

5. Rasmusson, "A Century of Swedish Theology," 131.

6. Rasmusson, "A Century of Swedish Theology," 131.

the idea of folk church because it has been developed in different ways in different cultural settings.[7] A central feature in the idea of folk church is, however, that the Church seeks to cater to the needs of the people who live in a given nation. Vikström argues, furthermore, that a folk church has a double loyalty: on the one hand it seeks to be loyal to its confessional tradition, on the other it also seeks to be true to the people who live in the geographical area in which the local churches minister.[8]

The second major notion that must be mentioned is the centrality of a creation perspective. Raunio maintains that "theology of creation" (*luomisen teologia*) has traditionally been a common denominator to Nordic Lutheran theologies.[9] Gustaf Wingren was one of the central advocates for a theology that emphasizes creation. Wingren reacted to theologies that accentuate Christology and ecclesiology over the doctrine of creation, as exemplified by Anders Nygren and Karl Barth.[10] For Wingren humans are in relationship with God by virtue of being created.[11] Such a theology is open to the idea that God is "at work" not only in the church but also outside it. This perspective implies a strong continuity between Christians and non-Christians.

The third theme is the stress on natural law. Natural law has been widely seen as the basis for ethics in our context.[12] Central to ideas of natural law is the assumption that all human beings have a sense of right and wrong. I will in this chapter discuss specific examples of natural law perspectives. Regarding the creation perspective and the assumption of natural law Vikström raises an important question: he asks, referring mainly to the Swedish situation, to what degree theological discourse that stresses creation and natural law has confused these with modernist understandings of reason and truth.[13]

7. Vikström, *Folkkyrka i en postmodern tid*, 10.
8. Vikström, *Folkkyrka i en postmodern tid*, 14.
9. Raunio, *Järki, usko ja lähimmäisen hyvä*, 48.
10. Rasmusson, "A Century of Swedish Theology," 141.
11. Rasmusson, "A Century of Swedish Theology," 141.
12. Raunio, *Järki, usko ja lähimmäisen hyvä*, 48. Raunio lists N. F. S. Grundtvig, Herbert Olsson, Lauri Haikola, Ragnar Bring, Gustaf Wingren, K. E. Løgstrup, Svend Andersen, Lennart Pinomaa and Jorma Laulaja among the central developers of Nordic theological and ethical thinking. (Raunio, *Järki, usko ja lähimmäisen hyvä*, 49.) Raunio also mentions the centrality of Luther studies in Nordic theology, in Finland pointedly expressed by Tuomo Mannermaa. (Raunio, *Järki, usko ja lähimmäisen hyvä*, 50.)
13. Vikström, *Folkkyrka i en postmodern tid*, 183.

The fourth typical element in Nordic Lutheran theologies that must be mentioned, if only in passing, is the notion of two regiments. This is the view in which God rules the world through two modes of government. Christian doctrine is understood to belong to the spiritual regiment, while morality belongs to the worldly regiment, since it by virtue of creation and natural law is a common human faculty. Despite the fact that the doctrine is central in many Nordic theologies it is not discussed extensively in this study.

Finally, by way of introduction to this chapter there are three clarifications that need to be made explicit. Firstly, I do not seek to relate Hauerwas's perspective to the ethics that people in the Nordic societies *de facto* display.[14] My task is defined as a conceptual one. Consequently the focus lies on relating Hauerwas's perspective to typical, mainly Lutheran, theological views in our context. Secondly, it should be noted that in the following several of the factors, for example, "church as social ethics" and "embodiment" are discussed in separate subchapters. This is done for practical reasons; despite these analytic demarcations the factors are closely interrelated. Thirdly, in this chapter I utilize a compare and contrast method between Hauerwas's views on the one hand, and samples of Nordic (with an emphasis on Finnish Lutheran) theology on the other.

CHURCH AS SOCIAL ETHICS REVISITED

Christian Narration

One central aspect of my account of Hauerwas's notion of church as social ethics has to do with the way life is narrated. Hauerwas, as I have tried to show, insists that Christian ethics requires the qualifier *Christian*.[15] It is a peculiarly Christian way of seeing life. The world, in the sense of the totality of the context is, on this view, explicitly narrated with the language of the Christian tradition.[16]

---

14. Such empirical studies have been done, see e.g. Gustafsson and Pettersson, *Folkkyrkor*.

15. Hauerwas, *The Peaceable Kingdom*, 17, 96.

16. The totality of the church's context can be, for example, the historical and cultural situations, demands, problems and opportunities in which the church finds herself. Indeed, what would be seen as a demand, problem or opportunity would be defined from within the Christian tradition.

To compare this perspective with some Nordic voices there is a difference to be observed. To put it bluntly: Nordic theology often works within a world that "science" gets to define.[17] Philosopher Sami Pihlström maintains that in Finland it has been common for Lutheran Christianity to try to co-exist peacefully with science.[18] This means that a scientific description of the world is given the interpretative prerogative, while theology's domain is that which science cannot study.[19] Questions in which theology may have some relevance include questions about the origin of life, the destiny of humankind and the like.[20] If Pihlström captures a typical Finnish/Lutheran perspective then theology is rendered a very marginal role. On this view theology can only make contributions in questions in which science remains silent. This would be a classic example of a "God of the gaps" perspective.

The perspective that Hauerwas's church as social ethics stands for is in noticeable contrast to Pihlström's description of theology's role in society. The late German theologian Dietrich Bonhoeffer can be instanced in order to explicate the contrast:

> If in fact the frontiers of knowledge are being pushed further and further back (and that is bound to be the case), then God is being pushed back with them, and is therefore continually in retreat. We are to find God in what we know, not in what we don't know.[21]

Bonhoeffer is, in other words, critical toward the idea that references to God are invoked only in the domains still unsubdued by (scientific) knowledge. In contrast to this Bonhoeffer claims that God is to be found in that which is known to us. The idea of God as a God in retreat would also be a strange description of the God that the Biblical texts reflect. Yet that is what the view that Pihlström takes to be typical of our context implies. The way I interpret Hauerwas on this point is that he would agree with Bonhoeffer. I think, furthermore, that Hauerwas would want to add that knowledge is never innocent. Some knowledges might, for example, involve epistemological assumptions that Christians would do well not to endorse. Privileging a scientific or secular description of the world,

---

17. An explicit example of this is Vikström et al., *Kyrkans budskap*, 18 that refers to "sociological facts" that tell us what the world is like.
18. Pihlström, *Usko, järki ja ihminen*, 63.
19. Pihlström, *Usko, järki ja ihminen*, 63.
20. Pihlström, *Usko, järki ja ihminen*, 63.
21. Bonhoeffer, *Letters and Papers*, 311.

furthermore, implies that such descriptions are neutral or objective; simply a matter of fact. It is, however, meaningful to explicitly acknowledge that all descriptions and knowledges rest on some premises. Because of this it is problematic to assume that one can draw a clear-cut line between "knowledge" and "faith."[22]

One example of an assumption that Christians would do well not to endorse might be the common idea that one's motherland is worth fighting for. It is, I would think, rather customary to assume that a border between two states is an important marker between people. It might be understood as common knowledge.[23] A Hauerwasian Christian would, however, question such knowledge for example by claiming that it is an artificial and often arbitrary boundary between people. Such a Christian would maintain that the church as a people that transcend national borders is more constitutive of a Christian's identity than is a national border. Hauerwas's notion of church as social ethics stands for this kind of narration.

On the view described by Pihlström, to display the contrast, the space given to theology is much more limited. On this view, Christians might, for example, assume the border between two nations to be a set "fact." Theology would then focus on more existential matters, such as, how to go on living with such a border etc. The perspective provided by Hauerwas is radical in that it creates its own analysis of a situation (its

---

22. I agree with Raunio when he suggests that from a late modern perspective the rationality of the natural sciences does not have to be wrong *per se*, it is just that various "areas of life" (*elämänalue*) may work with differing and yet legitimate premises. (Raunio and Luomanen, *Teologia*, 116.) To this I would add though that in a late modern context one cannot take such "areas of life" to mean a trenchant differentiation of society. Jose Casanova, for example, has argued that the idea of a separate religious sphere has become implausible. (Casanova, *Public Religions in the Modern World*, 19.) One of the reasons for this is that "religion" in Western contexts seems to be emerging in new venues that do not fit the idea of a "religious sphere." This can be seen, as was suggested in the introduction to the present study, in how literature, movies and music discuss religious themes in new ways. (See Kurtén, "Gud i Norden," 111–128. See also Henriksen, *På grensen til Den andre*.) Ward further argues that this is not a *return* of religion "but a new religiousness that is hybrid, fluid, and commercialized" (Ward, *The Politics of Discipleship*, 131.) I have elsewhere tried to show how these new religious expressions—that Ward calls "hybrid, fluid, and commercialized"—do not have to mean "shallow" phenomena. See Tolonen, "Post-Secular Alternative Politics."

23. I do not want to downplay the role that historical developments, past wars, and a sense of history and homeland may have to many if not most people. For the sake of this example, however, I do not discuss these highly complex issues. I do, nevertheless, think that Hauerwas makes an important point when he claims that Christians' first allegiance should be to the kingdom of God and not to the nation state. It seems to me that it is difficult to be both patriot and Christian.

own sociology if you will). The fact that such an analysis is narrated with the language of church can provide a perspective that might not occur to people who do not subscribe to such language. Moreover, a Hauerwasian perspective would not emphasize knowledge about a situation, but faithful living in the face of whatever situation the church finds herself in. Such living would embody the conviction that the border in the example is manmade and not a reason to take arms even if the situation would "call for it" (if one looked at the situation with common nationalistic assumptions). This kind of Christian life might to others seem rather passive. A Hauerwasian Christian would obviously also have to live with the border—since she does not assume she has the power to change such things. Her hands would, however, be tied in that she would seek to be loyal to God more than to the state.[24]

Considering the current scarcity of quarrels about national borders in the Nordic context there is another perhaps more relevant example of the perspective that Hauerwas's church as social ethics stands for. This example has to do with how mundane things such as politics and economics are understood. It is not a Nordic example, per se, but I think that it still makes a relevant conceptual point. In *Heal Thyself: Spirituality, Medicine, and the Distortion of Christianity* Shuman and Meador provide, as Hauerwas in the foreword puts it, "a theological reading of the political and economic practices that produce the distorted character of current medicine and theology."[25] *Heal Thyself* is an exercise in the kind of theology that does not assume an explicit or implicit God of the gaps strategy. A

---

24. Whenever Christian pacifism is discussed the example of "what would you do if someone threatened your family with a gun and you also had a gun" is sooner or later brought up. Both Yoder and Hauerwas have discussed this issue in several places (see e.g. Yoder and Baez, *What Would You Do?*, 144; Hauerwas, *Matthew*, 110; Hauerwas, *Dispatches from the Front*, 188.). Joan Baez shows how hypothetical questions about such a threatening situation lead to hypothetical answers: "Okay, you're a pacifist. What would you do if someone were, say, attacking your grandmother? . . . Say he had a gun, and he was about to shoot her. Would you shoot him first?" "Do I have a gun?" "Yes." "No. I'm a pacifist, I don't have a gun." "Well, say you do." "All right. Am I a good shot?" "Yes." "I'd shoot the gun out of his hand." "No, then you're not a good shot." "I'd be afraid to shoot. Might kill grandma." (Yoder and Baez, *What Would You Do?*, 62.) Through her witty style Baez shows that one cannot say for sure what one might do in a hypothetical crisis situation. Baez then goes on to ask why people are trained to kill for the sake of nation states. That is not a hypothetical question but a concrete one that opens up an important discussion regarding common assumptions and attitudes.

25. Shuman et al., *Heal Thyself*, xii.

"theological reading" indicates that the book attempts to provide a distinct perspective on these practices.[26]

The view that Pihlström describes might, on the contrary, assume non-theological descriptions of political and economic practices as givens and then reflect on theological matters within the "parameters" set up by other disciplines or "science." Finnish theologian Kari Kuula for one indicates that such an approach is not uncommon in our context. According to Kuula Lutheranism usually supports the existing social order and trusts the discernment of the legislators.[27] This would, as far as I can see, imply a theological approach that comes, roughly speaking, close to Pihlström's description.

Hauerwas's theology is a constructive amendment in that it stands for a distinct perspective. Hauerwas laments that

> Too often religious belief is presented as a primitive mythical worldview, or metaphysics, that cannot be considered true in any verifiable sense. It is assumed that religious language describes the world only indirectly, metaphorically, or poetically. (. . .) I contend that Christian convictions do not poetically soothe the anxieties of the contemporary self. *Rather, they transform the self* to true faith by creating a community that lives faithful to the one true God of the universe. When self and nature are thus put in right relation we perceive the truth of our existence.[28]

Hauerwas claims that Christian convictions "transform the self" so that human existence is seen in light of those convictions. Convictions, on this view, train the eye-sight of those that are "exposed" to Christian community. It may also be noted that whilst Hauerwas does not take Christianity to be "a metaphysics" he is not, as I understand him, to represent a theology altogether without metaphysics. This becomes clear in this quote when

---

26. To give an example of how the authors give a distinct perspective is the way that they discuss the topic of health. Instead of assuming popular beliefs about health the authors ask what "the place of health" is in a Christian life. See Shuman et al., *Heal Thyself*, 12–14.

27. Kuula, *Hyvä, paha ja synti*, 22.

28. Hauerwas, *The Peaceable Kingdom*, 16. (Italics mine.) The quote continues: "But because truth is unattainable without a corresponding transformation of self, 'ethics,' as the investigation of that transformation, does not follow after a prior systematic presentation of the Christian faith, but is at the beginning of Christian theological reflection." (16) This is a good overall description of Hauerwas's take on Christian ethics.

he says "When self and nature are thus put *in right relation* we perceive the truth of our existence."[29]

The question about narration is not, however, only relevant to the question of the relationship between theology and science, or between competing descriptions of practices such as politics and economics. There are, I would argue, more subtle ways to narrate things in ways that are, from Hauerwas's perspective, foreign to Christian tradition. I will in the following take an example from the Finnish Lutheran Church. Hytönen quotes John Vikström, who at the time was archbishop:

> In the leadership of the Church we have clearly acknowledged that it is possible to see our statements as an obstacle for development—the development that aims for the individual's greater freedom of choice. We have, nevertheless, thought that we have benefited the future of this land and people by upholding also communal values. This has made the concern about the future of the family a particularly central motif. A family based on marriage is obviously among the traditional values, but it is also in our view one of the most important building-blocks of this country, and therefore, one of the most important and most profitable investments.[30]

Note the argumentation in this quote: it is *not* primarily done with arguments or language that rise from Scripture, the Confessions, or the mandate of the church. Instead the interests of "land and people" are central. Vikström notes that the church has sought to thwart the development that seeks to increase the freedom of the individual by upholding "communal values" *because* it is in the best interests of "land and people." There is no mention here of what the church based on its own mandate might stand for. The family unit is, Vikström suggests, a "profitable investment" for the future. The capitalist-language is blatant. This may not be the only type of argumentation that Vikström uses but it is at least one kind that he uses. Talk about "values" can likewise be seen as an example of the church's acceptance of discourses and argumentation that is foreign to its own tradition. The idea that theological language must be translated into a more neutral language, for example, the language of values, is a liberal construct. Such translation, as I have sought to show previously in this

---

29. Hauerwas, *The Peaceable Kingdom*, 16. (Italics mine.) Elsewhere, as I have noted before, Hauerwas has claimed that he is not opposed to metaphysics, but he does not consider himself to have "a naturally metaphysical mind." (Hauerwas in conversation 2010/01/30.)

30. Hytönen, *Kirkko*, 32. My translation.

study, is problematic because it leads to reduction of Christian language and therefore also dims the unique perspective that Christianity can provide. Resorting to language that is at home in capitalism is surely, in a way, understandable to a wider audience but it can also be seen as being in great discord with the gospel.

This is, however, a very complex issue. The way I have interpreted Vikström above makes him sound more like a businessman than a bishop. One must, nevertheless, take into consideration the perspective that perhaps the talk about what is best for land and people is but an expression of Christian love for the neighbor. One may argue that the kind of Christian narration that Hauerwas calls for is implicit in every aspect of life in Nordic societies. Due to the long history of Lutheranism even the most hardnosed capitalist would, on this view, be shaped by Christian tradition. I do think that this is an important perspective that one should take into consideration. Vikström's words above are meaningfully interpreted with this perspective in mind. This interpretation would suggest that perhaps Vikström's language is not after all that foreign to the Christian tradition. Despite this concession I would argue that the distinctness of the church, nevertheless, gets lost in speech like this. The reason simply being the omission to use explicitly Christian language—though it might provide a unique perspective on the matter at hand. The church, furthermore, it can be argued, has a mandate of its own. Reducing this mandate to "whatever is best for land and people" is not, when approached in a postliberal mode, faithful to Christian tradition.[31]

I take Vikström's language to reflect typical Lutheran assumptions about the relationship between church and state. In other words, most functions in society are assumed to be shaped by Christianity. I do not here try to assess in what ways or to what degree it may or may not be faithful to the wider Christian tradition. For my purposes I simply want to show that Hauerwas's perspective provides a meaningful alternative for churches that seek to act in our context. It is an amendment to Lutheran perspectives in that it does not make Christianity and theology relevant only to existential matters, but to a matter that shapes the way a Christian sees the world. On this view theology has relevance for how the world—including science, politics,

---

31. It should also be noted that it is not self-evident what is "best for land and people." Whatever is considered best for land and people is necessarily judged within some narrative and it would be meaningful to acknowledge the assumptions involved in speech like this.

and economics—is understood, not just for how to understand the bits of our experience that science cannot account for.³²

Still another example from Nordic theological ethics that brings to the fore a similarity but also a difference between Nordic discourse and Hauerwas can be found in Swedish theologian Göran Bexell's *Kyrkan och etiken*.³³ Bexell argues that Christian (Lutheran) ethics is not something that can in all situations provide "solutions": it is, on his account, part of life that we have to live with tensions and dilemmas.³⁴ What Christianity, however, provides to this human situation is a disposition of perseverance and love.³⁵ Bexell maintains that such an "inner disposition" in the face of dilemmas "always has an impact on the situation in which the problem takes place."³⁶

Bexell's take on Christian ethics shows that it is not the case that Lutheran ethics makes the qualifier "Christian" altogether superfluous to ethics. In other words, though an emphasis on natural law downplays the need to talk about a distinct Christian ethics, Christian convictions still have a role to play in the shaping of a Christian's morality. Hauerwas makes the qualifier even more important. As I have tried to show earlier, the qualifier "Christian" is, for Hauerwas, essential to Christian ethics. A similarity between these two views is that Hauerwas could also claim that a disposition trained by the Christian story has an "impact" on difficult situations. I would, however, argue that Hauerwas's perspective goes an important step further: a narration of "the situation" done from the perspective of the Christian story may shed new light on what is happening in the situation; the situation is not only a given, but an event that calls for interpretation, which in turn can be done on various premises. As Hauerwas says, quoting Iris Murdoch: "I can only choose within the world I can *see*, in the moral sense of 'see' which implies that clear vision is a result

---

32. It must be specified that I am not here suggesting that one should on postliberal theological grounds reject, for example biological, geographical or astronomical findings. One should, therefore, make a distinction between scientific findings and the role that such findings receive in one's life. An extreme position would be one that makes "science" a worldview that is expected to "explain" life to us. Another extreme would be a complete ignorance of scientific findings. As far as I can see, a Hauerwasian account of human life does not subscribe to neither extreme.

33 Bexell and Asheim, *Kyrkan och etiken*.

34. Bexell and Asheim, *Kyrkan och etiken*, 44.

35. Bexell and Asheim, *Kyrkan och etiken*, 44.

36. Bexell and Asheim, *Kyrkan och etiken*, 44. My translation.

of moral imagination and moral effort."[37] The perspective that Hauerwas stands for has the potential to open up a new perspective.

This perspective is opened up through the insistence to use "Christian language" in describing the common practices of a church. To explicate on this I will instance an example: Hauerwas writes of a pastor at Broadway Methodist Church who used to call the congregation "a miracle."[38] Hauerwas first thought that to be an exaggeration but on further reflection he considered it an apt term for a group of people who would not otherwise gather. What joined the people was their

> determination to worship, convinced that through our presence to one another we were in the presence of God. As a result I am convinced that no theology or ethic is truthful that does not help people, such as those at Broadway, appreciate the significance of their worship. Indeed, I suspect much of the difficulty of current church life and our corresponding theology is that we have not paid serious attention to how difficult it is rightly to understand the common things we do as Christians—e.g., pray, baptize, eat meals, rejoice at the birth of a child, grieve at illness and death, reroof church buildings, and so on. In the absence of our ability to describe theologically the significance of these activities, we find we misdescribe and distort what we do by the necessity to resort to descriptions and explanations all too readily provided by our culture.[39]

There are four things that I want to reflect on with regard to this quote. Firstly, on Hauerwas's account Christians have a particular language that needs to be learnt in order for a church to be able to describe "what it is about" in a way that is faithful to its tradition. Worship is central in learning the language and the life in which such language is at home.

Secondly, in this quote Hauerwas displays his attempt to do theology in service of churches; he suggests that a truthful theology pays attention to worship and how language is used in worship. The "misdescriptions" that Hauerwas alludes to are attempts to explain what church is really about that are not informed by Christian tradition, such as "sociological and psychological explanations."[40] What follows from such explanations is that Christian practices such as prayer and baptism are reduced to some-

---

37. Murdoch, *The Sovereignty of Good*, 37 quoted in Hauerwas, *Wilderness Wanderings*, 155.
38. Hauerwas, *Christian Existence Today*, 123.
39. Hauerwas, *Christian Existence Today*, 123–124.
40. Hauerwas, *Christian Existence Today*, 124.

thing else than what they are considered to be in their proper context. This is an example of Hauerwas's attempt to do theology on its own terms, without giving interpretative privilege to other accounts of human life.

Thirdly, an attempt to give interpretative privilege to Christian language opens up for the critique that Hauerwas does not take seriously what we know through disciplines such as sociology and psychology.[41] Such a critique, furthermore, seems to render Hauerwas's project a "sectarian" one, especially if considered with an alleged natural law or "creation perspective" in mind. On this point it is important to recognize the fundamentally different premises at work: a Hauerwasian theology claims that a Christian is one who assumes that something decisive happened in the life, death and resurrection of Jesus that shapes how everything else is viewed, while other disciplines do not make such an assumption.[42] Another relevant perspective in considering the critique in question is to problematize the knowledge that is arrived at through the various disciplines. This would entail questioning the assumption that disciplines such as sociology and psychology indeed gets to the "facts" while theological claims necessarily must be interpreted to mean something else than what they seem to be claiming.

Fourthly, if Christians lose the ability to "talk right" they also lose their capacity to provide an alternative to the world. If Hauerwas is right in his claim that the world does not know that it is world without the church providing an alternative way of life, it seems crucial that church recovers and maintains its particular language. Without such a particular language church cannot aptly describe what it is about, and as a result cannot provide a meaningful alternative to the wider society.

If these points are reflected on in relation to our Lutheran folk church context some further considerations come into focus. Though Hauerwas's ecclesiology has some similarities with Luther's thought, there is an obvious tension between a Hauerwasian conception of church and a folk church. This tension has to do with the distinctness of the perspective that church on Hauerwas's account can provide. I would argue that the idea of a folk church effectively prevents a church to discover and live out its distinctness. What Hauerwas takes to be a particular life-shaping Christian story is not identical with a nation's story. This particularity is in our context thwarted because very few people in the folk church come

---

41. Grenholm's search for an "acceptable ethics" provides an example of such a critique, see Grenholm, *Bortom humanismen*.

42. Hauerwas and Swinton, *Critical Reflections*, 4.

together for worship in order to discover life in light of the conviction that God has acted decisively in Jesus.⁴³ In a folk church where the majority of "the folk" do not attend "the church" it seems to me to lead to a peculiar "syncretism" between a (Lutheran) Christian tradition and contemporary secular assumptions. If the folk church arrangement is reflected upon with Hauerwas's theological project in mind, one would have to conclude that a folk church in which the majority of the members do not attend worship cannot but antagonize the particularity of the Christian tradition, and as a result rob the world from seeing a particular alternative to its ways of life.

To sum up this discussion on narration, the crucial resource that I see in Hauerwas's theological approach lies in the claim that theology has a unique description of the world. Such a description could *from a mainstream perspective* be at least a corrective that might help the wider society identify and critique, for example, "epistemic violence" (Spivak) in an allegedly democratic society. An explicitly Christian perspective can, therefore, be seen as a means for society to be self-critical.⁴⁴

The relationship between the church and the wider society has similarities with that of the mainstream and the "subaltern" in postcolonial theorist Gayatri Chakravorty Spivak's sense. The subaltern refers, roughly, to "deprived others"; people who in various ways are cut off from power.⁴⁵ For Spivak the "Subaltern must always be caught in translation, never truly expressing herself."⁴⁶ The subaltern's language and knowledge are, in other words, marginalized by the mainstream—this is an expression of epistemic violence. bell hooks (Gloria Jean Watkins) also speaks tellingly of the relationship between the powerful and the subaltern:

> No need to hear your voice when I can talk about you better than you can speak about yourself. No need to hear your voice.

---

43. On the account presented here coming together for worship services is crucial to learning Christian language and life. While I do maintain this I would like to think that a "community of friends" can also to some degree act as a training ground for Christians: one can get to know exemplary Christians who can become a positive influence in one's life. Yet I would argue that a community of friends cannot replace a church, since the church through its liturgy can provide a constancy that friendships may not. Church, furthermore, especially the Eucharist, shows that people who otherwise would not gather come together.

44. Obviously Hauerwas would not want to make the church just a "means" for the betterment of society, but it is still, I would argue, one facet or possible "result" of his view.

45. The subaltern for Spivak is more sophisticated than that but this suffices for my brief reflection. See De Kock, "Interview," 46.

46. Spivak in Sharp, *Geographies of Postcolonialism*, 111.

> Only tell me about your pain. I want to know your story. And then I will tell it back to you in a new way. Tell it back to you in such a way that it has become mine, my own. Re-writing you I write myself anew. I am still author, authority. I am still colonizer the speaking subject and you are now at the center of my talk.[47]

hooks suggests that the story told in the subaltern's vernacular is not given legitimacy. It is rather re-interpreted in a different conceptual frame-work and told in a different language. This way the powerful gets to define what the subaltern is "really saying." What the subaltern says is not taken seriously. This, while borrowed from the field of postcolonial theory, seems to me to describe well what often takes place regarding religion in society: it is not uncommon that theological language is re-interpreted in, for example, anthropological or psychological terms. Central to postcolonial studies is to critique the mechanisms that dismiss the subaltern. Positively expressed it provides resources for the mainstream to be critical of its ways, for example, by recognizing some of the foundational premises of its thought. The perspective that Hauerwas represents with its stress on the uniqueness of the church's language could, I have suggested, provide something similar to the wider societal discourse.

Political Christianity

The perspective that Hauerwas stands for, I have suggested, provides a distinct Christian narration of the world. This implies that the understanding of politics, among other things, is also profoundly shaped by the Christian tradition. I will in the following try to show how a Hauerwasian perspective provides an amendment to typical Nordic and Lutheran ways of understanding the relationship between Christianity and politics.

A characteristic of our context that I want to discuss is the strong sentiment that religion is a private, not a political, thing. In Nordic societies it is customary to make a distinction between "private ethics" and "political ethics": in the former Christian faith may have a shaping role, whereas in the latter it has in most cases no relevance.[48] To what degree can this sentiment be explained with the impact of typical Lutheran theology? To put it differently, is the tendency to separate private ethics from political ethics fueled by Lutheran thinking? It seems to me that this is at

---

47. hooks, bell in Ferguson, *Out There*, 241–243.
48. Grenholm in Østnor, *Etisk pluralisme i Norden*, 242.

least part of the story.[49] Grenholm maintains that according to Lutheran theology the Church's task is both to proclaim the evangel and to clarify (the Lutheran conception of) "the law."[50] The Church as institution is not, however, to involve itself in politics—that is to be left to those with political power.[51] Grenholm notes, however, that contemporary representatives for the Nordic Churches may point out that the Church is to function as a critic of party politics and shape attitudes in questions such as justice, peace, environment and equality.[52] Grenholm claims that it is common in our context to have an "ethical dualism": private and social ethics are separate.[53] In Luther's thought this is seen in the distinction that he makes between a person's duties as a "person" and those that the same person has in his or her "office."[54]

The point that I want to make by referring to Grenholm's description of what he takes to be typical Lutheran ethical discourse is that it has an idea of politics that is given. On this view being a Christian does not seem to provide any distinct perspective on what politics is, other than the Lutheran conviction that those in power act within God's worldly regiment. While Lutheran theology, in Grenholm's description, allows for the Church to function as a critic of politics it, nevertheless, seems to assume that everyone understands the world (including politics) in the same way. I suspect, furthermore, that on Grenholm's account Lutherans assume an understanding of politics that disciplines other than theology get to define. To reiterate, the interpretative prerogative on the matter is, to recall Pihlström's description in the preceding subchapter, handed over to other than theological perspectives (for example, sociology or political science).

In Lutheran thinking it is difficult to talk about a relationship between Christians and the wider society because they are assumed to be

49. Another part of the story is the complex development in modernity in which religion in general came to be seen as working within a sphere of its own. Grenholm also makes these observations: he maintains that Lutheranism provides the ideological background to separating private and public/political ethics. Grenholm also thinks that an important aspect of the differentiation of society is the impact of the Enlightenment (esp. Kant), see 259–260. I do not, however, pursue this aspect any further in this study.

50. Østnor, *Etisk pluralisme i Norden*, 246.

51. Østnor, *Etisk pluralisme i Norden*, 246. Grenholm notes that this kind of two regiment thinking is not to be taken to assume a theocracy in which the state is in service of the Church. It is rather that the state is assumed to act on natural law. (See 247.)

52. Østnor, *Etisk pluralisme i Norden*, 250–251.

53. Østnor, *Etisk pluralisme i Norden*, 255, 261.

54. Østnor, *Etisk pluralisme i Norden*, 256.

so intimately intertwined. This is the case at least if one assumes a difference between Christian's ethics and ethics of those that are not Christians. The reason for this is simply that morality is seen as something that is based on a shared humanity, and as such the idea of a distinct Christian ethics becomes more or less nonsensical.[55] Hauerwas's perspective is different in that it claims that it is necessary to make a distinction between "church" and "world," as well as between Christian ethics and other ethics. I have argued (chapter 2) that the notion of church as social ethics necessitates a distinct Christian community. I also suggested that a stress on the distinctness of Christian community is in tension with the idea of a folk church. A folk church diffuses the distinctness of Christian community and language.[56] Lutheran folk church theology thus bereaves the church from its peculiar political aspect.

Hauerwas's perspective, in other words, calls into question the assumption that contemporary Nordic societies are profoundly shaped by Christian practices. The simple reason I say this is that our churches are unfilled most of the time. In Hauerwas's perspective, however, worship attendance is central to being a Christian.[57] A Christian who does not attend church is, to make an analogy, like a person who claims to practice the martial art of Brazilian jiu-jitsu (BJJ) but does not actually attend sparring sessions. The question about how much one should attend in order to be a practitioner is not a very meaningful one. If a would be BJJ-practitioner takes part in training he or she will quickly, on a very personal level, get some approximation as to whether he or she is a practitioner. If one does not, for example, know what to do when the opponent sets up a triangle-

---

55. Despite this the lifestyles of Christians and those that are not Christians may differ. Kuula claims that the basic difference according to Lutheran thinking has to do with *motivation*: a Christian seeks to do right for the benefit of "the neighbor" because it is God's will, whereas the non-Christian does it because s/he is forced to do so, or because s/he thinks it might be beneficial to her/him. (Kuula, *Hyvä, paha ja synti*, 23.) If this is the case one must conclude that it is not inconceivable in Lutheran thought that Christian convictions might shape a person's ethics. Kuula's remark is also a reminder of the fact that there are differing views among Lutherans regarding how far one wants to take the emphasis on a natural law that makes morality a universal phenomenon.

56. I am not suggesting that it is immediately clear what is and what is not "Christian language." Liturgy is clearly Christian language in that it narrates the world in a peculiar way. There are, however, many languages between liturgy on the one hand and, for example, political discourse that assumes that Christian convictions have no relevance whatsoever on the other. In a Hauerwasian perspective it takes initiation and training to recognize Christian language.

57. See e.g. Hauerwas, *Wilderness Wanderings*, 2–3; Berkman and Cartwright, *The Hauerwas Reader*, 530; Hauerwas, *In Good Company*, 250.

choke then one can safely conclude that one has no clue about the practice of BJJ. If one, furthermore, does not know what a triangle-choke is then one does not know the language used in BJJ. Learning the language and the practices of a tradition takes attendance and training. Other people's assessments about whether a person is a practitioner or not are not important. It is rather that the person undergoing training will, as time goes by, come to see that he or she has become a practitioner. This analogy also goes for the way Hauerwas sees Christianity.[58]

On Hauerwas's account Christianity has relevance not only to personal ethics but also to political ethics; the disconnection between the two is undone. If Christianity is taken to be primarily a way of life and not only a way of thinking it is, I have argued, inherently political. The notion of church as social ethic, therefore, brings about a distinct understanding of politics that seeks to be faithful to Christian convictions. An example of this is the disavowal of violence: a commitment to nonviolence can have very concrete public (political) repercussions, and not only in times of war. At the same time it must be maintained that it is not just the rejection of violence that makes Hauerwasian Christian ethics different from non-Christian ethics. The difference that this type of Christian ethics implies

---

58. One can also ask if it is possible to be fluent in BJJ based on earlier practice even if one is not currently actively pursuing the art. A question such as this is a reminder that when it comes to martial arts, as well as Christianity, one must approach the phenomenon in a more nuanced way. I am indebted to Patrik Hagman (a colleague in both theology and martial arts) for this point. With regard to Christianity this is an important clarification. It is unhelpful to categorize people into Christians and non-Christians, as if it was an unambiguous taxonomy. One should take into consideration that some might, for example, be proficient in the language of the church without current active participation in worship. Others again may be active but unfaithful to how language is used in the tradition. Then there is the question of whether it is meaningful in the first place to try to assess who is or is not a Christian. At least I would suggest that for Christians it is a pointless activity based on the Christian conviction that Christ came to tear down barriers between people (Gal. 3:28). If such lines must be drawn one way would be the approach that Bonhoeffer suggested: the border between church and world is to be drawn "from the outside." In other words, those who do not (wish to) belong to the church define the boundaries of church. (Gill, *The Cambridge Companion*, 10, 13.) I conclude that the fact that it is difficult and problematic to draw a line between Christians and non-Christians does not mean that one cannot do so under any circumstances. Even if it is problematic to make such distinctions (in the kind of "borderline cases" that I have mentioned) it does not mean that one cannot say that some seem to practice Christianity whereas others do not. Wielding such a taxonomy does not require the observant to claim s/he is able to judge who is or is not a Christian. I take it that there is a profound sense in which one must leave such judgment "up to God."

is difficult to account for in any comprehensive and detailed way because it is *ad hoc* in character. Someone schooled in Christian tradition sees any situation or development in a certain light; the ethical task is then to improvise and respond spontaneously to ethical demands (in Løgstrup's sense).[59]

There is a sense in which this is comparing apples and oranges: Hauerwas's notion of church as social ethics implies a divergent narration of what politics is, whereas in the Lutheran perspective is seems more given what politics is; it is taken to be that which we in everyday life call (party) politics. A Hauerwasian perspective does not entail a rejection of common politics; on this view people might well vote and be active in a political party. It does, however, include a distinct perspective, a wider understanding of politics. This has to do with the observation that people in society are not governed by party politics alone: there can be other kinds of disestablished politics that nevertheless has a profound impact on people's lives. Take the example of boycotting other than fair trade or locally produced foods. This would be, on a seemingly small-scale, an example of how ethical consumerism is a kind of politics. Another local example of alternative politics, which has already been mentioned, is the Lutheran church in Turku (Finland) that protected an immigrant from being deported. This case shows that there is room for such "civil disobedience" in a Lutheran context despite the idea that Christians are to submit to "the ruler" (Rm. 13). If that church, however, had operated with the common Lutheran assumption that the ruling authorities are in God's service (unless blatantly going against Scripture) then this act of alternative politics might not have occurred.

Grenholm's Hauerwas

I indicated above, regarding the understanding of politics, that there is an element of "comparing apples and oranges" involved: Hauerwas's notion of church as social ethics works with an understanding of politics that is

---

59. This does not have to mean that a Hauerwasian Christian would see *every* situation differently from non-Christians. The analogy with jiu-jitsu can also be recalled here: a threatening situation, for example, is often seen differently by someone trained in jiu-jitsu compared to someone who is not. The analogy is, as is often the case with analogies, limited at this point, because a martial art is not necessarily—though it can be—character shaping to the degree that it would shape how a person responds to any every-day situation. A pacifist martial artist may, of course, experience multiple difficulties in a threatening situation.

not "given" in the same way as it is often in typical Lutheran perspectives understood to be. The differing views on politics has an analogy in the way that typical Lutheran premises for ethics leads to a kind of reasoning that is rather different from the kind of reasoning that Hauerwas's perspective leads to. To expound on this I will relate Hauerwas's ethics to the ethics of Carl-Henrik Grenholm.

Grenholm's *Bortom humanismen*[60] is a study in Christian ethics that explicitly discusses Hauerwas's approach to ethics. In so doing he has been one of the central theologians to introduce Hauerwas to Nordic ethical thinking. Because of this and because my reading of Hauerwas differs from Grenholm's I will discuss *Bortom humanismen* to some length.[61] My argument is that Grenholm's problems with Hauerwas have mainly to do with differing understandings of both ethics and the perspective available to the ethicist. It is, therefore, of value to assess, firstly, his approach to ethics and, secondly, his treatment of Hauerwas.

In *Bortom humanismen* Grenholm seeks to provide an "acceptable understanding" of ethics.[62] He develops his understanding of ethics through a critical discussion with five approaches to ethics. He calls these rational natural law ethics, narrative virtue ethics, theocentric ethics, liberation ethics, and feminist ethics. Grenholm then proposes what an acceptable ethics might look like.

In his presentation Grenholm presents the following criteria for an acceptable ethical approach. Firstly, what he calls the "universalizability criterion." This entails the assumption that if something is morally right for someone in a given situation, it is morally right for everybody in similar situations. Secondly, the "consistency criterion," which means that an ethical model contains moral judgments that are non-contradictory. Thirdly, Grenholm suggests a criterion he calls "experience criterion": a credible ethical model should arrive at conclusions that are in agreement with "human observations and experiences." Fourthly, the "integration criterion," which refers to moral judgments that are in line with what we know about ourselves and our human existence. The integration criterion means that moral conclusions should be coherent with scientific findings.

---

60. Grenholm, *Bortom humanismen*. It has been used as a course textbook in the Nordic countries.

61. I approach Grenholm's book as an example of one typical Nordic response to the type of ethics that Hauerwas represents. My interest, therefore, does not lie in discussing Grenholm's theology as it is expressed in his other publications.

62. The following references to Grenholm are found, unless otherwise stated, in Grenholm, *Bortom humanismen*, 34–37.

Grenholm suggests that an acceptable ethics must be consistent with what is known of morality through sociological study. The fifth and final criterion Grenholm calls the "anthropological criterion" (*människosynskriteriet*). In other words, an acceptable ethical model must be in harmony with an acceptable view of the human being. Grenholm argues that a credible ethical model must be consistent with the understanding of the human being found in the Bible and later Christian tradition, as well as with contemporary human experiences and with what is known through scientific research. Grenholm then explains that these five criteria constitute the basis for his analysis of the various ethical outlooks that he critiques.

Grenholm's criteria for a credible ethical model raises some critical questions. There certainly is a need to assess different ethical outlooks. Yet it seems to me that Grenholm works with assumptions about the character and scope of Christian ethics that can be questioned.

The first criterion, the universalizability criterion, seems problematic and would require a more thorough discussion. What does it mean to say "if something is morally right for someone in a given situation, it is morally right for everybody in similar situations"? This point seems to presuppose some sort of ahistorical point of view in order to be meaningful. One can, of course, declare such a thing, as a way of suggesting something about the nature of morality, but the claim is a theoretical assumption that cannot be substantiated in any way. If such an objective view is not implied then how can it, from a contextual and subjective perspective, be known whether two seemingly similar situations are in fact similar? If one considers the fact that all humans are unique in their set of desires, needs, intentions and so on, that is, in the totality of their context, it becomes problematic to speak about "similar situations." It seems, therefore, that Grenholm is not consistent regarding the point of view available to the observer.[63] It fur-

---

63. This same critique has been put to Hauerwas, see Smith, "Hauerwas and Kallenberg," 305–326. Smith sets out to "argue that [Hauerwas and Kallenberg] most likely presuppose what they deny—an epistemic access apart from language to an objective, unconstructed world. Repeatedly, each author makes sweeping, generalized claims about the way the 'world' is. What are we to make of these strong opinions? We will see that they face a dilemma: either they presuppose access to the nature of a real world that exists determinately apart from language; or, they make general, even universal claims from within their localized, particular forms of life. If the former is the case, then this conclusion would be damaging to the core of their linguistic constructionism, or what I will also call their linguistic 'method.' But if the latter is the case, then their opinions are just the result of how each of their forms of life (which they do not specify in sufficient detail) has made its particular world by its use of language. Therefore, these latter kinds of claims are question-begging, and they are

ther seems that this criterion necessarily leads to an ethical outlook that simplifies what is going on in seemingly similar situations where people act in a seemingly similar way.

Grenholm's first criterion for an acceptable ethical model also sounds similar to Kant's categorical imperative. If it in essence ends up being the same as the categorical imperative, it seems like a contradictory criterion since Grenholm elsewhere dismisses a universalizing ethic based on reason.[64]

One critique that Grenholm's criteria, more specifically, the integration criterion, the anthropological criterion and the experience criterion (which all seem to be a form of integration criteria) invite has to do with contextuality. Experiences, interpretations of human existence, scientific findings and truth-claims are all informed by the context in which they are made. Though the determinative role of context is a truism, Grenholm suggests in a seemingly unproblematic way that what can be known about human existence through, for example, sociological research, is the truth. It is, however, problematic to imply that sociology is somehow objective, as if it was not informed by some ontological and epistemological assumptions.[65] Sociology, as well as other disciplines, has its narratives and traditions that instruct its conclusions of the world. A related critique is that it is not unproblematic to assume that all humans are alike, that is, that human experience is the same for everyone.

Grenholm also talks unabashedly about his approach to ethics as being in line with a Christian understanding of the human being. While he points out that a Christian anthropology maintains that we are both created and fallen beings he does not give any arguments for his conclusion. In

---

nothing but the viewpoints of some particular, discrete community, which renders them rather uninteresting for most readers."(305–6) Smith's reasoning does not, in my view, take sufficiently into consideration the role that tradition pays in Hauerwas's theology. Smith is, however, right in that the views that Hauerwas's interpretation of Christian tradition represents may not be interesting to all.

64. Grenholm, *Bortom humanismen*, 95.

65. John Milbank, for example, is a theologian who has suggested that theology should be critical of sociology. Milbank suggests that theology should insist on a sociological perspective that is shaped by theology. See Milbank, *Theology and Social Theory*, 110. The difference between Milbank and Hauerwas is fittingly summarized by Hauerwas as: "Milbank wants Christians to win . . . I think at best we should want as Christians to endure." (Hauerwas, *Performing the Faith*, 217.) Hauerwas's approach is in other words a more modest co-existence with other traditions of thought, whereas Milbank talks about "outnarrating" other accounts. See Milbank in D'Costa, *Christian Uniqueness Reconsidered*, 19, and Milbank, *Theology and Social Theory*, chapter 11.

other words, why would such a Christian view of the human have to lead to Grenholm's view of ethics? In order to make such a claim one would have expected a more thoroughgoing discussion of various theological anthropologies as well as of the fact that it is not unproblematic to assume that humanity is a unitary notion.

In the ethical outlook that Grenholm develops he distances himself both from a rationality-based natural law ethics as well as from a revelation-based narrative virtue ethic. His own contribution entails elements from both of these. It is an approach that maintains that both revelation in Christ and human experiences and rational reasoning contribute to moral judgments.[66] The arguments for this suggestion are that it is concordant with, firstly, a Christian anthropology and, secondly, with a modified ethical contextualism. The latter refers to an outlook that pays attention to the particularities of Christian ethics while maintaining the possibility for dialog between various outlooks in a pluralistic society.[67] Grenholm thus arrives at an understanding of ethics that is "beyond humanism" (*bortom humanismen*).

In summary of the first issue of this subchapter I conclude that giving criteria, such as the ones Grenholm gives, presuppose an overly optimistic modern view of the possibilities of rationality in ethical matters. It seems that despite Grenholm's critique of such optimistic accounts of rationality he, nevertheless, implicitly assumes what he critiques in his constructive proposal. These criteria, furthermore, presuppose a certain view of ethics in order to appear credible and rational. From this then follows that the criteria proposed by Grenholm are biased in a way that will logically dismiss the type of virtue ethic approach that Hauerwas represents. If one, however, accepts Hauerwas's understanding of the scope and task of Christian ethics his virtue ethics can be assessed rather differently.

The second issue of this subchapter has to do with Grenholm's explicit treatment of Hauerwas. Grenholm criticizes the type of narrative virtue ethics that Hauerwas represents. The first point of criticism is that "[Hauerwas's] ethical contextualism entails a refined epistemological relativism, according to which all the reasons people give for an acceptable moral judgment are specific to a certain social and cultural context."[68] The problem that Grenholm has with this is that it leads to too non-critical

---

66. Grenholm, *Bortom humanismen*, 269. Grenholm calls his approach to ethics "*teologisk anknytningsetik*," roughly translated "theological affiliation ethics."

67. Grenholm, *Bortom humanismen*, 270.

68. Grenholm, *Bortom humanismen*, 131. My translation.

a stance toward the moral views of one's own tradition. The question that must be raised is therefore: does the kind of perspective that Hauerwas stands for necessarily preclude self-critique? Even if one assumes a contextual perspective, as Hauerwas does, it does not have to mean that self-critique is impossible. What should also be noted is that Grenholm's objection seems to presuppose a context-free perspective. It approaches Hauerwas's ethical perspective from premises that are foreign to the way that Hauerwas seeks to discuss ethics. Grenholm's treatment of Hauerwas does not seem to take Hauerwas's claim to work in the service of a concrete tradition seriously. For Hauerwas Christianity is a given, in the sense that we do not get to make up what it is.[69] Grenholm points out above that in Hauerwas's approach "the reasons people give for an acceptable moral judgment are specific to a certain social and cultural context." This assessment of Hauerwas's stance does not take into consideration that the complex givenness that is the gospel can be seen to allow for a critical perspective on the context.

Grenholm's second point of criticism has to do with theological anthropology (*människosyn*). Grenholm suggests that a narrative virtue ethic has too pessimistic a view of the human being. He further states that this pessimism is not fully compatible with an understanding of the human being that Christian tradition represents. This entails, more specifically, incompatibility with the conviction that humans are created by God and as such have some moral knowledge independent of revelation in Christ.[70]

On this point my reading of Hauerwas differs from Grenholm's. In a Nordic context in which natural law thinking and an emphasis on the theological categories of "creation" and "redemption" has traditionally been common his concern is, however, understandable. In that perspective Hauerwas's theological anthropology might seem pessimistic. In Hauerwas's perspective it seems that the word "pessimism" used in this sense might be something of a mistake. Hauerwas is not suggesting that a non-Christian cannot have a good life or make good choices. In my reading Hauerwas simply wants to emphasize the role of tradition in narrating what is right and wrong. For a Hauerwasian Christian the tradition that informs her or him is "the story of Jesus," whereas for the non-Christian it might be some other more or less defined tradition.

"Creation" and "redemption" are, furthermore, not categories that Hauerwas operates with, since he claims that

---

69. Hauerwas, *Wilderness Wanderings*, 3.
70. Grenholm, *Bortom humanismen*, 131.

> such a dualism is based on a fundamental theological error. Not only does such a dualism presuppose, like natural law positions, a norm of justice apart from Christ, but it turns a condition made necessary by human sin into a theological principle that even determines the subsequent doctrine of God. [. . .] Lutheran theology wrongly attributed revelatory value to an autonomous sphere separate from Christ's redeeming work.[71]

This is a reminder of, not only the fact that Hauerwas is not Lutheran, but more importantly, the fact that context is next to everything in theological reflection: Grenholm has a set of premises and critiques Hauerwas out of that (Lutheran) theological context. While one can hardly completely distance oneself from one's context it is still important to seek to understand a provocateur as much as possible on her or his own grounds before passing judgment.

Grenholm, furthermore, suggests that Hauerwas's approach is incompatible with the observation that people representing different traditions and life-views might share ethical ideals and moral principles.[72] The way I interpret Hauerwas on this point differs from Grenholm. Emphasizing the role of a concrete tradition in ethics, as Hauerwas does, is "not to deny that all people may share important moral characteristics, but (. . .) [that] these shared characteristics are not of the sort that allows one to actually anchor morality in them."[73] The similarities that Grenholm refers to can, in other words be subsumed by Hauerwas's approach and the suggested incompatibility is, as far as I can see, ostensible. In an analogical way, on Hauerwas's account, it can be observed that different religions may have striking similarities. Despite this Hauerwas does not reduce them to "the same" but maintains that, for example, Buddhist compassion is not the same as Christian love in slightly differing guise.[74] Grenholm's observation concerning shared ethical ideals does not, therefore, have to be incompatible with Hauerwas's approach.

Grenholm, thirdly, understands the ethic that Hauerwas promotes as a secteristic one. With this he means to say that the particular form of Christian ethics that Hauerwas describes is not accessible to others than to those who "belong to church as fellowship."[75] The question of sectarian-

---

71. Hauerwas, *Vision and Virtue*, 205–206.
72. Grenholm, *Bortom humanismen*, 131.
73. Hauerwas, *Truthfulness and Tragedy*, 9–10.
74. Hauerwas, *Against the Nations*, 2.
75. Grenholm, *Bortom humanismen*, 131.

ism has already been discussed. Two questions, however, point to some of the issues that a more thorough discussion would entail: What is the narrative or tradition that generates this critique? Why is it assumed by Grenholm that Christians cannot be a distinct community?

A fourth problem that Grenholm has with Hauerwas is that his ethical outlook is "too limited" concerning the context in which we find ourselves.[76] Grenholm seems to read Hauerwas in a way that limits the context for ethics to the ecclesial. Grenholm adds that gender and social status also has an impact on our moral views and our understanding of what is rational in matters moral.[77] This appears, according to my reading of Hauerwas, to be a hasty conclusion. Hauerwas does in much of his writing emphasize the story of Jesus and the church that interprets it as the context that shapes moral convictions. This is by no means to be understood as the only story that informs moral judgment. Hauerwas indeed acknowledges that we are in fact shaped by many stories. This is exemplified, for example, by his text on being both Texan and Christian and his development of the topic entitled "On being a Christian and an American."[78]

A final remark on Grenholm's ethical approach is that he does not pay much attention to a community that seeks to embody a certain ethic. Instead he simply proceeds to give what appear to be "reasonable" criteria for an acceptable ethical model. The question about "reasonable" or "acceptable" *for whom* is not discussed. It seems to me that it has been quite common in the Nordic context to do theology in a way that does not assign a central role to the church. Is there not then the risk that such criteria are arbitrary, because they do not attend to real people and their lives? Grenholm seems to strive for an understanding of ethics where one can in principle assess moral judgments. He defines ethics as a theoretical reflection on morality.[79] I would, however, suggest that Grenholm does not take the peculiarities of contexts, traditions and individuals sufficiently into consideration (cf. Hauerwas's emphasis on concrete life-situations).

76. Grenholm, *Bortom humanismen*, 171, 189–190, 197.
77. Grenholm, *Bortom humanismen*, 170.
78. Hauerwas, *A Better Hope*, 24; Hauerwas, *Christian Existence Today*, 25–45. A more fruitful critical question that can be put to Hauerwas is whether he gives *enough* attention to such other stories? The roles that, for instance, national, ethnic or gender stories play in one's understanding of the story of Jesus may, after all be decisive. This question will not, however, be pursued further in this study since it is not a critique posed by Grenholm.
79. Grenholm, *Bortom humanismen*, 15.

While ethics can be defined as a theoretical reflection on morality, it does not have to lead to a kind of theorizing that has no need for a concrete community.

The conclusion that I arrive at regarding Grenholm's treatment of Hauerwas is that he critiques Hauerwas out of a set of premises that is different to the one Hauerwas works with. Grenholm intereprets Hauerwas from his Lutheran natural law perspective, which does not do justice to Hauerwas's contribution to theological ethics. Approaches to ethics that seek to "universalize" and "ahistorize" ethics, exemplify what Hauerwas calls "the standard account" of ethics.[80] In stark contrast to such approaches, Hauerwas claims that

> Christian ethics should begin with Christian convictions and how they shape our understanding of moral existence. To begin here is not to deny that all people may share important moral characteristics, but (. . .) [that] these shared characteristics are not of the sort that allows one to actually anchor morality in them[81]

This is an important remark considering the common assumption in Nordic contexts that a reasonable understanding of Christian ethics is or should be based on natural law. Hauerwas's perspective is, furthermore, coherent with his overall project in that it does not render the church unintelligible as I would argue Lutheran natural law thinking risks doing. Instead, the church has a central role in society because, as mentioned before, "without church the world cannot know that it is world."[82] In this perspective church can be an alternative in society exactly because it stands for a perspective that is not shared by everyone.

Another way to describe the differences in premises for theological thinking between Grenholm and Hauerwas is to talk about modern and late modern. Of these two paradigms Grenholm can be labelled a typically modern thinker while Hauerwas exemplifies a late-modern approach. This becomes evident, for example, in Grenholm's tendency to look for the objective and the universal, while Hauerwas focuses on the contextual and the particular.

---

80. Hauerwas, *Truthfulness and Tragedy*, 16.

81. Hauerwas, *Truthfulness and Tragedy*, 9–10.

82. E.g. Hauerwas, *The Peaceable Kingdom*, 101–102; Hauerwas and Willimon, *Where Resident Aliens Live*, 46.

Two Regiments

Hauerwas's contribution in the field of ethics can be further clarified by discussing it explicitly in relation to the Lutheran doctrine of two regiments. This is an understanding of the relationship of church and state that permeates Lutheran theology, which has consequences for a Lutheran understanding of ethics. I will here focus on how Luther's idea of the two regiments has generally been interpreted in Finland, and more specifically, on the repercussions for ethics that the doctrine has. I do not intend to go into details in my description of the doctrine.[83] The idea is simply to contrast Lutheran regiment theology with Hauerwas's notion of church as social ethics in order to show how the latter differs from the former.

According to the Lutheran doctrine of two regiments Christian doctrine and morality belong to different modes of God's government in the world. Doctrine and morality are, on this account, not to be mixed together. John Vikström can act as an example of this. Vikström maintains that the regiments must be kept separate and the state is not to give orders in issues related to people's relationship with God because it is the individual's business and not a public thing.[84] To express it differently, a distinction is made between *coram hominibus* and *coram Deo*: morality has to do with life before fellow humans, while faith (and doubt) is something that plays out before God. The Lutheran Church sees itself as an equal to other actors in society when it comes to moral issues: the Church does not claim to have any particular insight that is not available to all people. As a result of this Lutheranism usually supports the existing social order and trusts the discernment of the legislators.[85]

On this point I want to note that the doctrine of two regiments seems to lead contemporary Lutheranism toward a position that renders Christianity a personal and abstract matter. Separating life before God from life before humans risks pushing Christianity into a private religious sphere that is detached from other aspects of life in society. The radically political character of Christianity is toned down in Lutheranism to the degree that the Lutheran Church has accepted the modern division between private and public. Björn Vikström maintains that in folk church theology the

---

83. Luther's thought on the matter is complex as it involves several distinctions such as that between spiritual and worldly modes of governing, between spiritual and worldly kingdoms, and further, between the kingdom of God and kingdom of the devil. See e.g. Malysz, "Nemo iudex in causa sua," 363–386.
84. Hytönen, *Kirkko*, 286.
85. Kuula, *Hyvä, paha ja synti*, 22–23.

modern distinction between politics and religion has been interwoven with the Lutheran notion of the two regiments.[86] This has then resulted in a situation in which the privatization of the faith has been theologically secured.[87]

Hauerwas's approach to ethics provides on this point an amendment to Lutheran thought. A central difference between the Lutheran doctrine of two regiments and Hauerwas's perspective is that on Hauerwas's account the Christian faith is taken to be inherently political in character. Christian convictions cannot be relegated into a personal apolitical sphere. For Hauerwas "our convictions are in themselves a morality."[88] In other words, "life before God" and "life before people" cannot be separated meaningfully in Hauerwas's theology, as it is often done in Lutheran theology. The emphasis that Hauerwas lays on the public and political character of Christianity has strong similarities with how the early Christians understood their faith as inherently public and political.[89] This is an example of how Hauerwas draws on older Christian tradition in order to provide an account of Christianity that has the potential to be politically relevant in our day.

Relating Hauerwas's ethics—if only on a very general level—to some common views in our context exhibits the kind of contribution that Hauerwas's line of thinking can make to Nordic ethical discussion and to typical Lutheran theology: an emphasis on Christianity as embodied convictions. Christianity is in Hauerwas's writing primarily a way of living that personify Christian convictions instead of a way of thinking, or of having certain knowledge or a set of convictions.[90] Doctrine and ethics is not, in other words, radically separated, but the latter displays the former.

---

86. Vikström, *Folkkyrka i en postmodern tid*, 147. Vikström discusses mainly the situation in Sweden but I take this to be a valid point in other Nordic contexts as well.

87. Vikström, *Folkkyrka i en postmodern tid*, 147.

88. Hauerwas, *The Peaceable Kingdom*, 16.

89. Hauerwas and Wells, *Blackwell Companion*, 204–207.

90. Christian ethics, on this account, is not something that we should think about once we have gotten our beliefs "straight." (Hauerwas, *A Community of Character*, 90.) There is, in other words, a need not to separate theology and ethics but also not to completely equate them: both extremes "[distort] the nature of Christian convictions. (Hauerwas, *A Community of Character*, 90.) What I take this to mean is that Christianity is faithful to its tradition only when it is a lived and embodied experience. This does not, however, mean that Christians would not also *hold* certain convictions. In other words, Hauerwas's attempt not to separate creed from ethics does not end up with only ethics; creed is not done away with.

In contrast to Lutheran ethics Hauerwas insists that Christian ethics is not a natural law ethics but an ethic informed by the Christian tradition.

Church as social ethics is, therefore, in my view a feasible take on Christianity that provides a meaningful amendment to typical Nordic theological discourse. It is meaningful in that it does not accept the division between public and private. As such it is a more credible account of Christianity in a late modern context than are modern accounts that in various ways explicitly or implicitly accept Christianity as a personal or "internal" matter. Church as social ethics is, in other words, contextual in that it is an expression of a "new visibility of religion," typical to a post-secular situation.

Point of Contact

It seems that there are elements that make Hauerwas's perspective incompatible with Lutheran perspectives. Despite this I want to argue that there is a similarity that opens up for the possibility to envision a Hauerwasian perspective even in a Lutheran context. A central point of contact between these perspectives has to do with the understanding of church and world.

Hauerwas's conception of church and world, as something that cuts through all human beings—instead of a clear-cut distinction between Christians and non-Christians—can be seen as a point of contact between his ecclesiology and a Lutheran folk church ecclesiology. In Luther's thought Christianity in the world is like a field in which both good seeds and tares can be found. Luther maintains that heretics are not to be "uprooted," for "he who errs today may find the truth tomorrow. Who knows when the Word of God may touch his heart?"[91] Expressed in Hauerwasian terms: one should not be quick to judge what is "world," since "that in creation that has taken the freedom not yet to believe" may at some point change its disposition.[92]

As has been alluded earlier this "believing" in Hauerwas's (and Yoder's) thought is not to be understood as a pietistic inner experience of salvation, or a mere intellectual conviction. It is rather participation in

---

91. Luther, *Sermons*, 70.

92. Yoder, *The Original Revolution*, 116. Yoder here quoted from Hauerwas, *The Peaceable Kingdom*, 101. Luther, however, seems to make a distinction between "true" and "false Christians": "this parable [Matt 13:24–30] treats not of false Christians, who are so only outwardly in their lives, but of those who are unchristian in their doctrine and faith under the name Christian, who beautifully play the hypocrite and work harm. (Luther, *Sermons*, 70.)

a community that seeks to imitate Jesus. This implies a visible church; a gathering of those who see the need to undergo such discipleship. This is a contrast to the kind of folk church theologies that envision a church even without a concrete body of adherents. I referred above to Björn Vikström who claimed that in our context the privatization of the faith has been theologically secured.[93] Such folk church theology with its radical inclusiveness, so to speak, augments the church and minimizes the world. As a result it becomes difficult to speak about church as a body of people practicing discipleship.

Despite the way that Luther's thought has been developed in these folk church theologies I suggest that there are in Luther's theology resources for viewing the church as a community of participants. The fact that there are regular worship services in the Lutheran Church, furthermore, makes it possible for people to gather and form a Eucharistic community. Participation in worship is, on Hauerwas's account, the chief way to receive training in Christian language and practice. Consequently I suggest that even in folk church contexts there are resources, both theological and practical, that can allow for an appreciation for and appropriation of the kind of contribution that Hauerwas's theology stands for. Hauerwas's perspective does not, in other words, have to be seen as a completely foreign one in our context.

EMBODIMENT REVISITED

In the third chapter of this study I provided an extended example of how Hauerwas talks about the question of truth in a way that stresses embodiment. Truth, on this view, is not treated in an abstract manner, but the focus lies on truthfulness, that is, on how a community lives—or fails to live—truthfully to its convictions. In the following I will explore how this emphasis on embodiment may provide an amendment to some common ways of approaching ethics in our context.

Moral as Law vs. Story-Driven Ethics

Ethics in our context, Tage Kurtén argues, is often understood "as a system of norms and rules which allows for rational deliberations."[94] Kurtén calls

---

93. Vikström, *Folkkyrka i en postmodern tid*, 147.
94. Kurtén, "The Christian," 104.

this understanding of ethics "the "law-metaphor" of ethics and morality."[95] Philosopher Lars Hertzberg describes fittingly the kind of reasoning that such an understanding of ethics leads to:

> In Western culture the law has often become the model for our understanding of morality. Morality is seen as a question of determining whether these or those "principles," "norms," or "rules" are "valid" or not; for whom they are "binding" and so on. One asks whether it is "right" or "wrong," "permitted" or "prohibited" to act in this or that way; or whether we have these or those "responsibilities" and "rights."[96]

Hertzberg calls this the "judicial model" of ethics but he seems to make the same point as does Kurtén.[97] There are two aspects at play in this view: firstly the point that one assumes morality to depend on a system of norms or rules, and secondly, that rational reflection in relation to these rules is central to ethics. On this view ethics is dependent on an alleged "external" norm, which is understood as a law: if one in some way breaks the norm it would be "wrong," whereas if one in a given situation complies with the norm it would be "right." In contrast to this a Hauerwasian perspective does not assume such an external norm; the focus is rather on acting in a way that is coherent with the persons "story" that in the case of Christians is (more or less) shaped by Christian tradition. The "norm" on this view would be an internal one in the sense that it arises from within a person. I will return to this later.

To further elaborate on the law-metaphor of ethics and to clarify the relationship between Hauerwas's perspective and Nordic ethical discourse it is in order to present an example of a typical Lutheran perspective, namely, the idea of natural law. Though different emphases within Lutheran theology can be discerned the idea of a natural law is still a central view. Generally speaking the basic idea is that God has created human beings with an inherent moral capacity. Humans can according to this view by way of their intellect and their conscience know what is right and wrong.

---

95. Kurtén, "The Christian," 104.
96. Hertzberg in Kurtén and Molander, *Homo moralis*, 207. My translation.
97. Hertzberg in Kurtén and Molander, *Homo moralis*, 207. See also Torrkulla and Backström, *Moralfilosofiska essäer*, 8. The editors talk about a "standard view" (*standardbild*) of ethics where morality has to do with a "rule system" (*regelsystem*) that is external to our lives.

The Lutheran Church commonly grounds its moral teaching in the idea of natural law.[98] Bishop emeritus Jorma Laulaja is a good example of this:

> Distinguishing between right and wrong is common to all humans, as is the capacity to perceive beauty, fear or the need to live in community with other people. At the core of our moral sense is a similar law [. . .] Our common moral sense includes the same that Jesus taught in the Sermon on the Mount (Matt 7:12): 'So in everything, do to others what you would have them do to you.' Jesus added that this so-called Golden Rule 'sums up the Law and the Prophets': all of ethics.[99]

This raises the question what is here meant by "right and wrong"? If Laulaja would say "good and bad" I would not think it that problematic. Right and wrong, however, seems to imply that there is something that is "objectively" right or wrong, and the same cannot be said of beauty or fear: beauty is, according to an old adage, in the eye of the beholder, and the same goes for what we fear. From this perspective Laulaja's view does not seem coherent. What we hold beautiful or frightening is relative to our story (experiences, worldview, "taste" etc.) and good and bad is also something that receives its intelligibility through a narrative. The same does not, I would suggest, necessarily go for right and wrong.

If human beings have objective access to right and wrong the Church's "statements" (*kannanotot*) only tell people what they already know through their reason and conscience. Obviously, the Lutheran point is exactly this: Christian proclamation is to show how we "fall short." At the same time it must be noted that in the Lutheran perspective Christian convictions and ethics are not directly linked to each other: morality is a feature that all humans as creatures share. Hauerwas, however, is critical of natural law traditions that make religion nothing more than a "motivational component of morality."[100] The problem he sees with this is that "not only has the moral force of Christian convictions been lost, but the very nature of moral experience has been distorted."[101] One way to interpret Hauerwas's problem here is that he takes natural law perspectives

---

98. Hytönen, *Kirkko*, 17, 74.

99. Laulaja, *Elämän oikea ja väärä*, 18. My translation. Raunio values Laulaja's *Elämän oikea ja väärä* as a book that has had much influence in the recent ethical views of the Lutheran Church in Finland. (Raunio, *Järki, usko ja lähimmäisen hyvä*, 50.) This makes it a meaningful example for my purposes.

100. Hauerwas, *The Peaceable Kingdom*, 12.

101. Hauerwas, *The Peaceable Kingdom*, 12.

to be based on a false universalism. For Hauerwas moral experience is historical and contingent. Ethics is, therefore, narratively constructed. For Christians it is shaped by a distinct tradition. Hauerwas thus stands for a different perspective than does Laulaja.

Though Laulaja talks about natural law he also displays a sensitivity to actual life-situations. Laulaja explicitly states that he does not seek to provide an "ethical cookbook" that provides a "recipe" for all sorts of problems.[102] He emphasizes that what is right and wrong must be continually re-assessed because there is no once and for all answer: Laulaja compares morality to walking along a road: it is something than each and every one must do her/himself.[103] From this follows that there seems to be Lutheran views that do not interpret the natural law as a rigid law, comparable to, for example, traffic laws (which do not leave much room for interpretation). While the view presented by Laulaja does not necessarily see natural law as a rigid external law, I would argue that he, nevertheless, involves the kind of rational deliberation that Kurtén above describes. There seems to be an element of improvisation without ready-made guidelines for morally commendable behavior. Yet this improvisation is made in relation to an alleged natural law.

Another similar example of this typical Lutheran perspective is the bishops' address on family, marriage and sexuality, called *Rakkauden lahja* (The Gift of Love). In this document (most of) the bishops of the Finnish Lutheran Church state that in its official ethical statements the Church wants to emphasize "basic moral principles" over "detailed instructions that fit into all life situations."[104] This could also be interpreted in a way that creates a space for individual ethical assessment that is to some degree instructed by the subject's story. At the same time it must be noted that in their statement *Rakkauden lahja* the bishops also stress that the capacity for moral judgment is something that is given to all as it is based on reason and conscience.[105] The mention of reason in this context I take to be an indication of the kind of moral reflection that Kurtén and Hertzberg critique. It also seems that the natural law assumption in the bishops' address implies that it is clear to all what these "basic moral principles" are. On this view the moral task for the individual is to align oneself with such principles. This task involves the use of rational capacities. The bishops'

102. Laulaja, *Elämän oikea ja väärä*, 12.
103. Laulaja, *Elämän oikea ja väärä*, 12.
104. Paarma et al., *Rakkauden lahja*, 23. My translation.
105. Paarma et al., *Rakkauden lahja*, 23.

view, furthermore, seems to involve the very idea of an "external law" that Kurtén and Hertzberg, as well as Hauerwas, suggest gives us a wrong picture of the place that morality has in our lives.[106] This becomes rather obvious when the document talks about the need for "external norms" without which it would be difficult to distinguish good from bad.[107]

It must be noted that Kurtén's and Hertzberg's account of a law-metaphor is a critique that may be relevant to many (Lutheran) views but not necessarily all. The focus here is, however, on typical Nordic views, and therefore it is meaningful to discuss the law-metaphor of ethics. Both Laulaja and the bishops' address leave space for "ethical improvisation," that is, for a person to re-interpret the "rules" so that they are relevant in a given situation. Yet, on my reading, the point that Kurtén and Hertzberg make about the law-metaphor for ethics and following rational deliberations is relevant to these views.

It is now time to consider Hauerwas's understanding of ethics in relation to the law-metaphor or morality. Kurtén proposes that

> The alternative to a rejected liberal and rational way of reasoning is not another theoretical justification . . . The alternative is instead a rejection of the view that moral matters are open for deliberations and moral reasoning in the way supposed. Moral philosophy (including theological ethics) following this alternative line points to the role moral language plays in the life of every human being.[108]

Hauerwas's perspective on ethics can be seen as the kind of alternative that Kurtén here is describing. Hauerwas's approach is different from the moral as law view. Central to this alternative is that "right" and "wrong" is determined from within a person's story. The "criteria" for what is morally praiseworthy or blameworthy is "internal"; it flows from the subjects tradition shaped character.[109]

---

106. Kurtén, "The Christian," 104; Kurtén and Molander, *Homo moralis*, 219; Hauerwas, *Against the Nations*, 44. See also Hauerwas, *The Peaceable Kingdom*, 11.

107. Paarma et al., *Rakkauden lahja*, 22. My translation. It should be noted that the bishops here talk about secular laws (*maalliset lait*). Yet the point remains that on this view one is supposed to align oneself to an external moral criteria, which involves rational deliberations.

108. Kurtén, "The Christian," 104. Hertzberg also maintains that the judicial model distorts our understanding of the role of morality in our lives. (Kurtén and Molander, *Homo moralis*, 219.)

109. Hauerwas, *The Peaceable Kingdom*, 28–30.

Yet this personal story is not to be understood as the story of a modern independent individual: crucial to Hauerwas's perspective is that the self be trained by the Christian tradition. This training takes place in worship and in Christian community:

> As Christians we believe we not only need a community, but a community of a particular kind to live well morally. We need a people who are capable of being faithful to a way of life, even when that way of life may be in conflict with what passes as "morality" in the larger society. Christians are a people who have learned that belief in God requires that we learn to look upon ourselves as creatures rather than creators. This necessarily creates a division between ourselves and others who persist in the pretentious assumption that we can and should be morally autonomous. Of course Christians are as prone to such pretensions as non-Christians. What distinguishes them is their willingness to belong to a community which embodies the stories, the rituals, an others committed to worshipping God.[110]

On this view Christian community is essential for the shaping of Christian character. The quote also shows that Hauerwas understands Christian morality to differ from the moralities of those who are not Christians. The central difference is and follows from the Christian conviction that we are created by God. For Hauerwas theologians are to write, and to acknowledge that they write, out of such a distinct perspective and community.[111] Hauerwas's view is consequently different from the Lutheran assumption that morality and faith are separate domains. On the theologian's task Hauerwas comments:

> Their first task is not, as has been assumed by many working in Christian ethics and still under the spell of Christendom, to write as though Christian commitments make no difference in the sense that they underwrite what everyone already in principle can know, but rather to show the difference those commitments make.[112]

A protruding example of such a difference in Hauerwas's own writings is his insistence on nonviolence. In other words, moral life looks different to a Christian pacifist compared to someone not committed to pacifism. More specifically, the alternatives for morally acceptable behavior in a

110. Hauerwas, *Against the Nations*, 43–44.
111. Hauerwas, *Against the Nations*, 44.
112. Hauerwas, *Against the Nations*, 44.

given situation (e.g. a conflict) differs between the two. With this quote it also becomes obvious that Hauerwas thinks that Christian ethics brings a unique contribution to other ethical perspectives in society: Christian ethics is not for Hauerwas the same as every other ethic. On this view Christian convictions open up a new perspective that would not otherwise be available.

Hauerwas further claims that trying to reflect on ethics in a way that does not explicitly flow out of a tradition or community can distort the way "the moral life as well as moral rationality" is understood.[113] Ethics based on an alleged natural law, at least in some formulations, comes close to the kind of ahistorical ethics that Hauerwas is critical of.[114] Following his reading of Christian tradition (with the need for initiation), and Alasdair MacIntyre's emphasis on the unavoidability of tradition, Hauerwas above implicitly maintains that it is an illusion to do Christian ethics in a manner that seeks to bypass the role of tradition.

Hauerwas also, to continue comparing and contrasting his view with typical Lutheran perspectives, maintains that we do not get to make Christianity up: it "is a given, albeit a complex given."[115] Christians need, on this view, to be initiated into the Christian story. Therefore I would argue that Hauerwas's perspective is a "first-person perspective" (Kurtén), but one in which the "person" undergoes initiation and therefore transformation.[116] There is, according to Hauerwas, a distinct Christian way of seeing and living to be learned, which shapes the way an individual acts.[117] I would not,

---

113. Hauerwas, *Against the Nations*, 44. See also Hauerwas, *The Peaceable Kingdom*, 11–12.

114. In *A Peaceable Kingdom* Hauerwas suggests that there are two "dominant characteristics of recent ethical theory: (1) the stress on freedom, autonomy, and choice as the essence of the moral life; and (2) the attempt to secure a foundation for the moral life unfettered by the contingencies of our histories and communities." (Hauerwas, *The Peaceable Kingdom*, 6–7.) Natural law perspectives come close to what Hauerwas is critiquing insofar as they assume that there is a moral "law" that is by virtue of creation available to all. Such a natural law can in some perspectives be assumed to provide a foundation for a universal ethics, which is what Hauerwas is critical of.

115. Hauerwas, *Wilderness Wanderings*, 3.

116. A first-person perspective assumes that every "ethical situation" is unique because people are unique. Kurtén's view will be discussed further in the following subchapter.

117. This is not, however, to be understood in the way that there is only one kind of Christian life. It rather refers to ways of life in which different kinds of individuals are affected by the Biblical stories. It is a life that involves initiation into tradition, intuitive action in specific situations based on the subject's tradition-tempered character.

however, describe such Christian ways of life in terms of the law metaphor of morality. In other words, though a Christian in a Hauerwasian perspective needs to be schooled in and by the Christian tradition, it is not a set of rules that Christians should learn. It has to do with character shaping and a kind of virtue ethic in which the subject lives in tune with her/his tradition-conditioned self-understanding. It might be better described as an attitude or posture that one is invited to learn through initiation into the Christian tradition—rather that a system of rules.

Moral as Knowledge vs. Embodiment

Understandings of ethics that assume a natural law are and have been central to the way that ethics is understood in the Nordic contexts. Creation theology and natural law views have been prevailing but they are not the only perspectives in our context. What can be called the "faith-ethic tradition" has been seen as an alternative to the natural law approach.[118] It is an understanding of ethics where right and wrong is tied to the Christian faith and to Scripture. According to this view believers and believing communities have through Scripture access to privileged knowledge in ethical matters.[119] In some ways the faith-ethic tradition seems at first glance to come close to what Hauerwas stands for. Yet there is an important point to be made regarding the faith-ethic tradition.

What unites the faith-ethical tradition and Hauerwas's perspective is the idea that Christians stand for an ethic that is different from other ethics in society. What, however, makes it difficult to lump Hauerwas's perspective together with the faith-ethic tradition has to do with the role assigned to knowledge. Hytönen, for example, seems to be talking extensively about "knowledge" of right and wrong. This knowledge is arrived at either by way of natural law or, in the case of the "faith-ethic tradition," through the Biblical texts. Hauerwas's approach, however, differs in this regard. For Hauerwas theology and ethics are in a way interchangeable, because he stresses that faith and life cannot be separated.[120] This entails, in other words, that Christian convictions must be embodied in order not to be abstract. A pragmatic way to express this critique toward the faith-

---

118. Hytönen, *Kirkko*, 280. (*Uskoneettinen perinne.*)

119. See for example Niskanen, *Moraali*, 11–18; Simo Knuuttila in Peura, *Usko ja rakkaus*, 103–115.

120. Hauerwas, *Truthfulness and Tragedy*, 142–143. See also Forrester, *Forrester on Christian Ethics*, 174–175.

ethic tradition is in the form of the following question: What good is it to know what is good if one is not embodying that very conviction by acting accordingly?

Asking such a question points to the kind of contribution that Hauerwas's line of thinking can make to both the faith-ethic tradition and typical Lutheran theology: an emphasis on Christianity as embodied convictions. Christianity in Hauerwas's writing is a way of life that displays certain convictions, more than it is knowledge about right and wrong or about Christian convictions.[121]

Kurtén and Hauerwas

Tage Kurtén presents an understanding of ethics in an article entitled "Kärlekens lag eller den naturliga lagen? Biblisk moraltradition idag."[122] The view of ethics developed in this article is interesting for my purposes for three reasons. Firstly, Kurtén is among those who in the Nordic context have reflected on Hauerwas's theology.[123] Secondly, Kurtén discusses Hauerwas's perspective in a way that brings to the fore the difference between Hauerwas's view and typical Nordic ethical discourse. Thirdly, Kurtén's view draws extensively on Hauerwas's view. On this point I will, however, argue that the latter stresses a meaningful element that the former does not. Because of these reasons it is of value to discuss the perspective that Kurtén develops.

Kurtén presents his understanding of ethics in polemic with forms of rationalistic Kantian ethics and utilitarianism that seek to formulate ethical codes in a theoretical way. In contrast to such approaches Kurtén suggests that ethics is something that is manifested in concrete life situations in the encounter between people. Kurtén does this by taking his cue from both Danish theologian Knud E. Løgstrup and Hauerwas. For Løgstrup ethics is something that is grounded in everyday encounters between people. When two people meet an element of trust is present. This becomes evident for example when one trusts another to speak truthfully. One's trust presents an ethical demand on the person met. It is an implicit demand that is not based on any moral law. According to Løgstrup one cannot by way of moral theories or rationality grasp anything "behind"

---

121. Hauerwas, *Truthfulness and Tragedy*, 142–143. See also Forrester, *Forrester on Christian Ethics*, 174–175.

122. Hytönen and Rajala-Kejonen, *Bibeln*, 178–195.

123. See also Kurtén, "The Christian."

Hauerwas in a Nordic Setting

or "beyond" this ethical demand that is present in relationships. In other words, the ethical demand implicit in relationships is not an application or result of a more fundamental rule or law. Løgstrup sought to develop an understanding of ethics that is not specifically Christian, but something that is common to all people.[124]

One of the critical questions that Løgstrup's approach to ethics surfaces is: will not such an understanding of ethics be relativistic? In order to meet such a critique Kurtén introduces Hauerwas.[125] Hauerwas's strong emphasis on the role of tradition and the fact that we are all part of a social network becomes a resource. Tradition and social context give an individual a frame of reference for distinguishing between good and bad, right and wrong. The understanding found in Hauerwas of self as story interwoven into a network of social relations is not an objective foundation for ethics. Despite this it does not lead to arbitrariness but allows for informed judgment.

The understanding of self as story is central to the understanding of ethics that Kurtén develops. We all live in a story that is unique to each individual. The story is shaped by our upbringing, tradition, education, experiences etc.; it is not something that one can freely choose. In such a narrative view of the self ethics has to do with consistency in relation to one's own story. When a person acknowledges her story, various acts can be more or less harmonious with how she sees herself. The act of lying can, for example, be in dissonance or conflict with the kind of person one is. Kurtén notes that because stories are individual it follows that the conditions (for acting well or badly) are different from one person to another. Ethics, therefore, involves a first-person perspective. Because of this it becomes problematic, indeed an illusion, to view ethical rules as timeless.[126]

The question of relativism might seem to remain despite the appeal to tradition, social context and a narrative self. Kurtén anticipates this critique and allies himself with Hauerwas in maintaining that such a critique operates with a false premise. This false premise is the idea that there is an

---

124. Hytönen and Rajala-Kejonen, *Bibeln*, 181–182. Løgstrup's proposal can be found in Løgstrup, *Den etiske fordring*, 295. It has been argued that "Løgstrup's signal achievement, still relevant after more than forty years, is to escape relativism by locating the source of ethics outside of human invention without lapsing into foundationalism." (Jackson, "Reviews," 460.) One may wonder though to what degree Løgstrup's idea of an inherent trust in people holds in other contexts than the Nordic one. See MacIntyre's and Fink's introduction to Løgstrup, *The Ethical Demand*.

125. Hytönen and Rajala-Kejonen, *Bibeln*, 183.

126. Hytönen and Rajala-Kejonen, *Bibeln*, 187.

objective and non-contextual measure available. Kurtén further suspects that much of Finnish Lutheran theology on the Lutheran understanding of law might be functioning with the same modern rationalist assumption. If this is the case, Kurtén suggests, it "gives a false notion of our moral capacities."[127] I agree with Kurtén on his interpretation of Hauerwas: Hauerwas does not assume such an objective gauge to be available. Instead morality is shaped by a contextual tradition, and "moral choices" receive their intelligibility from within a tradition and a social context.[128]

I think that the view that Kurtén develops captures something important about the character of ethics. He stresses that it is not about an external law or a set of rules that one is supposed to relate to by way of rational reflection. Morally commendable behavior, rather, has to do with being "in tune" with the kind of person one is. The role of self as story is, in other words, accentuated.

If Hauerwas's ethics is compared to Kurtén's view, I suggest that an aspect regarding the shaping of a person's ethics comes into focus. This aspect is the role of Christian community. For Hauerwas it is in Christian community and collective worship that one learns the language and way of life of Christians.[129] This aspect is not entirely missing with Kurtén

---

127. Hytönen and Rajala-Kejonen, *Bibeln*, 185.

128. See e.g. Berkman and Cartwright, *The Hauerwas Reader*, 529–530. This idea of ethics without an alleged objective measure may give raise to critical questions. One might, for example, maintain that such an ethic will not help people to "run society." It must be noted, however, that such a critique is Constantinian in that it supposes that Christian ethics should contribute to the state's task. It may also assume ethics to be a universal and inherent human capacity. The scope of Hauerwas's ethics is narrower: I would describe it as an attempt to answer the question "how are we as Christians to live (act, speak, think etc.) considering that God raised Jesus?" This is also the reason why the common critique that Hauerwas endorses withdrawal from society is misdirected: on Hauerwasian grounds it is not the task of theology and ethics to make society "work." The obsession to be able to formulate an ethic that is universally available and valid has some typically modern characteristics. Yet I am not saying that we do not need laws in order for society to work. Some form of agreement on acceptable behavior is necessary for society to function but it is not in a Hauerwasian perspective the primary task of Christian ethics.

129. Hauerwas, *Vision and Virtue*, 20; Berkman and Cartwright, *The Hauerwas Reader*, 530–531. Hauerwas makes the point very clearly when he states that "Worshiping God with other people is absolutely essential to learning to live as a Christian. This is not work that can be done by yourself. It can only be in a community through which you are made part of an ongoing history, that you don't get to make up Christianity. It is received. 'Jesus is Lord' is going to make my life quite dysfunctional in relationship to a good deal of American practice. Being a Christian should just scare the hell out of us." It's like on Sunday we need to rush to gather for protection. That we

but it is attenuated compared to Hauerwas's heavy stress on the role of community.[130]

If ethics is to be understood "in the first person," as Kurtén puts it, what consequences does it have for the understanding of Christianity? Is there a risk to overemphasize one's own story and downplaying the role of the biblical story? If it is the case, as Hauerwas claims, that "we do not get to make Christianity up," there should be a way to have the biblical story critique and even correct one's own story.[131] To further reflect on the perceived difference in Kurtén's and Hauerwas's perspectives I will give an example.

A person, P1, is part of a church community. P1 has a story of his own that intersects with an understanding of the story of Jesus. There are also other persons in the community, P2, and P3, who also have their own stories (depending on their upbringing, experiences, and education etc.) that include their view of the story of Jesus. Since all of these, P1, P2, and P3, belong to the same church it can be assumed that there is an understanding of the story of Jesus that is at least partly shared by all of these persons. I am not suggesting that they have the same experience, since everyone is unique. I do, however, think that if people share the language of a community then they also, to a considerable degree, share the meanings and interpretations of the community, despite the fact that people in community tend to have personal opinions and deviations from the community's assumed perspective.

---

believe that God was in Christ reconciling the world is craziness; it's gonna make your life really weird. You just need to get together to . . . on Sunday, to be pulled back in to the reality of God's Kingdom, which I believe we do. I mean it's there in baptism, in the proclamation of the Word, and Eucharistic celebration." (Hauerwas, "The System vs. The Kingdom.")

130. Kurtén speaks about the role of social context (*sociala sammanhanget*). (Kurtén and Molander, *Homo moralis*, 73.) Kurtén is on this point inspired by Wittgenstein, who maintained that human language and life are social in character. (Kurtén, "Teologi mellan ontologi och antropologi," 23, 25.) Kurtén does not, however, explicitly talk about the role of church as does Hauerwas.

131. Hauerwas maintains that "I have little use, however, for the easy affirmation of variety in Christian tradition or for appeals to pluralism to legitimate the view that theologians get to decide what they want Christianity to be. The Christian tradition is a given, albeit a complex given, that invites and requires, rather than inhibits, argument." (Hauerwas, *Wilderness Wanderings*, 3.) The argument that Hauerwas here talks of I take to be the kind of interpretative work that must be done in each time and place where the church finds herself. Such work is necessary in order that Christian tradition finds a meaningful, contextual expression in a given context.

If P1 were to act in a way that is in dissonance with the church community's story of Jesus, would it, for example, be possible to have any sort of accountability or "church discipline" between the members within Kurtén's view? Is it possible that P2 and P3 could rebuke an inconsistency in P1's behavior, because of the fact that they are well schooled and rooted in the shared understanding of the story of Jesus? This seems to be possible in Hauerwas's thought considering his stress on the role of those who are more experienced in what a life shaped by the story of Jesus is like.[132]

Obviously, P2 and P3 might perceive the wrong act in question differently than P1 because of differing personal stories, and further, because of the fact that they do not immediately see the intention that P1 had in mind when he committed the act. Consequently P2 and P3 should not jump to conclusions about what indeed has taken place in the life of P1. Kurtén points out that a person who seeks to tell others what to do reveals something about his/her own moral stature.[133] I agree, but I would still argue that there might be situations in a church community where a person has unmistakably gone wrong. This means that the person has acted in a way that is in disagreement with how the story of Jesus is interpreted in the community that the person belongs to. Such a situation needs then to be faced, in order that the community would be truthful to itself and to the surrounding society.[134] This is clearly a very delicate matter since confronting and rebuking people can easily be an act of selfishness or just another power struggle.[135] If one, however, perceives Christianity as a way of life that needs to be learnt, which Hauerwas does, it is something that at times may involve some form of communal discipline.

I agree with Kurtén that ethics should not be primarily seen as a question of rational deliberation about rules, but I also suggest that Hauerwas's stress on the role of Christian community is meaningful. It is meaningful if one takes Christianity to be a way of life that takes initiation. I conclude that there is an observable difference between Hauerwas and Kurtén when

---

132. Hauerwas speaks of the need to correct people who live in an unfaithful way. He also maintains that Christians "need to establish a context where they can have real disputes with others." (Berkman and Cartwright, *The Hauerwas Reader*, 323, 532.)

133. Hytönen and Rajala-Kejonen, *Bibeln*, 194.

134. Rebuking someone is not the same as policing over other people. The motive for this kind of confrontation is faithfulness to a tradition that seeks to learn to speak truth. See Hauerwas, *Christian Existence Today*, 89–96.

135. Examples of ways that communal disciplining can go wrong are plentiful. Henriksen mentions quenched desire and the use of shame as problematic approaches. (Henriksen, "Shame, Desire and Marginality," 75–90.)

it comes to the shaping of a person's ethics. Kurtén is inspired by Hauerwas's virtue ethic with its rejection of moral as law, but the former does not emphasize the "social situatedness" of the moral subject in as concrete a way as does the latter.

CONSTANTINIANISM AND NONVIOLENCE REVISITED

Constantinianism and nonviolence will here be discussed together. The reason for this is that the alternative to Constantinianism that Hauerwas envisions implies a rejection of violence and coercion. We saw in the fourth chapter of this study that Hauerwas follows Yoder in maintaining that one cannot create a consistent anti-Constantinian model.[136] If one were to provide such an alternative it would too in some regards be Constantinian. Whatever an anti-Constantinian ecclesial strategy might be it is necessarily *ad hoc* in character. What amounts to Anti-Constantinian and nonviolent practices is, in other words, determined contextually in specific situations. The task here is, therefore, to enquire what this disposition might contribute to a Nordic context with regard to the notion of witness.

I suggested that Hauerwas's account of Constantinianism is best read as a "heuristic tool"; as short-hand for the altered status of Christianity. The remark that it took courage to be a Christian *before* Constantine and courage to be a pagan *after* Constantine supports such an interpretation.[137] Constantinianism is, in other words, a typifying way to talk about the change in Christianity's status in society. While the notion can be seen as a simplification of history, it can still be seen as *part* of the story of what happened at the time of Constantine, and more specifically, a part of the story that has relevance for the Christian community.[138] Hauerwas is explicitly trying to tell a Christian story, not a neutral observer's story. This

---

136. Hauerwas, *The State of the University*, 69 quoting Yoder and Cartwright, *The Royal Priesthood*, 250.

137. Hauerwas and Wells, *Blackwell Companion*, 42.

138. Swedish theologian Ola Sigurdson, for example, suggests that religious *pluralism* was the result of the Edict of Milan, rather than Christianity. (Sigurdson, *Det postsekulära tillståndet*, 202.) This could be interpreted to imply that Hauerwas's take on Christianity before and after Constantine is a simplification: perhaps the role of Christianity in society did not, after all, change as radically as Hauerwas suggests. If this is the case then Constantinianism might not be a historically meaningful notion. This does not, however, in my view have to imply that one could not still talk about Constantinianism as a type or model for a certain kind of ecclesial strategy.

goes to say that Hauerwas is seeking to draw out some implications of the historical development around Constantine, and then to use the resulting account as a tool or type for identifying a certain kind of Christian activity in contemporary society.

There is another factor that needs to be accentuated in an attempt to assess the contribution of Constantinianism. This point can be illuminated by asking questions such as: What is the relevance of Hauerwas's notion of Constantinianism in a Nordic folk church setting? Does Christianity in Nordic contexts resort to some forms of Constantinianism, and more specifically, is the (Finnish) folk church arrangement a Constantinian venture?

Questions such as these bring to the fore the temptation to call "this that." It is a complicated matter to, as it were, pair conceptual ideas with empirical reality. In this project I have, however, defined my task as a conceptual one. In other words I focus on the use of language; logical presuppositions and coherence (or lack of it), rather than on sociological or historical analysis of our context. As a result I do not find it meaningful to claim that, for example, the Lutheran folk church arrangement in Finland, in its entirety, is a Constantinian project.

Despite this it can be observed that some manifestations of Christianity in our context displays features that might contain Constantinian assumptions. One example of what I call a "Constantinian trait" is the work of the Christian Democratic Party in Finland. The party stands for "values" that are understood to reflect Christian convictions. These values are seen as essential in order for life in society to be good, and therefore, the party pursues these values in its program.[139] This comes close to Hauerwas's description of Christians who do not trust God to be able to maintain a witness to God's kingdom without the help of Christians lobbying the state to reinforce Christian convictions through laws.[140] A Hauerwasian critique of such a view of Christian politics would entail paying attention to its inherently albeit subtly violent disposition. The problem, according to a Hauerwasian interpretation, is that it coerces others to act a bit more "Christianly."

Another example that brings to the fore the kind of perspective that an awareness of Constantinianism entails can be found in Finnish Lutheran theology as represented by the bishops' address *Rakkauden lahja*:

---

139. The Christian Democrats, "Christian Democracy."
140. Hauerwas and Willimon, *Resident Aliens*, 80–81.

Hauerwas in a Nordic Setting

> In addition to conscience external laws and common norms, which represent broader than individual convictions, are needed both in the spiritual and the societal life. They are more than the sum of common opinions: they must when necessary be able to pierce through delusive common opinions. Without the support of external norms it can become difficult to distinguish between good and bad. The task of secular laws is to, through decrees and even restraint, steer communal life in the right direction.[141]

This can be interpreted to contain a Constantinian trait in that it wants to force life in society in what is taken to be "the right direction." Commonly a society is assumed to need laws and regulations, and I do not wish to argue otherwise, but in a Hauerwasian perspective it is not the task of Christians to provide or struggle for such laws.[142] The way that the bishops argue is, it seems to me, Constantinian in that it assumes that "worldly laws" steer the common life of citizens in the "right direction." As referred to earlier, Hauerwas notes that "the view that what God is doing is being done primarily through the framework of society as a whole and not through the Christian community is the presumption that lies behind the Constantinian accommodation of the church to the world."[143] On this view, the church has a mandate of its own that cannot be assumed to be furthered by other bodies in society.

The way that *Rakkauden lahja* reasons, it seems to me, fits Hauerwas's abovementioned characterization of Constantinianism. The stress on external laws that are needed to guide us in the "right direction" (whether "right direction" is defined from within Christian tradition or a universal natural law perspective) falls under the label Constantinianism: it implies that the church is optional for whatever God may be doing in society.

Hauerwas suggests, as seen in chapter four, that failing to make a distinction between church and world has had severe consequences (Christological and ecclesiological) for the shape that Christianity takes.[144] After Constantine conversion to Christ and discipleship became optional for being a Christian. I stated above that I do not suggest that the folk church

---

141. Paarma et al., *Rakkauden lahja*, 22. My translation.

142. The kind of libertarian socialism and anarcho-syndicalism that Noam Chomsky embraces exemplify visions of a secular society that assign in some ways a differing role to laws and regulations. See e.g. Pateman, *Chomsky on Anarchism*.

143. Hauerwas, *With the Grain of the Universe*, 221 referring to Yoder and Cartwright, *The Royal Priesthood*, 198.

144. Hauerwas, *The State of the University*, 66.

arrangement in its *entirety* is Constantinian. Despite this I think that some folk church theologies do include a strong Constantinian element.

A telling example of this comes from Sweden. In Sweden "folk church theology" has been developed in a direction that views the Lutheran Church as highly inclusive, or as it is often called, an "open folk church."[145] Ola Sigurdson helpfully asks whether this "openness" means that the Church accepts any convictions (or lack thereof) that "the folk" may underwrite as valid expressions of Lutheran Christianity?[146] If this is the case then it implies that people's convictions are reduced to something irrelevant.[147] Sigurdson wonders whether it is at all possible to *disagree* with the Church if, as seems to be the case in an "open folk church," anything and everything is included as a valid expression of Christianity?[148] A Church that is so inclusive that it absorbs every attempt to heresy would involve an element of Constantinian coercion. There *should* be a possibility to dissent from what is taken to be Christianity.[149]

Moreover, in such a situation it is difficult to imagine any meaningful distinction between church and world. If the Lutheran Church in Sweden makes "member of the Church" equal to "Christian" then the visibility of the church is done away with. A Church with a large member-base but few participants in worship, which is typical of Nordic folk churches, becomes a community without community; a body without a body. Such a community and such a body is, in other words, nothing more than a theological construct without any meaningful referent.

In a situation such as the one in the example from Sweden, Hauerwas's perspective provides an important critique. The insistence on a distinction between church and world challenges forms of Christianity that embraces as Christians even people who do not consider themselves Christians or undergo Christian initiation (discipleship). On this point an anti-Constantinian approach would involve a rejection of the subtle coercion that this kind of "open folk church" thinking harbors. The perspective that Hauerwas stands for adds, in my view, an important, aspect to Nordic

---

145. Sigurdson, "Vilka är vi nu?," 62. This does not, of course, mean to say that the "open folk church" is the only kind of folk church theology in Sweden. For a brief summary of the Swedish views see e.g. Wrede, *Folkkyrkan*. See also Vikström, *Folkkyrka i en postmodern tid*.

146. Sigurdson, "Vilka är vi nu?," 64.

147. Sigurdson, "Vilka är vi nu?," 64.

148. Sigurdson, "Vilka är vi nu?," 64.

149. Obviously it is by no means obligatory to be a member of the folk churches. Consequently it is a subtle form of coercion that we are concerned with here.

theologizing. This aspect is the attention given to rejection of coercion, or positively expressed, the affirmation of nonviolence.

To conclude I would suggest that discussing a concept such as Constantinianism can have very practical ramifications. More specifically, describing and analyzing a notion can identify central themes and issues that concrete Christian communities might do well to grapple with. In the case of my account of Constantinianism, it might, so to speak, suggest part of the agenda in the task of interpretation carried out by local churches. To reiterate this point with regard to my overall task: Reflection on the notion of Constantinianism can help a Christian community identify possible Constantinian traits in its life and ministry.

The notion of Constantinianism can, I have suggested, be a resource for churches that seek to communicate a Christian tradition in our context in that it can function as a tool for critical self-reflection. By paying attention to practices that might explicitly or implicitly rely on existing power structures, such as the state, to support the Christians' task, Christian communities can be more truthful to their tradition. Unchecked traits of Constantinianism, on the other hand, leads Christian communities into incoherence: a message of God's love told coercively cannot but be self-defeating.

Chapter 6

Conclusion

IN THE PRESENT STUDY I have claimed that a postsecular situation, characterized by both declining memberships in established Churches as well as a new visibility of alternative religious expressions, opens up a need to reflect on alternative ways of understanding Christianity in its context. The overarching theme of this study has been Christian witness. I have stated that in a postsecular situation a Christian church, even a folk church, cannot assume a position of majority or power. How to understand Christianity as a community that is neither in power nor a majority becomes a relevant question. I have suggested that the theology of Stanley Hauerwas provides a meaningful perspective in an attempt to understand Christianity in its context, and more specifically, Christian witness. I have related my reading of Hauerwas to some typical Nordic theological emphases. This has been done in order to bring to the fore some crucial aspects of—what in the introduction's task description was called—*a feasible account of Christian witness that pays regard to the altered conditions for the use of religious language*. A central change in the conditions for the use of religious language is, as has already been alluded to, that Christian communities cannot any longer assume to be a majority or in a position of power.

What remains to be done is to summarize the considerations of this study and in so doing articulate a feasible account of Christian witness. To be clear I must maintain that due to the character of the following account it can only be, as it were, a silhouette of a feasible account of witness. The reason being, as has been pointed out before, that the central notions in Hauerwas's theology involve *ad hoc* elements. What follows is, therefore, an account of some central aspects that churches that seek to be witness in a postsecular Nordic context might do well to grapple with.

I have suggested that Hauerwas's theological perspective is an amendment to the way that Christianity in its context, or more specifically expressed, Christian witness, has often been understood in Nordic Lutheran theological discourse. This amendment emerges from relating the three main ideas of this study to typical Nordic perspectives. These three interrelated ideas are, as the structure of this study insinuates, the notions of (1) church as social ethic, (2) embodiment, and (3) Constantinianism and nonviolence.

(1) Church as social ethic was seen as a resource in that it, firstly, provides a distinctly Christian narration of the world. Typical Lutheran perspectives, it was suggested, tend to limit the scope of theology and Christian faith to existential matters. Lutheran theology, therefore, tends to act in a world in which the sciences are given the interpretative privilege. A postliberal perspective, however, seeks to provide its own reading of the world, and as such, theology is not relegated only to domains of life that the sciences cannot study. This implies that postliberal theology claims to provide a unique vision of life. A unique perspective on life carries potential to serve as a means for society to reflect self-critically on its practices and politics. Identifying "epistemic violence" was mentioned as an example of the kind of societal self-critique that the church by virtue of being a "subaltern" could provide to the wider society. Secondly, church as social ethic stands for a distinct alternative politics. This was seen as an amendment to typical Nordic perspectives in that it undoes the disconnection between "personal ethics" and "political ethics." Thirdly, it was observed that the understanding of church and world provides a point of contact between Hauerwas's and Luther's thought. This, it was suggested, makes it possible to appropriate Hauerwasian insights within a Lutheran context. At the same time it must be kept in mind that the doctrine of the two regiments as well as the stress on Christianity as a personal matter creates a real tension between Hauerwasian and Lutheran perspectives. Another point of tension is the reluctance and difficulty in Lutheran folk church theology to make any kind of distinction between church and world. This, I have argued, robs the world from the distinct perspective that the church might offer. At the same time it was suggested that on this exact point Luther's thought might provide an opening for making a distinction between church and world.

From these considerations follow that the notion of church as social ethic suggests that Christian witness is indistinguishable from the life of Christian communities: church not only has a social ethic but it is a social ethic. Similarly, witness requires Christian communities that display, not only talk about, an alternative way of life.

(2) The embodied character of Hauerwas's project was also seen as a contribution to a relevant Nordic conception of witness. This contribution lies in an understanding of ethical life that emphasizes the social character of human life. Morality is not, on this view, primarily application of some abstract ahistorical laws, as in some Lutheran perspectives, but something more concrete and contextual. Morality reflects the kind of person one is, and the kind of person that one is, is shaped by our social context (other people, community). A Hauerwasian understanding of ethics is, therefore, highly critical of contemporary individualism. The inherently social character of human life has ramifications for Christian witness. As a result, a feasible understanding of witness takes it to be a communal phenomenon. On this view, witness is what happens when a Christian community displays an alternative way of life.[1] Witness is, therefore, a very concrete matter.[2]

(3) Constantinianism and nonviolence, it was suggested, brings in a distinct perspective to typical Nordic Lutheran theological discourse. This perspective insists on a distinction between church and world and on nonviolence as the form that witness takes. Peaceableness is the body-language of a community without which there can be no witness. Coercive or violent witness is, on this view, an oxymoron.[3] My account of Constan-

---

1. This is not to say that all alternative forms of life are witness. What we are concerned with here is the kind of witness that is formed by Christian tradition.

2. I here recall the words of Acts 4:20 "for we cannot stop speaking about what we have *seen* and *heard*" and 1. John 1:3 "what we have *seen* and *heard* we proclaim to you also, so that you too may have fellowship with us; and indeed our fellowship is with the Father, and with His Son Jesus Christ." (NASB, italics mine.)

3. If one nevertheless wants to talk about witness in terms of violence, it must be asked wherein the violence lies. Nonviolent witness does not, on the view assumed in this study, coerce "the other" into accepting the tacit claims made by the witness. If the other, that is, the person who encounters a community of witness, were to be drawn to that community it is possible to think that it is Christian tradition that lays claims on the person (rather than the witness). To clarify, communication of a Christian tradition can be seen as a triangular event, not just a dialog between the witness and the other. Such a triangular event involves three parts, the witnessing community, Christian tradition and the other. It is here assumed that Christian tradition "is something" and not just a social and historical construct, though it obviously is that too.

tinianism and nonviolence, furthermore, challenges the subtle coercion that an "open folk church" thinking involves. The notion of Constantinianism can also function as a tool for self-critique of Christian community: reflecting on Constantinianism can help identify otherwise undetected forms of coercion.

All of these considerations (1, 2, 3) involve an attempt to view Christianity as an alternative society in society, and as such a minority that cannot rely on power in order to coerce others to accept their claims. With this these ideas, to recall my task description, pay regard to a central aspect of the altered conditions for the use of religious language.

A venue for *further study* would be to relate Hauerwasian postliberalism to Nordic free church theologies. For example, Pentecostalism or The Evangelical Free Church could in the case of Finland provide more indigenous ways to see Christianity as a counter-society in society.[4] Another area of study that I did not enter has to do with asceticism. Hauerwas's theological project includes only few explicit references to asceticism.[5] Asceticism can, however, be seen as implicit in much of Hauerwas's theology.[6] This is obviously a venue for further study, which relevance is by no means limited to the Nordic context.

A central feature that has surfaced throughout the whole study is the centrality of embodiment for Christian witness. Christian convictions are on this view inseparably intertwined with Christian life. To put it in Hauerwas's words:

> The task of Christian ethics is to help us see how our convictions are in themselves a morality. We do not first believe certain things about God, Jesus, and the church, and subsequently derive ethical implications from these beliefs. Rather our convictions embody our morality; our beliefs are our actions. We Christians ought not to search for the "behavioral implications"

---

4. It must be noted, however, that the pietistic emphasis on personal salvation that these denominations often exhibit is, from the perspective of the present study, problematic. The reason for this is that pietism displays some typically modern characteristics. Christian faith in these denominations is often, as far as I can see, made a "spiritual" and personal, rather than a public and political thing. The perspective assumed in this study is critical of the modern idea of a differentiated society, with a separate sphere for religion. Yet I must point out that one should not be too hasty to declare that denominations such as the abovementioned *only* stand for personal and apolitical convictions. This is precisely why I think that it would be interesting to relate Hauerwasian perspectives to free church theologies.

5. For the most obvious mention see Hauerwas, *The Peaceable Kingdom*, 150.

6. Hagman, "To Travel in One Place."

of our beliefs. Our moral life is not comprised in beliefs plus decisions; our moral life is the process in which our convictions form our character to be truthful.[7]

This perspective is, as I have suggested, an amendment to how theological ethics in our context often emphasizes knowledge about Christian convictions and their "application." To reflect on this quote with the overarching theme of witness in mind, one could say that witness is what happens where convictions are embodied. I have attempted to show that each of the central ideas in this study—a Hauerwasian Christian ethics, the stress on embodiment even in talking about a topic such as truth, as well as the notions of Constantinianism and peaceableness—exemplify the embodied character of the kind of postliberal theology that this study has discussed.

---

7. Hauerwas, *The Peaceable Kingdom*, 16.

Bibliography

Ahlqvist, Marjo, et al. *Flumen Saxosum Sonans: Studia in Honorem Gunnar af Hällström.* åbo Akademi, 2010.
Aristotle. *Metaphysics.* Nuvision, LLC, 2005.
Asad, Talal. *Formations of the Secular: Christianity, Islam, Modernity.* Stanford, CA: Stanford U. P., 2003.
Barth, Karl. *Church Dogmatics I/1.* Edinburgh: T & T Clark, 1995.
Bavister-Gould, Alex. "The Uniqueness of After Virtue (or 'Against Hindsight')." *Analyse & Kritik* 30 (2008) 55–74.
Berkman, J., and Michael Cartwright. *The Hauerwas Reader.* Durham, NC: Duke University Press, 2001.
Bevans, S. B., and Roger Schroeder. *Constants in Context: A Theology of Mission for Today.* Maryknoll, NY: Orbis Books, 2004.
Bexell, Göran. *Svensk moralpolitik: några moraliska frågors behandling i riksdags- och regeringsarbetet sedan 1950-talet.* Lund: Lund U.P., 1995.
Bexell, G., and Ivar Asheim. *Kyrkan och etiken.* Stockholm: Verbum, 1992.
Bonhoeffer, Dietrich. *Letters and Papers from Prison.* New York: Macmillan, 1972.
Bosch, David Jacobus. *Transforming Mission: Paradigm Shifts in Theology of Mission.* Maryknoll, NY: Orbis Books, 1991.
Brown, Peter Robert Lamont. *The Rise of Western Christendom: Triumph and Diversity, A.D. 200–1000.* Malden, MA: Blackwell, 2003.
Bruce, Steve. *God is Dead: Secularization in the West.* Oxford: Blackwell, 2002.
———. *Religion in the Modern World: From Cathedrals to Cults.* Oxford: Oxford U. P., 2002.
Brunner, Emil. *The Word and the World.* New York: C. Scribner's Sons, 1931.
Casanova, José. *Public Religions in the Modern World.* Chicago, IL: University of Chicago Press, 1994.
Cavanaugh, William. "Does Religion Cause Violence?" Online: http://ebookbrowse.com/cavanaugh-does-religion-cause-violence-pdf-d16518674.
———. *The Myth of Religious Violence: Secular Ideology and the Roots of Modern Conflict.* New York: Oxford University Press, 2009.
———. "Discerning: Politics and Reconciliation." In *The Blackwell Companion to Christian Ethics,* edited by Hauerwas, S., and Samuel Wells, 211–233. Malden, MA: Blackwell, 2004.
Cavanaugh, W. "Stan the Man: A Thoroughly Biased Account of a Completely Unobjective Person." In *The Hauerwas Reader,* edited by Berkman, J., and Michael Cartwright. Durham, NC: Duke University Press, 2001.
Clapp, Rodney. "What Would Pope Stanley Say?" Online: http://www.booksandculture.com/articles/1998/novdec/8b6016.html.

Bibliography

Crittenden, Jack. *Beyond Individualism: Reconstituting the Liberal Self*. New York: Oxford University Press, 1992.

Crowder, Colin. *God and Reality: Essays on Christian Non-realism*. London: Mowbray, 1997.

D'Costa, Gavin. *Theology in the Public Square: Church, Academy, and Nation*. Malden: Blackwell, 2006.

———. *Christian Uniqueness Reconsidered: The Myth of a Pluralistic Theology of religions*. Maryknoll, NY: Orbis Books, 1990.

Davaney, S. G., and Delvin Brown, "Postliberalism." In McGrath, A. E., and Duncan B. Forrester. *The Blackwell Encyclopedia of Modern Christian Thought*. Oxford: Blackwell, 1993.

De Kock, Leon. "Interview with Gayatri Chakravorty Spivak: New Nation Writers Conference in South-Africa." *A Review of International English Literature* 23/3 (1992) 29–47.

Ferguson, Russell et al. *Out There: Marginalization and Contemporary Cultures*. Cambridge, MA: The MIT Press, 1990.

Forrester, Duncan B. *Forrester on Christian Ethics and Practical Theology: Collected Writings on Christianity, India, and the Social Order*. Farnham, England: Ashgate, 2010.

———. "Social Justice and Welfare." In *The Cambridge Companion to Christian Ethics*, edited by Robin Gill, 195–208. Cambridge, U.K.; NY: Cambridge University Press, 2001.

Frei, Hans W. *The Eclipse of Biblical Narrative: a Study in Eighteenth and Nineteenth Century Hermeneutics*. New Haven: Yale University Press, 1974.

Gill, Robin. *The Cambridge Companion to Christian Ethics*. Cambridge, U.K.; NY: Cambridge University Press, 2001.

Gregersen, Niels Henrik. "The Fluid Mission of the Church." In *Walk Humbly with the Lord: Church and Mission Engaging Plurality*, edited by Mortensen, V., and Andreas Nielsen, 74–84. Grand Rapids, MI: W. B. Eerdmans, 2011.

Grenholm, Carl-Henric. *Bortom humanismen: en studie i kristen etik*. Stockholm: Verbum, 2003.

Gustafson, James. "The Sectarian Temptation: Reflections on Theology, the Church and the University." *Proceedings of the Catholic Theological Society* 40 (1985) 83–94.

Gustafsson, G., and Thorleif Pettersson. *Folkkyrkor och religiös pluralism – den nordiska religiösa modellen*. Stockholm: Verbum, 2000.

Habermas, Jürgen. *Mellan naturalism och religion: filosofiska uppsatser*. Translated by Eva Backelin. Göteborg: Daidalos, 2007.

Hagman, Patrik. "To Travel in One Place: Openings for a New Asceticism in the Theology of Stanley Hauerwas." *Political Theology* 13:1. (2012).

———. *Om kristet motstånd*. Stockholm: Artos & Norma, 2011.

———. *The Asceticism of Isaac of Nineveh*. Oxford; New York: Oxford University Press, 2010.

Hauerwas, Stanley. *A Better Hope: Resources for a Church Confronting Capitalism, Democracy, and Postmodernity*. Grand Rapids, MI: Brazos, 2000.

———. *A Community of Character: Toward a Constructive Christian Social Ethic*. Notre Dame, IN: University of Notre Dame Press, 1981.

———. *After Christendom? How the Church Is to Behave If Freedom, Justice, and a Christian Nation Are Bad Ideas*. Nashville, TN: Abingdon, 1991.

———. *Against the Nations: War and Survival in a Liberal Society*. Notre Dame, IN: University of Notre Dame Press, 1992.

———. "Beyond the Boundaries: The Church Is Mission". Paper presented on 2010/01/28 at the Church & Mission in the Third Millennium conference in Århus, Denmark. (Later published in Mortensen and Nielsen, *Walk Humbly with the Lord*, 53–73.)

———. "Burke lecture." Online: http://www.youtube.com/watch?v=FPPJCkfxdTs.

———. *Character and the Christian Life: A Study in Theological Ethics*. Notre Dame, IN: University of Notre Dame Press, 1994.

———. *Christian Existence Today: Essays on Church, World, and Living in Between*. Grand Rapids, MI: Brazos, 2001.

———. *Curriculum vitae*, 2011.

———. *Dispatches from the Front: Theological Engagements with the Secular*. Durham, NC: Duke University Press, 1994.

———. "Failure of Communication or A Case of Uncomprehending Feminism." *Scottish Journal of Theology* 50/2 (1997).

———. "Faith Fires Back: A Conversation with Stanley Hauerwas." Online: http://www.dukemagazine.duke.edu/dukemag/issues/010202/faith.html.

———. *Hannah's Child: A Theologian's Memoir*. Grand Rapids, MI: W. B. Eerdmans, 2010.

———. *In Good Company: The Church as Polis*. Notre Dame, IN: University of Chicago Press, 1995.

———. *Matthew*. Grand Rapids, MI: Brazos, 2006.

———. *Naming the Silences: God, Medicine, and the Problem of Suffering*. Grand Rapids, MI: W. B. Eerdmans, 1990.

———. On Prayer. Online: http://www.youtube.com/watch?v=gYRk3uPVhvY.

———. *Performing the Faith: Bonhoeffer and the Practice of Nonviolence*. Grand Rapids, MI: Brazos, 2004.

———. *Sanctify Them in the Truth: Holiness Exemplified*. Nashville, TN: Abingdon, 1998.

———. *The Peaceable Kingdom: A Primer in Christian Ethics*. Notre Dame, IN: University of Notre Dame Press, 1983.

———. *The State of the University: Academic Knowledges and the Knowledge of God*. Malden, MA; Oxford: Blackwell, 2007.

———. "The System vs. The Kingdom." Online: http://www.youtube.com/watch?v=M6Dr1QLiaAo.

———. "The Testament of Friends." *Christian Century* 107/7 (1990) 212–16.

———. *Truthfulness and Tragedy: Further Investigations in Christian Ethics*. Notre Dame, IN: University of Notre Dame Press, 1977.

———. *Unleashing the Scripture: Freeing the Bible from Captivity to America*. Nashville, TN: Abingdon, 1993.

———. *Vision and Virtue: Essays in Christian Ethical Reflection*. Notre Dame, IN: Fides, 1974.

———. *Wilderness Wanderings: Probing Twentieth-Century Theology and Philosophy*. Boulder, CO: Westview, 1997.

———. *With the Grain of the Universe: The Church's Witness and Natural Theology. Being the Gifford Lectures Delivered at the University of St. Andrews in 2001*. Grand Rapids, MI: Brazos Press, 2001.

Bibliography

Hauerwas, Stanley et al. *The Wisdom of the Cross: Essays in Honor of John Howard Yoder.* Grand Rapids, MI: W.B. Eerdmans, 1999.

Hauerwas, S., and John Swinton. *Critical Reflections on Stanley Hauerwas' Theology of Disability: Disabling Society, Enabling Theology.* Binghamton, NY: Haworth, 2004.

Hauerwas, S., and Jean Vanier. *Living Gently in a Violent World: The Prophetic Witness of Weakness.* Downers Grove, IL: IVP Books, 2008.

Hauerwas, S., and Paul Wadell. "Review of *After Virtue.*" *The Thomist* 46/2 (1982).

Hauerwas, S., and Samuel Wells. *The Blackwell Companion to Christian Ethics.* Malden, MA: Blackwell, 2004.

Hauerwas, S., and William H. Willimon. *Resident Aliens: Life in the Christian Colony.* Nashville, TN: Abingdon, 1989.

———. *Where Resident Aliens Live: Exercises for Christian Practice.* Nashville, TN: Abingdon, 1996.

Hays, Richard B. *The Moral Vision of the New Testament: Community, Cross, New Creation: a Contemporary Introduction to New Testament Ethics.* San Francisco, CA: Harper, 1996.

Hedenius, Ingemar. *Tro och vetande.* Stockholm: Bonniers, 1949.

Heelas, Paul. *The Spiritual Revolution: Why Religion is Giving Way to Spirituality.* Malden, MA: Blackwell, 2005.

Heelas, P., and Linda Woodhead. *Religion in Modern Times: An Interpretive Anthology.* Malden, MA: Blackwell, 2000.

Helander, Eila. *Muutoksen tulkkina: kirkot ja uskonnollinen elämä osana yhteiskuntaa.* Helsinki: Kirjapaja, 2003.

Helsingin Sanomat, 2007/09/09. Online: http://www.hs.fi/kotimaa/artikkeli/Kirkkoherra+Lehikoinen+Seura-kunta+ toimiavoimesti+toisin+kuin+Ulkomaalaisvirasto +/1135230310278.

Henriksen, Jan-Olav. "Mission: Invitation to Community." In *Walk Humbly with the Lord: Church and Mission Engaging Plurality,* edited by Mortensen, V., and Andreas Nielsen, 70–73. Grand Rapids, MI: W. B. Eerdmans, 2011.

———. *På grensen til Den andre: om teologi og postmodernitet.* Oslo: Ad Notam Gyldendal, 1999.

———. "Shame, Desire and Marginality: Considerations on Challenges to a Contemporary Theology about Human Experience." *Nordic Journal of Religion and Society* 21/1 (2008) 75–90.

Hobson, Theo. 2007. "Against Hauerwas." In *New Blackfriars* 88/1015 (2007) 300–12.

Hytönen, Maarit. *Kirkko ja nykyajan eettiset kysymykset.* Tampere: Kirjapaja, 2003.

Hytönen, M., and Eivor Rajala-Kejonen. *Bibeln och kyrkans tro i dag: synodalavhandling 2004.* Tammerfors: Kyrkans forskningscentral, 2004.

Jackson, Timothy P. "Reviews." *Modern Theology* 14/3 (1998) 459.

Jeffner, Anders. *Theology and Integration: Four Essays in Philosophical Theology.* Uppsala: Acta universitatis Upsaliensis, 1987.

———. *Vägar till teologi.* Älvsjö: Skeab, 1981.

Jenson, Robert W. *Systematic Theology. Volume 1: The Triune God.* New York, NY: Oxford University Press, 1997.

Jokinen, Heidi. "The Church Does (Not) Apologize: The Evangelical Lutheran Church in Finland and the Civil War of 1918." In *Crisis and Change: Religion, Ethics and Theology under Late Modern Conditions,* edited by Henriksen, J. O., and Tage Kurtén, 91–111. Newcastle upon Tyne, UK: Cambridge, 2012.

Jones, L. Gregory, et al. *God, Truth, and Witness: Engaging Stanley Hauerwas.* Grand Rapids, MI.: Brazos, 2005.

Katongole, Emmanuel. *Beyond Universal Reason: The Relation Between Religion and Ethics in the Work of Stanley Hauerwas.* Notre Dame, IN: University of Notre Dame Press, 2000.

Ketola, Kimmo. "Spiritual Revolution in Finland? Evidence from Surveys and the Rates of Emergence of New Religious and Spiritual Organisations." *Nordic Journal of Religion and Society* 20/1 (2007) 29–40.

Kingwell, Mark. *A Civil Tongue: Justice, Dialogue, and the Politics of Pluralism.* University Park, PA: Pennsylvania State University Press, 1994.

Knight, Kelvin. *The MacIntyre Reader.* Notre Dame: University of Notre Dame Press, 1998.

Knuuttila, Simo. *Järjen ja tunteen kerrostumat.* Helsinki: Suomalainen teologinen kirjallisuusseura, 1998.

Kurtén, Tage. "Gud i Norden. Teologi och empiri." *Tidskrift for teologi og kirke* 2–3/75 (2004) 111–28.

———. "Teologi mellan ontologi och antropologi." *Kirke og kultur* 103 (1998) 17–27.

———. "The Christian Living in Two Worlds? Religious Contributions to the Legitimacy of a Nordic Democratic Society." *Studia Theologica. Nordic Journal of Theology* 61/2 (2007) 91–12.

———. "Vad innebär sanning i ett religiöst sammanhang?" In *Tro och mångfald. Religionsmöten och religionsteologi i Norden*, edited by Yvonne Terlinden et al. Borgå: Tema Nord, 2005.

Kurtén, T., and Joakim Molander. *Homo moralis: människan och rättssamhället.* Lund: Studentlitteratur, 2005.

Kuula, Kari. *Hyvä, paha ja synti: Johdatus Raamatun etiikkaan.* Helsinki: Kirjapaja, 2004.

L'Arche International. "Beginnings." Online: http://www.larche.org/l-arche-since-its-beginnings.en-gb.22.10.content.htm.

———. "Communities." Online: http://inter.larche.org/f/nf4261ai.

Laulaja, Jorma. *Elämän oikea ja väärä: eettiset valinnat tänään.* Helsinki: Kirjapaja, 1994.

Lindbeck, George A. *The Nature of Doctrine: Religion and Theology in a Postliberal Age.* Philadelphia: Westminster, 1984.

Lindfelt, Mikael, et al. *Mot bättre vetande: festskrift till Tage Kurtén på 60-årsdagen.* Åbo: Åbo Akademi, 2010.

Løgstrup, Knud Ejler. *Den etiske fordring.* København: Gyldendal, 1957.

———. *The Ethical Demand.* Notre Dame, IN: University of Notre Dame Press, 1997.

Lovin, Robin W. *Christian Realism and the New Realities.* New York: Cambridge University Press, 2008.

Luomanen, Petri. *Teologia: Johdatus tutkimukseen.* Helsinki: Edita, 2001.

Luther, Martin. *Sermons of Martin Luther.* Forgotten Books, 2007.

Lutz, Christopher Stephen. *Tradition in the Ethics of Alasdair MacIntyre: Relativism, Thomism, and Philosophy.* Lanham, MD: Lexington Books, 2004.

MacIntyre, Alasdair. *After Virtue: A Study in Moral Theory.* London: Duckworth, 1985.

———. *Selected Essays.* Cambridge, UK; New York: Cambridge University Press, 2006.

———. *Whose Justice? Which Rationality?* London: Duckworth, 1988.

Bibliography

Malysz, Piotr J. *"Nemo iudex in causa sua* as the Basis of Law, Justice, and Justification in Luther's Thought." *Harvard Theological Review* 100 (2007) 363–86.

Mannermaa, T., and Kirsi Stjerna. *Christ Present in Faith: Luther's View of Justification.* Minneapolis MN: Fortress, 2005.

Marion, Jean-Luc. *God Without Being: Hors-Texte.* Chicago: The University of Chicago Press, 1991.

McCarthy, Colman. "'America's best theologian' walks pacifist road," 1–5. Online: http://fredericksburg.com/News/FLS/2003/042003/04202003/944336/index_html

Milbank, John. *Theology and Social Theory: Beyond Secular Reason.* Oxford: Blackwell, 1993.

Mortensen, V., and Andreas Nielsen. *Walk Humbly with the Lord: Church and Mission Engaging Plurality.* Grand Rapids, MI: W. B. Eerdmans, 2011.

Murdoch, Iris. *The Sovereignty of Good.* New York: Routledge, 1970.

Nation, M., and Samuel Wells. *Faithfulness and Fortitude: In Conversation with the Theological Ethics of Stanley Hauerwas.* Edinburgh: T&T Clark, 2000.

Newbigin, Lesslie. *The Open Secret: An Introduction to the Theology of Mission.* Grand Rapids, MI: W.B. Eerdmans, 1995.

Niebuhr, H. Richard. *Christ and Culture.* New York: Harper, 1951.

Nikolajsen, Jeppe Bach. *Redefining the Indentity of the Church: A Constructive Study of the Post-Christendom Theologies of Lesslie Newbigin and John Howard Yoder.* PhD thesis, MF Norwegian School of Theology, 2010.

Niskanen, Heikki. *Moraali, harkinta, yhteisö: tutkimus Amerikan evankelis-luterilaisen kirkon eettisistä kannanotoista 1987–94.* Helsinki: H. Niskanen, 2000.

Ollenburger, Ben C., et al. *A Mind Patient and Untamed: Assessing John Howard Yoder's Contributions to Theology, Ethics, and Peacemaking.* Telford, PA; Scottdale, PA: Cascadia; Copublished with Herald, 2004.

Olsson, Herbert. *Grundproblemet i Luthers socialetik.* Lund: Håkan Ohlsson, 1934.

Paarma, Jukka, et al. *Rakkauden lahja: piispojen puheenvuoro perheestä, avioliitosta ja seksuaalisuudesta.* Helsinki: Kirjapaja, 2008.

Pateman, Barry. *Chomsky on Anarchism.* Oakland, CA: AK Press, 2005.

Peura, Simo. *Usko ja rakkaus: luterilaisen teologian mahdollisuudet tänään.* Helsinki: Suomalainen teologinen kirjallisuusseura, 1989.

Pihlström, Sami. *Uskonto ja elämän merkitys: näkökulmia uskonnonfilosofiaan.* Helsinki: Suomalainen teologinen kirjallisuusseura, 2010.

———. *Usko, järki ja ihminen: uskonnonfilosofisia esseitä.* Helsinki: Suomalainen teologinen kirjallisuusseura, 2001.

Pinches, Charles Robert, et al. *Unsettling Arguments: a Festschrift on the Occasion of Stanley Hauerwas's 70th Birthday.* Eugene, OR: Cascade, 2010.

Pope John Paul II. *Catechism of the Catholic Church.* Online: http://www.vatican.va/archive/ENG0015/__P29.HTM.

Rasmusson, Arne. "A Century of Swedish Theology." *Lutheran Quarterly* XXI/2 (2007) 125–62.

———. *The Church as Polis: From Political Theology to Theological Politics as Exemplified by Jürgen Moltmann and Stanley Hauerwas.* Lund; Bromley, Kent, England: Lund University Press; Chartwell-Bratt, 1994.

Raunio, Antti. *Järki, usko ja lähimmäisen hyvä: tutkimus luterilaisen etiikan ja diakonian teologian perusteista.* Helsinki: Suomalainen teologinen kirjallisuusseura, 2007.

Raunio, A., and Petri Luomanen. *Teologia: johdatus tutkimukseen*. Helsinki: Edita, 2010.
Reinders, Hans S. "The Meaning of Sanctification: Stanley Hauerwas on Christian Identity and Moral Judgment." In *Does Religion Matter Morally? The Critical Reappraisal of the Thesis of Morality's Independence from Religion*, edited by Albert. W. Musschenga, 141–72. Kampen: Kok Pharos, 1995.
Reynolds, Jack. "Jacques Derrida." In *Internet Encyclopedia of Philosophy*. No Pages. Online http://www.iep.utm.edu/derrida/#SH2a.
Hick, John. "Believing—and Having True Beliefs." In *Is God Real?*, edited by Runzo, Joseph. Basingstoke: Macmillan, 1993.
Ryman, Björn et al. *Nordic Folk Churches: A Contemporary Church History*. Grand Rapids, MI: W. B. Eerdmans, 2005.
Saarinen, Risto. *Sosiaalietiikka ja uskonnon eetos: teologisia tutkielmia*. Helsinki: Suomalainen teologinen kirjallisuusseura, 1999.
Sharp, Joanne P. *Geographies of Postcolonialism: Spaces of Power and Representation*. Los Angeles; London: Sage, 2009.
Shuman, Joel, et al. *Heal Thyself: Spirituality, Medicine, and the Distortion of Christianity*. Oxford: Oxford University Press, 2003.
Sigurdson, Ola. "Att söka sanningen. Om Anders Jeffner och Ingemar Hedenius." *Svensk Teologisk Kvartalskrift* 76 (2000) 14–18.
———. *Det postsekulära tillståndet: religion, modernitet, politik*. Göteborg: Glänta production, 2009.
———. "Vilka är vi nu?" *Svensk Teologisk Kvartalskrift* 76 (2000).
Sigurdson, O., and Jayne Svenungsson. *Postmodern teologi: en introduction*. Stockholm: Verbum, 2006.
Smith, R. Scott. "Hauerwas and Kallenberg and The Issue of Epistemic Access to an Extra-Linguistic Realm." *The Heythrop Journal* 45/3 (2004) 305–26.
———. *Virtue Ethics and Moral Knowledge: Philosophy of Language after MacIntyre and Hauerwas*. Aldershot, Hants, England; Burlington, VT: Ashgate, 2003.
Somerville, Gerald. "On *Whose Justice?*". Online: http://web.ukonline.co.uk/gerald.somerville/amwjcom.htm#ch18.
Soskice, Janet Martin. *Metaphor and Religious Language*. Oxford: Clarendon, 1985.
Stout, Jeffrey. *Blessed Are the Organized: Grassroots Democracy in America*. Princeton, NJ: Princeton University Press, 2010.
———. *Democracy and Tradition*. Princeton, NJ: Princeton University Press, 2004.
Svenungsson, Jayne. *Guds återkomst: en studie av gudsbegreppet inom postmodern filosofi*. Lund: Lunds universitet, 2002.
Taylor, Charles. *A Secular Age*. Cambridge, MA: Belknap, 2007.
The Christian Democrats. "Christian Democracy." Online: http://www.kristillisdemokraatit.fi/KD/www/en/our_goals/christian_democracy/index.php.
Thomson, John B. *The Ecclesiology of Stanley Hauerwas: a Christian Theology of Liberation*. Aldershot: Ashgate, 2003.
Tillich, Paul. *Systematic Theology: Volume 1*. Chicago: The Chicago University Press, 1973.
Tolonen, Miika. "Post-Secular Alternative Politics: The Case of L'Arche." In *Crisis and Change: Religion, Ethics and Theology under Late Modern Conditions*, edited by Henriksen, J. O., and Tage Kurtén, 77–89. Newcastle upon Tyne, UK: Cambridge, 2012.

Bibliography

Torrkulla, G., and Joel Backström. *Moralfilosofiska essäer*. Göteborg: Thales, 2001.
Trakakis, Nick. *The End of Philosophy of Religion*. London; New York: Continuum, 2008.
Troeltsch, Ernst. *The Social Teaching of the Christian Churches*. Chicago: University of Chicago Press, 1931.
Uskonopin kongregaatio. "Vastauksia joihinkin kysymyksiin, joita on esitetty tietyistä kirkkoon liittyvistä opinkohdista." Online: http://www.catholic.fi/docs/cdf_070710.htm
Vainio, Olli-Pekka. *Beyond Fideism: Negotiable Religious Identities*. Burlington, VT.: Ashgate, 2010.
Vikström, Björn. *Folkkyrka i en postmodern tid: tjänsteproducent i välfärdssamhället eller engagerande gemenskap?* Åbo: Åbo Akademi, 2008.
Vikström, John, et al. *Kyrkans budskap till individ och samhälle: två betänkanden utarbetade på uppdrag av biskopsmötet i Finlands evangelisk-lutherska kyrka*. Helsinfors: Församlingsförbundet, 1973.
Vilppula, Anne. *Suomen laki II, 645/1985, vapautuslaki*. Helsinki: Talentum, 2009.
von Stosch, Klaus. *Glaubensverantwortung in doppelter Kontingenz: Untersuchungen zur Verortung fundamentaler Theologie nach Wittgenstein*. Regensburg: Ratio Fidei 7, 2001.
Ward, Graham. *The Politics of Discipleship: Becoming Postmaterial Citizens*. Grand Rapids, MI: Baker, 2009.
Wittgenstein, Ludwig. *Philosophical Investigations*. Oxford: Blackwell, 1997.
Wrede, Gösta. *Folkkyrkan i framtiden*. Stockholm: Verbum, 1992.
Yoder, John Howard. *The Christian Witness to the State*. Newton, KS: Faith and Life, 1964.
———. *The Original Revolution: Essays on Christian Pacifism*. Scottdale, PA: Herald Press, 1972.
———. *The Politics of Jesus: Vicit Agnus Noster*. Grand Rapids, MI: W. B. Eerdmans, 1994.
———. *The Priestly Kingdom: Social Ethics as Gospel*. Notre Dame, IN: University of Notre Dame Press, 1984.
Yoder, J. H., and Joan Baez. *What Would You Do? A Serious Answer to a Standard Question*. Scottdale, PA: Herald, 1992.
Yoder, J. H., and Michael Cartwright. *The Royal Priesthood: Essays Ecclesiological and Ecumenical*. Grand Rapids, MI: W. B. Eerdmans, 1994.
Yoder, John Howard, et al. *The Jewish-Christian Schism Revisited*. Grand Rapids, MI: W. B. Eerdmans, 2003.
Yong, Amos. *In the Days of Caesar: Pentecostalism and Political Theology*. Grand Rapids, MI: W.B. Eerdmans, 2010.
Østnor, Lars. *Etisk pluralisme i Norden*. Kristiansand: Høyskoleforl., 2001.

www.ingramcontent.com/pod-product-compliance
Lightning Source LLC
Chambersburg PA
CBHW071444150426
43191CB00008B/1238